NO MORE PEACE

NO MORE PEACE

Abolition War and Counterrevolution

OLIVER BAKER

UNIVERSITY OF CALIFORNIA PRESS

University of California Press
Oakland, California

Library of Congress Cataloging-in-Publication Data

Names: Baker, Oliver, 1984– author.
Title: No more peace : abolition war and counterrevolution / Oliver Baker.
Description: Oakland : University of California Press, [2025] | Includes
    bibliographical references and index.
Identifiers: LCCN 2024033960 (print) | LCCN 2024033961 (ebook) |
    ISBN 9780520401839 (cloth) | ISBN 9780520401846 (pbk.) |
    ISBN 9780520401853 (ebook)
Subjects: LCSH: Counterrevolutions—United States—History. | White people—
    United States—History. | Slavery—United States—History. | Abolitionists—
    United States—History. | Capitalism—Social aspects—United States—History. |
    Racism—Economic aspects—United States—History. | Indigenous peoples—
    United States—History.
Classification: LCC E184.A1 .B234 2025 (print) | LCC E184.A1 (ebook) |
    DDC 305.800973—dc23/eng/20241126
LC record available at https://lccn.loc.gov/2024033960
LC ebook record available at https://lccn.loc.gov/2024033961

34 33 32 31 30 29 28 27 26 25
10 9 8 7 6 5 4 3 2 1

Contents

Introduction

ABOLITION WAR AND WHITE COUNTERREVOLUTION

Class Struggles of Antebellum Racial Capitalism

DURING HIS TENURE in Kansas, John Brown made racists afraid. But fear was the least of their problems when dealing with Brown's abolition war strategy. In August 1855, when he learned of proslavery aggressions in the new territory, Brown left his farm in the Adirondack Mountains of New York State for the prairies of Kansas to join his sons and other abolitionists in armed resistance to slavery. When proslavery Missourians invaded Kansas to impose slavery, they did not anticipate encountering abolitionists, who shot back. For years Brown, like many abolitionists, had been organizing in preparation for crises like what was unfolding in Kansas. These conflicts were opportunities to gain ground on the enemy, slavery.

The following spring and summer, Brown led an abolition militia in a campaign to rout Missouri "border ruffians" from the territory. These efforts culminated in the Battle of Osawatomie on August 30, 1856, where Brown's militia drew national recognition as a formidable military force confronting slavery power. Four hundred proslavery Missourians descended on the town of Osawatomie to lay waste to Brown's base of operations, the first stop in their trek to raze the major free-state towns in Kansas. When they approached Osawatomie, the Missourians were intercepted by Brown's son, Frederick. Before he could take cover, the Missourians ruthlessly shot him point blank, killing him instantly. When John Brown, who was not at Osawatomie at the time but nearby, learned of the attack, he rallied his small guerrilla forces, around forty men, and mounted a counterattack. Although greatly outnumbered and outmatched, Brown's forces proved deadly, fearless, and stubborn, only retreating when they ran out of ammunition. After Brown's forces escaped into the brush by crossing the nearby Marais des Cygnes River, the Missourians set fire to the small cluster of buildings at Osawatomie. While proslavery forces burned the town and forced abolitionists to retreat, Brown's guerrilla tactics demonstrated that armed abolitionists were a deadly enemy, not to be underestimated. That Brown with only a few dozen fighters could mount such a challenge to a much larger and powerful enemy shattered the confidence of proslavery forces that they would be able to seize control of the Kansas territory. Armed abolition had raised the cost of expanding slavery into Kansas territory.[1] Though in the preceding months Missourians had easily sacked the free-state stronghold of Lawrence and intimidated free-state supporters, they began to fear abolitionists and take flight following their run-ins with Brown's abolition militia.

Brown later reflected on the battle and his plans going forward. Referring to the destruction of Osawatomie, he told his son Jason: "God sees it. I have only a short time to live—only one death to die, and I will die fighting for this cause. There will be no more peace in this land until slavery is done for. I will give them something else to do than extend slave territory. I will carry the war into Africa."[2] Brown's assertion that peace and slavery could not coexist illustrated his understanding of slavery as a war on Africans. He would later write in the preface to his "Provisional Constitution," a document proposing the establishment of an abolition government that could centralize and direct his abolition war strategy, that "slavery throughout its entire existence in the United States is none other than a most barbarous unprovoked and unjustifiable War of one portion of its citizens upon another portion."[3] It was a war of capital accumulation perpetrated by one class against another. Those who waged this war had initiated the violence, not those fighting against it. Brown suggested that social peace in a class society premised on slavery was illusionary. True peace could only arrive when the class war of slavery was resolved through the overthrow of one class by another. To call for peace between slavery and abolition to preserve the union, which was the common refrain before and after the violent clashes in Kansas, was to condone the violence of slavery and delegitimize the struggle of the enslaved to liberate themselves. Brown's promise to end slavery through violent means—through abolition war—was precisely his commitment to peace.

This vision of armed abolition going on the offensive to take the fight to slavery's doorstep embodies an underappreciated history of revolutionary insurgency in antebellum America that was formative in the shaping of US racial capitalism. This was the history of what I refer to as *abolition and anticolonial wars* waged by the enslaved and colonized to overturn slavery and settler colonialism. Abolition and anticolonial wars were the numerous rebellions, insurrections, revolts, raids, slave rescues, fugitive flights, maroon societies, land defenses, and armed campaigns of North America whose partisans considered US class society an enemy to defeat as a requisite for emancipation and self-determination. These were not movements seeking to reform US institutions. Rather, they were wars for liberation whose aim was to overthrow or win autonomy from US class society. *No More Peace* studies the relationship between abolition and anticolonial wars and the development of US racial capitalism's modes of repression.

I argue that this revolutionary character of abolition and anticolonial wars called into existence what I refer to as *white counterrevolution* (a term adapted from the work of Gerald Horne), which served as the linchpin structure of repression securing slavery and settler colonialism.[4] As class movements, abolition and anticolonial wars produced critical insights about white counterrevolution precisely through their militant confrontation with it. White counterrevolution formed from the forging of alliances across class and difference among Europeans to protect slavery and settler colonialism from liberation struggles of the enslaved and colonized. It was a mass-based project to harness the power of widespread participation by Europeans in carrying out anti-Black and anti-Indian repressive violence. The necessity to save capitalism from abolition and anticolonial wars compelled settlers and enslavers to construct white counterrevolution. By demonstrating how abolition and anticolonial wars forced the making of white counterrevolution to protect class society, *No More Peace* illuminates how slavery and settler colonialism were always uncertain projects—constantly vulnerable to defeat, collapse, and ruin at the hands of those who resisted.

Brown's warning of "no more peace in this land until slavery is done for," which anticipated the chant often heard today in the streets of "No Justice, No Peace," was also a promise that abolition war's fight in Kansas was to stop slavery's expansion. Historians Gerald Horne and Walter Johnson argue that the proslavery South had pursued territorial expansion in response, in part, to the threat of abolition. Encompassing more territory allowed slavery to amass greater political, economic, and military power to combat growing abolition power.[5] The efforts of Missourians to seize Kansas territory for slavery was a preemptive expansion to head off the rising tide of abolition. In this way, Brown's promise also spoke to abolition war's role in the movement of the struggle between Black revolution and slavery. As shown in chapter 4, Brown was merely one among many partisans carrying out abolition war, whose tradition was slave revolts, maroon communities, the Underground Railroad, Black community-defense vigilance committees, slave rescues, and other forms of Black militancy that deployed collective force to abolish slavery. While often exceptionalized as a singular leader, Brown had made himself into a student of and soldier for Black liberation.[6] His radicalism flowed from his choice to put the politics of Black insurgency in command of his strategy. As a war of liberation, abolition war functioned in terms of what Karl Marx, a contemporary of Brown, called a "locomotive of history."[7] It drove forward slavery's reactionary developments in a dance between enemies.

The same could be said of Indigenous anticolonial wars. Just as they had done since the inception of settler colonization, Indigenous nations of North American waged defensive wars to protect their territories and maintain governance over their land bases. Among the major wars during this period were Tecumseh's War (1811–1813), the Creek War (1813–1814), the Black Hawk War (1832), the Seminole Wars (1817–1821, 1836–1842, 1855–1858), and the wars of Indigenous nations of the western seaboard resisting waves of genocidal settler invasions that resulted in the establishment of Oregon and Washington territories (1846) and the state of California (1850). There were also intersections between abolition and anticolonial wars during this period. The Great Dismal Swamp maroon society of southern Virginia and northern North Carolina was an experiment among displaced Indigenous people (many of whom were Tuscarora), Black maroons, and poor whites combining to win autonomy from US class society.[8] As chapter 2 explores, the Seminole Wars witnessed Seminoles, Black Seminoles, and Black maroons joining in coalitional armed resistance to Florida's settler plantation society. In Kansas, John Brown worked with leaders of the Sac, Fox, and Ottawa nations, who offered him resources and sanctuary when his militia needed to escape from proslavery forces. While this assistance is often overlooked, without it Brown's guerrilla campaigns likely would have failed because they depended on tactical retreat after engaging enemy proslavery forces. The Sacs, Foxes, and Ottawas saw in abolition war an alignment with anticolonialism.[9] When Brown's abolition militia later attacked Harper's Ferry, Virginia, to seize the federal arsenal and initiate a protracted guerrilla campaign to topple slavery, proslavery leaders believed that Brown had collaborated with the Pamunkey Tribe and enslaved Africans in an insurgent united front. Historian John Stauffer notes that one proslavery reporter suggested Brown modeled his campaign after the Second Seminole War of Florida, seeking "to make the Alleghany and Cumberland Mountains and the Dismal Swamp his everglades."[10] In all these cases, abolition and anticolonial wars posed alarming challenges to the viability of US class society. In the dialectic of resistance and repression, they served as the motor forces in the development of the repressive structures that came to enforce racialized settler capitalist social relations. The threat of abolition and anticolonial wars ending the projects of slavery and settler colonialism to win Black and Indigenous liberation compelled the construction of white counterrevolution.

I conceptualize white counterrevolution as more than simply a periodic protection or restoration of the status quo in response to punctuated revolutionary insurgencies or seizures of power. In Marxist thought, Karl Marx, Friedrich Engels, and Vladimir Lenin theorized counterrevolution as a campaign of reactionary bourgeois forces to restore capitalist power in the wake of the proletariat's revolutionary seizure of state power.[11] In this formulation, counterrevolution is a momentary reactionary strategy to unravel revolutionary victories and reassert bourgeois power over the working class. In what follows, I theorize white counterrevolution as a structure that arose intertwined with capitalism's relations of production as they developed in the context of North American slavery and settler colonialism. It was not solely an episodic policy or campaign to crush revolutionary activity; it was a structure baked into the modes of reproducing racial capitalism. I identify and examine two pillars of white counterrevolution: *white alliance policing* and *settler mass militarism.* These formations developed together and worked in tandem to form the structure of white counterrevolution. I contend that gaining this critical view of the history of white counterrevolution comes from the study of the forces that prompted its construction, namely the abolition and anticolonial wars of antebellum America.

At times the study of settler colonialism and slavery is done one-sidedly or without a view of how peoples' struggles to emancipate themselves from dispossession and exploitation determine the character of these structures of violence. Settler colonialism and slavery are theorized as already fully devised and completed projects unleashed on those whom they target, rather than as continuously developing counterformations to the resistance of the targeted.[12] In other words, the role of class struggle is often not foregrounded in the study of the development of US racial capitalism. Class struggle is considered a framework only applicable to the history of wage labor's fight for emancipation from capitalism. The fights for liberation from slavery and settler colonialism in North America are often viewed as prehistories to the class struggle proper of capitalism's industrial proletariat. Yet class struggle is neither a one-way fight for freedom of the exploited nor contained by the history of European wage labor.

Class struggle is the historical movement of the social antagonism or material power imbalance between classes within the organization of a society's mode of production. In the *Communist Manifesto*, Marx and Engels defined class struggle in terms of a war between the "oppressor and oppressed" who "carried on an uninterrupted . . . fight that each time ended, either in a revolutionary reconstitution of society at large, or in the common ruin of the contending classes."[13] This war between classes, Nick Estes and Roxanne Dunbar-Ortiz explain, "operates on different scales, between boss and worker, oppressor and oppressed, and between colonizer nation and colonized nation."[14] While Marx and Engels applied their theory of class struggle to the European context to understand the relationship between wage labor and capital, they also were just as interested in the history of capital's wars of primitive accumulation—settler colonialism and slavery—beyond Europe and the national liberation struggles of the enslaved and colonized.[15] During the period of primitive accumulation, European nations colonizing and enslaving Indigenous, African, and other oppressed nations was a form of class oppression. The wars of the enslaved and colonized to defeat primitive accumulation have formed the history of class struggle between imperial nations and oppressed nations. Theorist Domenico Losurdo argues that Marx and Engels, in their analysis of the Irish and Polish national liberation struggles of their time, theorized national liberation as a form of class struggle on capitalism's international scale in which nations grow rich from the exploitation of other nations, while within those imperial nations of the metropole capitalist classes exploit for profit their own working classes.[16]

The foundational work of C. L. R. James, Frantz Fanon, Walter Rodney, Sylvia Wynter, Cedric Robinson, and other scholars of anticolonialism and Black liberation struggle have developed Marxist analysis of class struggle on this international scale beyond the context of the European proletariat to develop historical materialist critiques of slavery, settler colonialism, and bourgeois humanism.[17] In recent years scholars of Indigenous studies and Black studies such as Roxanne Dunbar-Ortiz, Gerald Horne, Manu Karuka, Nick Estes, Christina Heatherton, Bernadine Hernández, Charisse Burden-Stelly, Glen Coulthard, Nikhil Pal Singh, Geo Maher, and Iyko Day, among others, have reinvigorated the study of anti-capitalist struggle within the traditions of Black, Native, and colonized peoples' liberation movements.[18] Joining these conversations, No More Peace examines the history of abolition and anticolonial wars as the story of antebellum America's class struggles on the international scale of primitive accumulation or imperialism. Those who engaged in these class movements for national liberation from slavery and settler colonialism produced understudied forms of thought pivotal for understanding not only US racial capitalism's modes of repression, essential to its reproduction and expansion, but also revolutionary theory and strategy not typically recognized in the traditions of anti-capitalist critique.

"I HAINT GOT NO HEART TO GO AND SEE THE SUFFERINGS OF MY PEOPLE PLAYED ON DE STAGE"

A leader for John Brown in the strategy of abolition war was Harriet Tubman. As discussed in chapter 4, if anyone at that time had a grasp on the class struggle of racial capitalism, it was Tubman. In the years after she liberated herself from slavery, Tubman worked for a time at a Philadelphia hotel. She labored as a domestic worker not only to eke out a living in the North, but also to save money to fund her Underground Railroad raids into the South to liberate others. This was a theme of Tubman's life: saving any extra wages to finance her revolutionary work and later, in her senior years, mutual aid projects supporting the poor and excluded, many of whom were former fugitive slaves and, after emancipation, refugee freedmen. She famously purchased a small farm and transformed it into a mutual aid center, which she named the "John Brown Hall" after her fallen comrade.[19] While she was working as a cook in the Philadelphia hotel, Tubman's coworkers asked if she wanted to join them to see a dramatic performance of Harriet Beecher Stowe's popular antislavery novel *Uncle Tom's Cabin*. Tubman rejected the offer. Her first biographer, Sara Bradford, recounts the conversation:

> While Harriet was working as a cook in one of the large hotels in Philadelphia, the play of "Uncle Tom's Cabin" was being performed for many weeks every night. Some of her fellow-servants wanted to go and see it. "No," said Harriet, "I haint got no heart to go and see the sufferings of my people played on de stage. I've heard 'Uncle Tom's Cabin' read, and I tell you Mrs. Stowe's pen hasn't begun to paint what slavery is as I have seen it

as the far South. I've seen de *real ting*, and I don't want to see it on no stage or in no teater."[20]

Tubman rejected *Uncle Tom's Cabin* because it overrepresented Black suffering. Perhaps Tubman believed, like fellow Black abolitionist Martin Delaney, that Stowe's narrative strategy of liberal humanism commercialized and thus mystified slavery's violence.[21] Anticipating Saidiya Hartman's critique of liberalism's representation of Black suffering, Tubman might have felt that Stowe's narrative represented the enslaved as suffering objects, available for repairing white psyches, rather than as revolutionary actors like herself, challenging slavery's power through armed guerrilla warfare.[22] In other words, dwelling on Black suffering for the sake of eliciting white pity was divorced from the trenches of abolition war in which Tubman was embedded. Tubman had seen the "real ting" of slavery not only because she had lived and already suffered from it but because she had struggled to defeat it. Tubman's rejection of Stowe's overrepresentation of Black suffering in *Uncle Tom's Cabin* becomes, I suggest, a call to foreground or begin with Black revolutionary struggle in the study of slavery over the tendency to see only Black suffering.

Years later Tubman would command a Black army in a guerrilla raid against Confederate forces in South Carolina. This was the famous Combahee River raid. Her official coleader in the raid, whom she personally selected to carry out her plan, was Union colonel James Montgomery, an abolition war veteran who had fought alongside and learned from John Brown in Kansas territory. The raid successfully liberated around eight hundred enslaved people, seized enemy property, and destroyed enemy infrastructure. In a dictated letter sent to her friend and supporter Bostonian abolitionist Frank Sanborn, Tubman reflected on the raid. She offered a representation of the enslaved's participation in the raid:

"I nebber see such a sight," said Harriet; "we laughed, an' laughed, an' laughed. Here you'd see a woman wid a pail on her head, rice a smokin' in it jus as she'd taken it from de fire, young one hangin' on behind, one han' roun' her forehead to hold on, t'other han' diggin' into the de rice-pot, eatin' wid all its might; hold of her dress two or three more; down her back a bag wid a pig in it. One woman brought two pigs, a white one, an' a black one; we took 'em all on board; named de white pig Beauregard, an' de black pig Jeff Davis. Sometimes de women would come wid twins hangin' roun' der necks; 'pears like I nebber see so many twins in my life; bags on der shoulders, baskets on der heads, and young ones taggin' behin', all loaded; pigs squealin', chickens screamin', young ones squallin."[23]

Here Tubman's representation of the enslaved speaks to her interest in centering Black revolutionary struggle. She represents their escape as chaotic and even comical, but she is not condescending. It is a celebratory representation. It is a representation of victory—of the enslaved struggling and winning. It is not of defeat or a dwelling on and thus fetishizing of Black suffering. Rather, Tubman depicts the image of the enslaved—in particular, enslaved women and children—participating as partisans in a raid that left their exploiters, abusers, and brutalizers destroyed, running for their lives. Tubman was interested in representing rehearsals for Black revolution and what it achieved over watching scenes of Black subjection depicted on stage for the consumption of white audiences.

No More Peace follows the lead of Tubman's method of analysis, in which she foregrounded revolutionary struggle, whereas often it is disavowed or overshadowed by critiques of power that see modern systems of domination as omnipotent projects in their success at neutralizing resistance. Studying how abolition and anticolonial wars gave rise to white counterrevolution is not to suggest that these wars were destined to end in defeat at the hands of violent repression. Rather, this focus on how white counterrevolution emerged and consolidated in response to the revolutionary orientation of abolition and anticolonial wars is precisely the study of how racial capitalism was always an embattled and uncertain project—itself susceptible to defeat and failure. The structures of repression that promise to uphold racial capitalism had to be built in response to revolutionary struggle. Illuminating how abolition and anticolonial wars conjured white counterrevolution makes legible the unfinished, contingent, and fragile character of racial capitalism that its ideologies disavow. I use an interdisciplinary approach blending historical analysis, literary critique, and theory to study a series of flashpoints in the history of abolition and anticolonial wars and white counterrevolution of the antebellum nineteenth century. I study the archives of these historical flashpoints, offering close readings of the writings, speeches, documents, narratives, and representations of these movements' partisans. *No More Peace* is grounded in Black radical thought, abolition theory, Indigenous critiques of settler colonialism, and historical materialism.

ABOLITION WAR AND WHITE ALLIANCE POLICING

One of the most significant moments in the history of abolition war was Nat Turner's insurrection. On August 21, 1831, Nat Turner led a revolt that attacked and terrorized the enslaver class of Southampton County, Virginia. While the insurrection started with only a handful of people, it would amass up to seventy partisans at its peak. Turner and his fighters kick-started the insurrection by assailing several local plantations in the Cross Keys area, where they killed enemy masters and their families, expropriated arms and supplies, and unleashed a debilitating panic among the white community. Turner had planned to then cut his way to the county seat of Jerusalem only a few miles away to seize weapons from its arsenal to distribute among his growing abolition army. If he could not hold the newly liberated area of Southampton County after taking Jerusalem, Turner intended to retreat to the nearby Great Dismal Swamp, a long-established maroon society, from which he could recruit more followers, sponsor further uprisings, and wage guerrilla attacks on slavery. Although after a few days the uprising was defeated by white militias—and over the ensuing days and months Turner and other insurrectionists were captured and executed by the state, their bodies mutilated and turned into war trophies by whites, then stolen by medical students for experiments—the insurrection's contribution to Black revolution far outweighed the state repression and white terror that followed.[24]

Turner's insurrection was guided by how he theorized abolition war. After his capture, local attorney and opportunist Thomas Grey interviewed Turner to glean a confession to sell to the public for profit. The interview was submitted to the court as Turner's confession to the crimes for which he stood trial. After Turner's conviction and sentencing to be hanged, Grey quickly published the interview as *The Confessions of Nat Turner* (1831). It circulated widely. Turner outmaneuvered his interviewer, making use of Grey's platform to articulate a revolutionary critique of slavery and theory of abolition war strategy. In *Confessions*, Turner describes slavery as a racialized class war accelerating toward a final reckoning: "I had a vision—and I saw white spirits and black spirits engaged in battle, and the sun was darkened—the thunder rolled in the Heavens, and blood flowed in streams—and I heard a voice saying, 'Such is your luck, such you are called to see, and let it come rough or smooth, you must surely bare it.'"[25] Turner concludes that it would take a war of liberation to end slavery's war against Africans. He articulates this through the language of liberation theology. He believed God had called him as a leader destined to overthrow slavery: "I heard a loud noise in the heavens, and the Spirit instantly appeared to me and said the Serpent was loosened, and Christ had laid down the yoke he had borne for the sins of men, and that I should take it on and fight against the Serpent, for the time was fast approaching when the first should be last and the last should be first."[26] His vision foresaw the enslaved overturning the class rule of enslavers, the enslaved conquering enslaver power.

Anticipating Marx and Engels by a decade, Turner argues that the class society of slavery engendered its own gravediggers in the enslaved. When Grey asks Turner if he received outside help or was providing help to others waging abolition war, trying to uncover a potential larger conspiracy, Turner teaches him about the dialectics of class war: "I questioned him as to the insurrection in North Carolina happening about the same time, he denied any knowledge of it; and when I looked him in the face as though I would search his inmost thoughts, he replied, 'I see sir, you doubt my word; but can you not think the same ideas, and strange appearances about this time in the heavens might prompt others, as well, as myself, to this undertaking.'" Where there was slavery, it would create the conditions for the enslaved to revolt for its overthrow. While Turner's insurrection is often described as an "intimate rebellion" in which the enslaved warred against their enslavers, with whom they were forced to live and labor closely, the two classes lived in different worlds or zones of existence, as Frantz Fanon would later theorize.[27] The stolen labor and lives of the enslaved created the world of the enslaver. Turner sees that as slavery's gravediggers, the enslaved must seize the means of the world that their exploitation produced in order to end that world: "And on the appearance of the sign (the eclipse of the sun last February), I should arise and prepare myself, and slay my enemies with their own weapons." In response to Turner's articulation of abolition war, Grey mocks Turner by reminding him that his capture and pending execution indicate his analysis and strategy have failed him. "*Ques.* Do you not find yourself mistaken now?" Famously, Turner responds, "Was not Christ crucified[?]" While Turner did not seek martyrdom for the sake of it, he well knew the risks of insurrection. He and his costrategists had painstakingly planned the uprising for months. In fact, the time spent debating strategy and tactics had caused Turner to fall ill. His ill health delayed the uprising, deferring it from July 4, 1831, to its later date in August. His response to Grey that his capture and pending execution prove Turner is on the right side of history mocks the white supremacist attorney's ignorance of the historical and political meaning of Turner's actions. Turner knew his contribution to abolition war would inspire higher levels of armed insurgency.

What Black Panther Party leader Fred Hampton would say many years later about the relationship between the revolutionary and the revolution applied to Turner just as much is it did, tragically, to Hampton himself: the white ruling class might have killed the revolutionary Turner, but they could not kill the revolution his actions advanced.[28] Turner's insurrection catalyzed the emerging abolition movement. It inspired those advocating for immediate abolition and accelerated the movement toward revolutionary abolition. Impacted by the Southampton uprising and other slave revolts, radical Black abolitionist Henry Highland Garnet called for a general strike among the enslaved that, he envisioned, would lead to mass insurrection as the first step in the revolutionary overthrow of slavery.[29] Less than thirty years later, modeled after Turner's strategy and answering the call to ignite mass insurrection, John Brown and Harriet Tubman, as discussed in chapter 4, would organize a guerrilla campaign to raid the federal arsenal at Harper's Ferry. Their plan was to seize the state's cache of weapons and distribute them among the enslaved in surrounding areas, followed by establishing maroon camps as rear bases in the Appalachian Mountains, from which a growing abolitionist army could launch guerrilla attacks on the South to overthrow slavery.

Turner's insurrection also greatly impacted the future of slavery and how it would be enforced. In the following months and years, enslavers were compelled to consider pathways going forward that they otherwise would not have entertained. Turner's insurrection had made losing one's life a potential cost of doing business for enslavers. And dying for slavery was not in the business plan for most enslavers. In the

Virginia legislative sessions and in the wider white enslaver community, some proposed plans for the immediate emancipation, coupled with African colonization of the enslaved to remove them from the state. African colonization was the movement to export formerly enslaved Africans to colonies in Africa. If slavery were to be abolished to prevent further insurrections, African colonization would ensure that formerly enslaved Africans would not be incorporated into US society. Others proposed gradual abolition.[30] Like previous insurrections, slave revolt made slavery not worthwhile to maintain as a mode of economy. Proposals to remove Africans, whether through immediate emancipation combined with African colonization or through gradual abolition, were submitted to save enslavers from disasters like what Turner's insurrection had unleashed on Southampton County.

Still, others homicidally proposed genocide as the solution to slave revolt. They called for the enslaved to be exterminated in retaliation for waging insurrection. Many enacted this sanguinary desire in the vigilante terror campaigns immediately following the revolt, in which hundreds of enslaved and free persons of African descent in the surrounding area were ruthlessly murdered as collective retribution.[31] However, these proposals were rejected by most enslavers because such "solutions" for preventing revolt threatened to eliminate the primary source of wealth of the plantation economy on which enslavers depended for their existence as a capitalist class, namely the enslaved African workforce. Instead of devising ways to remove enslaved Africans, many enslavers demanded the white community be better organized as an anticipatory policing force to prevent and repress Black insurrection. Enslavers chose to intensify and enlarge what was already a strategy under construction since the inception of slavery: the organization of whites into a policing community to guard against revolt.

This range of responses reveals how Turner's insurrection forced enslavers to see the revolutionary character and trajectory of slave revolts. If white supremacy had blocked them from seeing this before through what theorist Geo Maher calls the "colonial blindspot," in which "the very same dehumanization used to justify racial-colonial domination blinds those at the top to the inevitability of resistance from below," Turner's insurrection compelled enslavers to contend with enslaved Africans as revolutionary actors.[32] The Southampton uprising brought to the surface and pushed forward the class war of slavery. While it advanced Black revolution, the revolt also spurred the expansion of white alliance policing that worked both to restore stable capital accumulation in Southampton and to better prevent revolt in the future. *White alliance policing* is the collaboration across class and difference among European settlers to repress slave revolt and fugitivity. Turner's insurrection demonstrated that it was slave revolt's potential to bring catastrophic loss and destabilization to the operations of capitalist social relations to the point that their very reproduction was under threat that compelled the making of white alliance policing. Maintaining formal standing armies was insufficient and too costly for the job of policing and repressing slave revolt. Instead, it would require harnessing the power derived from the collective and widespread participation of all the free or nonenslaved persons to carry out this duty. This was what Virginia enslavers went to work repairing, retooling, and further consolidating in the aftermath of Turner's insurrection to ensure anti-Black accumulation would be protected and upheld going forward.

This response to Turner's insurrection was but one flashpoint in the longer history of the construction of white alliance policing. Yet as I explore in chapter 1, it was these moments, when Black abolition war erupted and either overcame white alliance policing or when white alliance policing failed to preemptively stop revolt, that I am interested in examining. They reveal much about how white alliance policing had to be built in the first place and its points of weakness or where it momentarily lost to abolition war. Alongside insurrection, Black fugitivity was also a strategy of abolition war in which programs like the Underground Railroad functioned as a guerrilla campaign in enemy territory.

The actions of the enslaved escaping from slavery and those who assisted them functioned as military strikes against slavery's power. They depleted it of capital and labor power, while also strengthening abolition war's rear bases in the North with new recruits. White alliance policing was thus developed to manage both revolt and fugitivity as strategies of Black abolition war.

INDIGENOUS ANTICOLONIALISM
AND SETTLER MASS MILITARISM

Settler societies, like the United States, take homicidal pleasure in turning the people they colonize into war trophies. It has been a sadistic but common practice. Historian Roxanne Dunbar Ortiz documents how Andrew Jackson, when leading state militias to repress Muskogee (Creek) resistance, ordered his soldiers to skin the bodies of those murdered to make into bridles and reins for their horses as trophies of conquest.[33] At the inception of settler colonialism in North America, leaders of the Plymouth colony including William Bradford and Edward Winslow ordered their military captain Myles Standish to commit a preemptive massacre of Massachusetts people for daring to defend their land and people from settler aggressions. In 1623, only a few years after the founding of the Plymouth colony, a neighboring settlement was established twenty miles north named the Wessagusset colony. There, settlers failed to produce their own food and began to defraud and steal from the Massachusetts tribe. Concerned that the Massachusetts would wage an attack on all English settlements, possibly leading to the liquidation of the fledgling British settler colonialism, Standish called for a meeting with the Massachusetts leader Wituwamat under the guise of updating trade negotiations. The meeting became a massacre. Standish stabbed Wituwamat to death, followed by his militia murdering several other Massachusetts people. Standish removed Wituwamat's head, and after his return to the Plymouth colony, it was impaled on top of the settlement's fort. The severed head remained there for years to terrorize local Indigenous tribes and discipline settlers to support colonial violence.[34]

As explored in chapter 2, through deception and lies the US military in Florida captured and imprisoned the insurgent Seminole leader Osceola. He would die of sickness while being held captive, after which a US army physician removed Osceola's head for "phrenological study," and it was proposed to exhibit the preserved head in New York City as a trophy.[35] The same violence was directed at the Mexican anticolonial fighter Joaquín Murieta of post-1848 California, a figure who is examined in chapter 2 as well. After a white militia murdered Murieta, they cut off his head, preserved it in a jar, and took it on tour to surrounding settlements, selling tickets to view it. Afterward Murieta's head was put on display in a museum in San Francisco. Like Nat Turner, he suffered the fate of whites turning his body parts into trophies. Like slavery, settler colonialism has also been a war of capital accumulation, but targeting Indigenous nations. While turning anticolonial and abolitionist rebels into war trophies was intended to mark the triumph of this war, in truth this practice indexed a tacit acknowledgment of the irrepressible resistance of the enslaved and colonized. Settlers need war trophies to affirm their power in the face of how Indigenous anticolonialism promised to materially end occupation and conquest. War trophies convinced settlers that settler colonialism was legitimate, invincible, and inevitable to disavow Indigenous resistance's reminder that it has never been a secure project.

In his anti-imperialist study of the history of the transcontinental railroad, Manu Karuka theorizes US capitalism as "continental imperialism." Returning to Lenin's theory of imperialism, Karuka explains that nineteenth-century US capitalism operated in the mode of imperialism through its settler colonization of Indigenous territories well before the point at which Lenin saw capitalism evolve into imperialism on a global scale at the turn of the century. "The colonization of

North America, and of the Plains in particular, anticipated and triggered many of the global dynamics that Lenin analyzed. . . . [V]iewed from Indigenous places [US] capitalism actually began in an imperial mode—capitalism is imperialism."[36] As a form of continental imperialism, US capitalism has always been a war machine targeting Indigenous nations for destruction.[37] Whereas war trophies celebrated settler imperial war as "civilization" conquering "savagery," Indigenous anticolonialism has illuminated how imperial war has been a struggle between classes and not a completed project. Settler colonialism has been the history of class struggle between Indigenous anticolonialism and settler capital. Indigenous nations have waged campaigns to defend land bases and maintain collective social relations against the incursions of imperial war.

Yet Indigenous anticolonialism has not merely been the struggle of Indigenous peoples against settler colonialism. Rather, it has been both the fight to defeat colonization *and* the effort to maintain the future-oriented development of Indigenous collective life opposed to capitalist social relations. In his study of the Oceti Sakowin's resistance to US imperialism, Nick Estes explains that "ancestors of Indigenous resistance didn't merely fight *against* settler colonialism; they fought *for* Indigenous life and just relations with human and nonhuman relatives, and with the earth."[38] Similarly, Joanne Barker, in her study on the settler state's repression of Indigenous resistance, argues that Indigenous governance is incompatible with capitalism. Against capitalism's atomization of social relations and violent class structure, Indigenous governance is rooted in "relationality and responsibility within and across species, territories, and waters" and "upholds values of reciprocity, generosity, and cooperation."[39] As such, Indigenous governance has always existed as an alternative to class society. "It is an insistence," Barker writes, "that things do not have to be the way they are, that another way is not only possible but already being lived out through other understandings of land and water, kin relationships, and territorial-based practices."[40]

When viewed this way, Indigenous governance possesses a revolutionary character in relation to US class society. It aspires to maintain and win collective life beyond capitalism. In *The Red Nation Rising*, Nick Estes, Melanie Yazzie, Jennifer Denetdale, and David Correia write that

> as anti-colonial movements the world over have demonstrated, the colonial relation—who stole the land, who works it, how it became a commodity—is the capital relation. Anti-colonial struggles are the strongest forms of class struggle. These struggles seek the annihilation of the ruling class *and* the working class, because a classless society subordinates no one group to another. However, decolonization requires the annihilation of the settler's privileged position and the recuperation of Native nationhood, where classes would cease to exist, and land and wealth would be restored not according to privilege but according to Native relations premised on reciprocity, equality, and justice.[41]

Due to their revolutionary character, Indigenous governance and anticolonialism face naked retributive violence from the state. "It is the very viability of this alternative to state control," writes Barker, "that the state responded and continues to respond [to] with such violent, suppressive force."[42] Barker explains that the state's tactic for legitimizing this reactionary violence is to characterize Indigenous governance and anticolonialism as terrorism, to deem Indigenous rebels murderable.

Building on Barker's analysis, I suggest that if Indigenous anticolonialism is not only the fight against, but also for an alternative to, class society, settler colonialism might be thought of as a war to accumulate that is conducted as a counterrevolution against Indigenous governance. If settler imperial expansion "proceeds through the nexus of war and finance," as Karuka contends, it is warfare whose mode or orientation is counterrevolution in relation to the noncapitalist social relations and governance of Indigenous peoples.[43] In the context of the class struggle between wage labor and capital, counterrevolution is understood as a strategy that the bourgeois class activates in response to specific moments of the proletariat's revolutionary insurgency or seizure of power. Yet as I examine in chapter 2, settler colonialism has functioned from its inception as an anticipatory or preventative counterrevolutionary war against noncapitalist Indigenous governance precisely because this form of governance relates as a viable alternative for collective life, already in positive form, to capitalism. If settler colonialism expropriates Indigenous land to secure a base for its accumulation processes, it also wages this war of expropriation as the fight to vanquish a competing political and economic system whose presence as a viable alternative threatens its hegemony and legitimacy.

Here I build on Karuka's important work on the relationship between Indigenous social relations and US countersovereignty. Karuka argues that "to focus on expansion is to focus on adaptation to prior and ongoing modes of relationship. The peculiarity of American institutions is the face of adaption and reaction to Indigenous modes of relationship. This adaptation and reaction are what I am referring to as 'countersovereignty.'"[44] Joining this conversation, I contend that settler colonialism as anti-Indian counterrevolution depends on what I refer to as settler mass militarism. I define *settler mass militarism* as the project of making all settler-citizens into anti-Indian combatants tasked with conducting, either directly or indirectly, anti-Indian counterrevolution to advance settler colonialism. Like white alliance policing, settler mass militarism is also a cross-class endeavor unifying European workers with capital, but with the slightly different yet interrelated objective of repressing Indigenous anticolonialism and governance. Like Black revolution of abolition war, it was the revolutionary threat of Indigenous anticolonialism as a viable alternative political economy to settler class society that invoked the creation and development of settler mass militarism. The Indigenous anticolonial wars of the antebellum nineteenth century threw into sharp relief this dialectic of Indigenous anticolonialism—as the assertion of noncapitalist governance and political economy—and the consolidation of settler mass militarism.

COUNTERREVOLUTION AND REPRODUCTION

W. E. B. Du Bois and, more recently, Gerald Horne have offered significant contributions to the work of conceptualizing the relationship between race and counterrevolution. In *Black Reconstruction*, Du Bois traces how Black worker resistance precipitated the Civil War, won emancipation, and momentarily achieved a dictatorship of Black labor over slavery capitalism housed in the Reconstruction program.[45] Black labor's power over southern capital laid a foundation for the potential consolidation of abolition democracy. However, this trajectory was interrupted by capital's campaign to restore its lost power. Du Bois describes this response as a counterrevolution of property that ultimately defeated Black labor's dictatorship and its march toward abolition democracy. Reconstruction had held the potential for the revolutionary transformation of North America and beyond. Du Bois reads this potential where other historians saw in Reconstruction only failure or worse inevitable defeat. By reading the class struggle between emancipation and racial capitalism, Du Bois reveals both how Black labor served as a revolutionary actor and how capital could restructure and adapt to mount a counterrevolutionary restoration of power. In this counterrevolution of property that united Southern and Northern capital against Black labor, poor whites, Du Bois points out, lamentably pledged loyalty to capitalism over the commitment to working-class objectives of a Black Reconstruction. This betrayal bolstered the counterrevolution of property and struck a blow against the project of abolition democracy.

Historian Gerald Horne has centered counterrevolution in his work on the history of settler colonialism and slavery. Horne details how early settler colonialism from the sixteenth to seventeenth centuries encountered formidable rebellion from enslaved Africans and Indigenous nations. As a result, European settlers were moved to develop a Pan-European unity of whiteness to band together despite their differences of religion, ethnicity, and class with the common objective of upholding settler colonialism and slavery. Horne argues that the American revolution was less a progressive development than a reactionary settler rebellion against British mainland authorities to obtain the capacity to wage counterrevolution to repress Black and Native resistance to settler colonialism and slavery.[46] Both Horne and Du Bois concentrate on specific periods of white counterrevolutionary activity. Counterrevolution is conceived as reactive to episodic eruptions of revolutionary victories by the enslaved and colonized. I extend the work of Du Bois and Horne by understanding white counterrevolution as *both* reactive and anticipatory. It is reactive in how Black rebellion and Indigenous anticolonialism waged insurgencies challenging US class society requiring counterrevolutionary repression and containment. White counterrevolution is also anticipatory in the way that it organizes modes of policing and militarism that are preventative of potential insurgencies. Its anticipatory character presumes insurgencies for collective life will always surface from the conditions of racial capitalism itself. The construction of white alliance policing and settler mass militarism indexes a need to head off the always present danger of irrepressible revolutionary ruptures.[47]

This theory of white counterrevolution helps us think through debates about capitalism's reproduction and expansion in Marxist thought. For Marx, capital accumulation transforms from the stage of primitive accumulation to mature industrial forms when the relations of production reproduce their own presuppositions, operating within an enclosed circuit of production and circulation that not only accumulates surplus value for the sake of it—the distinguishing trait of capitalism—but also, at the same time, reproduces the process itself. The production processes become, at the same time, the reproduction of the social system of capitalism. When the relations of production reproduce their own conditions of possibility—workers receive the product of their labor to satisfy their needs, and capital accumulates a portion of value to replenish spent fixed capital—Marx calls this *simple reproduction*. When the relations of production reproduce their own presuppositions with the addition of extracting surplus value through the exploitation of labor power, capitalism uses this added surplus value to expand its capacity to accumulate further surplus value. Marx calls this *expanded reproduction*. The process repeats on larger scales.

Expanded reproduction is also the level of capitalist maturation at which the state's use of direct force is no longer needed as a principal vehicle for upholding capitalism's relations of production. At the level of expanded reproduction, workers are fully absorbed by capitalist production or forced to depend wholly on wage labor for the reproduction of their lives. In these conditions, workers are principally controlled by what Marx referred to as the "silent compulsion" of abstract economic power rather than the direct force of the state. Marx writes, "The organization of the capitalist process of production, once fully developed, breaks down all resistance. The constant generation of a relative surplus population keeps the law of supply and demand of labour, and therefore keeps wages, within narrow limits which correspond to capital's valorization requirements. The silent compulsion of economic relations sets the seal on the domination of the capitalist over the worker. Direct extra-economic force is still of course used, but only in exceptional cases."[48] In mature or fully developed capitalism, it is only when workers dialectically transform their association as those subjected by the capitalist production process into conscious collective resistance that capital must command the power of the state to deploy direct force to repress worker struggles, such as by breaking strikes or criminalizing union activity. However, as Marx contends, this use of force is exceptional, unlike when it was primary during the stages of primitive accumulation. State violence is only introduced in times when worker resistance poses risks to the reproduction of the relations of production. Marx implies that capitalism's expanding reproduction on greater scales hinges on a corresponding rise in the silent compulsion of economic power. While the state remains the sole purveyor of force protecting the relations of production from worker resistance, this role fades into the background in proportion to the full development of capitalism's production process centered around the exploitation of wage labor. Theorists who foreground the European industrial proletariat in the critique of capitalism surmise that capital's interest in scaling up its capacity to exploit labor power without the costly use of direct force to control workers was what drove it to turn to wage labor over formal slavery.[49] This view ignores, however, how Black rebellion was the force that incurred these costs that drove capitalists to transition to wage labor as an alternative source of value.[50]

Following Marx's own observation that capitalism develops differently across contexts, or as he says, "the history of [capitalist] expropriation assumes different aspects in different countries, and runs through its various phases in different orders of succession, and at different historical epochs," in North America it has not been strictly state violence or the silent compulsion of economic power that reproduces capitalist social relations. Rather, it has been the project of white counterrevolution, whose pillars of white alliance policing and settler mass militarism operate beyond centralized state violence.[51] What I mean by this is not simply white vigilantism. The cross-class unity and mass character underpinning white counterrevolution are the base from which the state draws its power to repress in the first place. The state tries to centralize the execution of white counterrevolution through its formal institutions of the police, prisons, and military. However, white alliance policing and settler mass militarism are broader and deeper than these formal state institutions. They exist at the level of the social, where the imperative to guard against Black revolution and Indigenous anticolonialism has organized the very form of US society. It is not just the centralized state that deploys force to reproduce capitalism. White counterrevolution at a mass level performs this work that extends state power but also operates independent of it. Historically, white workers face silent compulsion and exceptional uses of state violence to contain their resistance. The enslaved and colonized have confronted white counterrevolution as a form of mass violence that also becomes centralized by the state. In this aspect I build on the work of Dylan Rodríguez, who theorizes whiteness as the long history of "white reconstruction" that deploys anti-Black and racial-colonial domestic warfare to ensure the ascendancy of white being in the face of abolitionist and anticolonial resistance.[52]

COUNTERREVOLUTION AND FREE LABOR

The study of white counterrevolution also helps intervene in debates about the role of whiteness in mediating the relationship between European workers and capitalism. Foundational works of the critical study of whiteness have explored the causes for poor, landless, and exploited European workers to support capitalism, settler colonialism, and slavery over building working-class unity with fellow exploited and dispossessed people like enslaved Africans or colonized Indigenous people. In recent years this issue has reemerged in mainstream discourse with the rise of reactionary Far Right political figures, like Donald Trump, who appear to court the support of the so-called white working class. Theodore Allen's influential study *The Invention of the White Race* posits that early capitalism's ruling class fashioned whiteness as a tool of social control over the working class, at the time composed of both English and African bond laborers. Surveying the conditions of seventeenth-century chattel bond labor in the Virginia colony with special attention to Bacon's rebellion of 1676, Allen maintains that elite planters governing the colony invented the white race to be a cross-class political standing conferring privileges on English workers over

African workers. These privileges, which marked English workers as members of the "white" race, secured their loyalty to the planter class. The planter class sought this loyalty in response to European and African workers uniting in Bacon's rebellion against the colony's authorities. While Bacon's rebellion, as discussed in more detail in chapter 1, was more of a settler revolt by one faction of settler property owners to expropriate Indigenous land, which precipitated an intra-settler division among the planter ruling class over how to conduct settler imperial expansion, Allen maintains that the combination of English and African workers in support of one faction of the ruling class against another was enough to alarm the planter elite to devise a better strategy of social control over the working class.[53] "White skin privilege," as Allen characterizes it, worked to deradicalize European workers from rebelling going forward. It neutralized their desire to rebel against unfair laboring conditions and severed their radical combination with enslaved Africans.[54] While Allen acknowledges that membership in the white race required that the English workers help in the policing of enslaved Africans, his project is more concerned with elucidating the role of whiteness in removing European workers from revolutionary anti-capitalist struggle.

David Roediger conceptualizes whiteness as a form of psychological compensation offsetting the white worker's subjection to wage labor exploitation. Roediger studies how Northern white labor of the antebellum period confronted the ills of burgeoning industrial production by appealing to white supremacy for immunity from magnified forms of capitalist domination. White workers legitimated their demands for immunity from capitalist domination against Black subjugation. They deserved protection from proletarian life not because they opposed capitalism but because they were not "Black." White workers deemed wage labor unjustified "white slavery," a grievance premised on assuming blackness equaled enslavement. Roediger notes that the cry of white slavery would eventually give way to defining wage labor as un-enslaveable free labor reserved for whites to maintain a racial hierarchy between white and Black labor in the job market and workplaces of Northern waged work. Like Allen, Roediger seeks to explain how whiteness worked to neutralize white labor's potential rebellion against capitalism during a time of newly intensified capitalist domination.[55]

The response to this work by Allen and Roediger, and that of Noel Ignatiev, Alexander Saxton, Cheryl Harris, and others has emphasized the attention to whiteness as privilege, symbolic value, and property that prevents white workers from engaging in revolutionary struggle.[56] Such attention, I contend, has overshadowed these works' interest in the history of whiteness in the contexts of repressing Black and Indigenous revolutionary struggle. The analytic of white counterrevolution of this study—which as mentioned owes much to Gerald Horne's work and is a return to Du Bois's foregrounding of counterrevolution—regrounds the study of whiteness as a reactionary project born from the contexts of US class society's imperative to manage Black revolution and Indigenous decolonization. This regrounding of whiteness in the history of anti-Black and anti-Indian counterrevolution helps us better see the location of whiteness within the logic of the social reproduction of racial capitalism. When whiteness is conceptualized as the vehicle for deradicalizing the white proletariat, it is often understood as a conscious tactic of the ruling class that, when recognized as such, white workers can individually refuse in order to engage in revolutionary struggle. Ignatiev's slogan that "treason to whiteness is loyalty to humanity" remains a revolutionary call for white workers to betray how whiteness conscripts them to be loyal to class society, while also historically helping with the latter's enforcement.[57] However, what the history of white counterrevolution demonstrates is that whiteness is more than a conscious tactic for controlling white workers. Rather, it is baked into capitalism's development as a repressive structure maintaining the reproduction of racialized class society. As I explore in chapter 3, one of my aims in the study of white counterrevolution is to understand how it structured European workers' confrontation with maturing forms of capitalism in the mid-nineteenth century. These workers participated in white alliance policing and settler mass militarism to conduct white counterrevolution. In turn, white counterrevolution structured how they responded to the growth of wage labor and the intra-white settler conflict this produced between white labor and capital.

ANTI-CAPITALIST NINETEENTH-CENTURY AMERICA

No More Peace also contributes to the rediscovery of the revolutionary anti-capitalist character and trajectory of nineteenth-century abolition and anticolonialism. Often abolition and anticolonialism are viewed through the lens of civil rights. They are considered important stages in the long history of marginalized people fighting to win rights and representation in US democracy. While abolition and anticolonialism certainly contained a diversity of strategies, tactics, and positions, historians have emphasized the civil rights framework for understanding these movements. I foreground the currents of revolutionary insurgency in the history of antebellum abolition and anticolonialism that emerged materially from the conditions of racial capitalism. As such, I write a history of abolition and anticolonialism that reveals how such movements contained organic forms of revolutionary anti-capitalist struggle in North America that have not been recognized in scholarship. Just as Marx and Engels theorized communism as the movement taking root among European workers during this same period to seize power from the bourgeoisie and impose a worker-governed society to usher in a classless future, abolition and anticolonial wars were campaigns to win an alternative society organized around collective life. With this as their trajectory, abolition and anticolonialism produced theorists of revolutionary anti-capitalism who are not typically considered within this tradition. Abolition and anticolonial war thinkers were anti-capitalist and anti-imperialist theorists whose understanding of racial capitalism and revolutionary strategy not only anticipated but also, as studied here, expand Marxist thought of later traditions.

I join scholars who have recently written histories or theorized the revolutionary anti-capitalist character of nineteenth-century social movements of the enslaved and colonized. Christina Heatherton's *Arise!* argues that the ascendency of US imperialism from the nineteenth to twentieth centuries dialectically gave rise to an overlooked revolutionary proletarian internationalism rooted in the worker and peasant resistance of the Mexican revolution.[58] Nick Estes's *Our History Is the Future* writes the history of Indigenous anticolonialism of the Oceti Sakowin nation from the nineteenth century to recent land defense campaigns against extractive industries at Standing Rock, North Dakota.[59] Bernadine Hernández's *Border Bodies* examines the lives and struggles of nineteenth-century Mexicana, Nuevomexicana, Californiana, and Tejana women and their resistance to capitalism and colonialism. Hernández argues that these women's bodies were crucial to US capitalism's conquest of the West and Southwest, in which gender and sexual violence was used to expand capitalist relations of production and reproduction.[60] Holly Jackson's *American Radicals* rediscovers a radicalism among the various social reform movements of the antebellum period, arguing that they aspired for revolutionary transformation.[61] Like these studies, *No More Peace* demonstrates that nineteenth-century abolition and anticolonialism were not movements of a precapitalist history, as they are sometimes characterized by some traditions of Western Marxism. Rather, they compose the history of class struggle of capital's period of primitive accumulation, which did not end but is ongoing, in the way that anti-Black accumulation and settler colonialism are continuous in their role as the foundations of modern US racial capitalism.

No More Peace also illuminates an archive of nineteenth-century representations and thought produced by militant social movements whose insights are pressing and relevant for understanding many of the contradictions of modern US racial capitalism and its terrain of class struggle in our contemporary era. We are in a period when the dialectic of resistance and repression has sharpened. Recent decades have witnessed progressive uprisings catalyzed by Black, Indigenous, and colonized peoples' struggles. They have been met by spiraling global state violence, militarism, counterinsurgency, and deadly insurgent white nationalism. Marx was right in his prediction that the internal accumulation crisis of capitalism would catch up with its capacity for expansion. As many scholars emphasize, Western capitalism has entered a stage of terminal crisis in which large portions of the working class are excluded from waged labor and treated as surplus humanity or waste standing in the way of the profit motive; environmental destruction is creating an unhabitable planet; and imperialist wars, both direct and hybrid, have raged to resolve the problem of capitalism's accumulation crisis, and perhaps more principally, to destroy competing economies, especially ones that seek to provide for the needs of people and the planet over profit. A theory of white counterrevolution becomes pivotal for understanding how capitalism responds to the forces that threaten its stability and legitimacy. It teaches us that capitalist power will navigate the current conditions of crisis and rebellion through the strategies and tactics developed during its long history of white counterrevolution. The project forged to manage Black revolution and Indigenous anticolonialism is, in turn, deployed against all people striving to achieve alternative futures.

CHAPTER OVERVIEW

Chapter 1 studies slave revolt and fugitivity as strategies of abolition war to illuminate the history of the consolidation of white alliance policing during the antebellum period. I examine the Stono rebellion of 1739, in which enslaved Africans held captive in the British colony of South

Carolina led a powerful revolt that momentarily cleared the way to escape to Spanish-controlled Florida territory, where they were promised freedom. While their escape was thwarted by colonial militias, the revolt shook the foundations of the colony. This led British settlers to fashion the infrastructure of a white alliance policing that would serve as a model for decades to come. From there, I examine in further detail Nat Turner's insurrection and how, as mentioned, it both paralyzed and compelled a retooling of white alliance policing. Turner's insurrection also accelerated abolition organizing. The Underground Railroad expanded, and abolition propaganda and print culture amassed greater power and thus influence. I study the period of anti-abolition mobs of the 1830s and the later passing of the Fugitive Slave Act (1850) as expressions of a hardening and nationalizing of white alliance policing trying to curb revolt and fugitivity from erupting into Black revolution. The chapter culminates with a reading of the Black abolitionist Martin Delany's *Blake; or, The Huts of America* (1859), which synthesizes the history of slave revolt and fugitivity by imagining the enslaved from the US South to Cuba conspiring to wage Black revolution. Delany's representation of international Black revolution maps the dialectic of Black rebellion and white alliance policing. Through this, the novel illuminates the linchpin role of white alliance policing in the enforcement of US racial capitalism. The novel also envisions how abolition war led by slave insurgency held the potential for attacking the weak points of white counterrevolution through internationalism.

Chapter 2 examines two flashpoints in the history of Indigenous anticolonial war during the antebellum period and what they reveal about the role of settler mass militarism in conducting anti-Indian counterrevolution. The first flashpoint was the Second Seminole War of Florida (1835–1842), in which Seminoles, Black Seminoles, and Black maroons united to wage an insurgency to repel Florida settler planters and US military forces as they refused to submit to the Indian removal policy of the 1830s. Known as the "Florida War," the Second Seminole

War ended in the defeat of the US regular army, as the Seminole insurgency could not be successfully repressed. US leaders debated the role of settler mass militarism in their strategy of anti-Indian counterrevolution, with many complaining that it should have been bolstered in Florida because the regular army alone had failed to subdue the Seminoles. I explore this anxiety related to the lack of a mass base of settlers in Florida and how, as a result, US leaders called for settlers to be hailed as armed combatant occupiers essential to anti-Indian counterrevolution, to avoid defeat going forward.

From there, I study Indigenous land defense and Mexican anticolonialism in what became California following the US imperial seizure of Mexico's territories in the Southwest after 1848. This was a period that witnessed settler colonialism in its most naked form. Rushes on land and gold became genocidal campaigns to eliminate Indigenous peoples and dispossess Mexican populations. This flashpoint serves as a counterpoint to the Second Seminole War, in that settler mass militarism was the vanguard force leading the US settler colonization of Indigenous California rather than the US state's regular army. I elucidate that this context best demonstrates how settler mass militarism was marked by a democratic, cross-class, grassroots collaboration among settlers. That is, it was through democratic participation and grassroots mobilization that settlers performed counterinsurgent warfare against Indigenous and Mexican anticolonialism. The chapter culminates with a reading of Cherokee author John Rollin Ridge's novel *Joaquín Murieta* (1854), which dramatizes the historical events of its titular character's anticolonial insurgency against invading US settlers in the years following 1848. Ridge's novel is famous for its sensational form as a precursor to what later became the western dime novel. While the novel is rife with ideological and formal contradictions related to its representation of anticolonial resistance, I read them as productive rather than limiting. These contradictions crystallize the dialectic of anticolonial war and settler mass militarism, which in dominant narratives is often disavowed to legitimize settler violence as self-defense, while demonizing anticolonial resistance to settler colonization and genocide. Through its contradictions, Ridge's novel exposes settler violence as reactionary and thus illegitimate in its role of advancing white counterrevolution, challenging narratives that portrayed settlers as victims of anticolonial wars rather than the aggressors who introduced the violence in the first place. I also study how Ridge represents the autonomous character of settler mass militarism in relation to the state, revealing how such autonomy defies the oversight of the state in waging anti-Indian war in ways that prove destabilizing to the legitimacy and reproduction of US settler society.

Chapter 3 studies how white counterrevolution recursively determined European workers' confrontation with their increased absorption in capitalist production of the later decades of the antebellum period. I argue that the cross-class alliances of white counterrevolution engendered among European workers an aspiration for white equality, a dream of European labor to be a coruler in the governance of capital. This was a utopian demand, I suggest, that exceeded what David Roediger has called a *herrenvolk republicanism*, in which a shared white racial standing legitimated the class inequality between white labor and capital. I trace the history of the aspiration for white equality within the labor movements of antebellum America. It was during this moment that white counterrevolution, I contend, formed a tension with emerging industrial capitalism. The aspiration for white equality emerging from the cross-class alliances of white counterrevolution was shattered by industrializing capital that increasingly sourced European workers as an exploitable labor force. This contradiction between the aims of industrializing capital and the aspiration for white equality came to spawn, I reveal, the monster of white insurgency in which European workers waged reactionary attacks on the state to bend it to their aim of securing white equality. I locate white insurgency erupting in the vigilante filibustering movements to establish white equality in Central America and the murderous anti-union draft riots of New York City. These moments of white insurgency form a prehistory to contemporary forms of insurgent white nationalism that have arisen in recent years in response to this continuous contradiction between the aspiration for white equality and the logics of value made worse in our period of deindustrializing capital.

Chapter 4 investigates the revolutionary insurgency of abolition war during the 1850s, focusing on the campaigns of John Brown and Harriet Tubman. I argue that the partisans of abolition war held and enacted a revolutionary theory of racial capitalism, white counterrevolution, and Black revolution. I look at John Brown's campaign from Kansas to Harper's Ferry as a group of abolition war thinkers who conceptualized the enslaved as the pivotal vanguard force stitching together and driving forward abolition war toward the revolutionary end of overthrowing racialized class society. I offer a close reading of Brown's plan at Harper's Ferry and Osborne Anderson's memoir of his experience as a leader in Brown's campaign. They envisioned a strategy of what I call a *dictatorship of abolition over slavery* that paralleled European communism's theory of a dictatorship of the proletariat and anticipated Du Bois's concept of abolition democracy that unfolded later through the Reconstruction program. I also read Harriet Tubman's theory of slavery and her guerrilla raids on the South in the Underground Railroad. I show that she understood slavery as a Manichean relationship for which only abolition war was the answer. Her raids as strikes against slavery were rehearsals for the general strike of the enslaved that, as Du Bois detailed, would take place at the onset of the Civil War. I read Brown and Tubman's campaigns as composed of thinkers who should be seen as practicing a historical materialism paralleling but also stretching European Marxism at the time. They theorized that Black revolution was the vanguard force for consolidating an international movement whose trajectory was not merely the abolition of formal slavery but the overturning of the class rule of US capitalism premised on slavery.

The conclusion reflects on how the period of abolition and anticolonial wars and white counterrevolution provides relevant insight for understanding our present era, marked by abolition and anticolonial rebellions, white reactionary backlash, and global counterrevolutionary state violence. I examine how contemporary capitalism depends on white counterrevolution to manage its worsening accumulation crisis. The strategies for managing abolition and anticolonial wars of the nineteenth century are the foundations of how US class society today represses anti-imperialist resistance in the context of worsening crises. I also trace how white counterrevolution explains the rise of insurgent fascism today and its relationship to the state. I reflect on how the critical view of white counterrevolution helps us grasp the latent fragility of racial capitalism. The necessity to construct, deploy, and renew white counterrevolution reveals the very presence of movements with the capacity to win collective life. Abolition and anti-imperialism are the unfinished movements of abolition and anticolonial wars of the nineteenth century. Their origins in revolutionary war for alternatives to class society are a reminder for us today that reform is counterinsurgency or what revolutionary abolitionist George Jackson simply called fascism, and that the myths of the inevitability and invincibility of class society that proliferate today merely hide its true nature as a paper tiger.

1

SLAVE REVOLT, FUGITIVITY, AND WHITE ALLIANCE POLICING

IN HIS FAMOUS STUDY of the Haitian Revolution, C. L. R. James notes that when the enslaved launched their first waves of revolt, they turned the enslavers' plantations to ashes. Fire was their weapon of choice. Haiti's Black proletariat destroyed rather than seized the island's means of production. It was a military choice. The enslaved knew, better than anyone, that destroying the enslaver's means of production was a death knell to the enemy's capacity to maintain slavery and contain the revolt. The destruction of the plantation factories would also combat efforts to restore enslaver power on the island. Following the principles of guerrilla warfare, the enslaved hit the enemy where it hurt, to weaken them, creating a more equitable terrain on which to wage a protracted war of liberation. James also tracked how Haiti's white planter class, in their lust for profits, blindly ignored the warning signs of impending revolt and continued to import enslaved Africans while intensifying the use of terror and brutality to enforce plantation discipline.[1] "Haiti was a volcano," writes Geo Maher, "because those in power, like so many afflicted by the white blind spot born of colonial domination, simply could not grasp so 'unthinkable' an event or the vastness of its implications."[2] The numbers of enslaved grew out of proportion to the minority planter class. The enslaved took advantage of the island's disproportionate class structure. The enslavers could call in a standing army from across the Atlantic, but by the time French military forces arrived, Haiti's Black revolution was well underway. It could not be halted. As smoke billowed from razed plantations and enslavers scrambled to flee the island, the white world beyond Haiti observed with consternation the unfolding revolt and its success in upending slavery.

George Washington's presidency spared no expense in providing resettlement assistance for fleeing enslavers routed from Haiti. In February 1793 Washington approved a bill that secured $15,000 in treasury funds in "support of such of the inhabitants of Saint Domingo, resident within the United States." Weeks earlier, members of Congress had written a letter to Washington imploring him to approve the funding to secure aid for French enslavers who had been "driven from St[.] Domingo by the Savage Barbarity of the People of Colour." They saw it as a grave injustice that Black revolt had reduced French enslavers and their families to destitution: "Men Women and Children most of them a few Months since in the highest Affluence who are destitute of every necessary of Life." Aiding French enslavers fulfilled the US obligations "to Humanity, to Christian Charity and to [its] National Character." That is, it was an act of white solidarity.[3] The newly formed United States was skilled at this practice of white solidarity. It was what set US enslavers apart, we could say, from French enslavers in Haiti. White solidarity emerged from the need of enslavers to harness their class power to guard against the resistance of the enslaved and colonized in North America. In US racial capitalism, slavery and settler colonialism grew together. The enslaver was also the settler, which is to say, not only a trafficker of enslaved Africans but a permanent occupier of Indigenous lands. The intertwined relationship between enslavement and settler colonialism required strong alliances among Europeans to guard against the resistance of those whom these projects targeted. In US class society, white alliances have been formidable and have proven an effective tool for preventing revolutionary revolts like that in Haiti. This chapter explores white alliances and their role in the reproduction of US class society. I examine the relationship between abolition wars and what I call white alliance policing to historicize and theorize how enslaved Africans' struggle for liberation shaped US capitalism's structures of repression and enforcement, which reproduce its social relations.

In *Black Reconstruction*, Du Bois offers a foundational critique of this relationship between policing and whiteness. He identifies the white proletariat's alliance with enslavers in protecting slavery from Black rebellion: "The system of slavery demanded a special police force and such a force was made possible and unusually effective by the presence of the poor whites."[4] With this assistance of poor whites, US enslavers, despite fears of the Haitian Revolution spreading to North America, "were nevertheless able to stamp out slave revolt.... [T]he whole white South became an armed and commissioned camp to keep Negroes in slavery and to kill the black rebel."[5] Recently, historian Gerald Horne has theorized whiteness as a pan-Europeanism forged in early capitalism to unify people across class and difference to guard settler colonialism and slavery against Black and Native insurgency.[6] European proletarians were just as, or perhaps more, useful to the ruling class as a policing force for early capitalism than they were as exploited laborers.[7] As Horne explains, "The enslaved produced wealth and the Europeans became more useful as occupiers of indigenous land and monitors of indigenes and the enslaved and the like."[8] Joining these conversations, this chapter argues that abolition war, through its strategies of slave revolt and fugitivity, gave rise to white alliance policing, which in turn functioned as slavery's vital structure of repression, securing capital accumulation. White alliance policing was executed through two strategies. The first was what I refer to as *prison guard whiteness*, whose task was to police slave revolt. The second was *slave catcher whiteness*, which repressed Black fugitivity. Prison guard and slave catcher whiteness can be best understood by examining key flashpoints when they were consolidated and refined in response to slave revolt and fugitivity. These flashpoints were the Stono rebellion (1739), Nat Turner's insurrection (1831), and the emergence of a more centralized abolition movement, including the expansion of the Underground Railroad from the mid-1830s to early 1840s.

Following the study of these flashpoints, I offer a reading of Black abolitionist Martin Delany's novel *Blake; or, The Huts of America* (1859) that imagines enslaved Africans of Cuba and the US South organizing mass insurrection to decimate slavery. While Delany is often recognized for advocating Black emigration beyond North America, leading scholars to read his novel in this context, he was also a coconspirator with John Brown's campaign of armed abolition insurgency in North America. As such, I read Delany's novel as a response to conversations on North American abolition war strategy among its partisans. One concern was the question of slavery's strategies of repressing armed abolition. Delany's *Blake* intervenes in this conversation by offering a critical reflection on white alliance policing and its role in upholding slavery, suggesting that its mass character made it slavery's linchpin strategy of repression for securing capital accumulation from revolt and fugitivity. The novel also reflects on how abolition war held the potential to outmaneuver and undermine white alliance policing to create openings for free workers to join the enslaved in pursuing revolutionary aims. This chapter's focus on Black abolition war and its constitutive role in the making of white alliance policing offers an expanded understanding of whiteness that looks beyond the analytics of white skin privilege and whiteness as a psychological wage, which remain touchstones in the critical study of whiteness. It also contributes to abolition theory's understanding of the modes of enforcement, repression, and counter-insurgency of capitalism that secure its power, authority, and continued existence.[9]

SLAVE REVOLT AND PRISON GUARD WHITENESS

Slavery was a war of capital accumulation against Africans. As Walter Rodney argues, Europe's theft of Africans and their labor delivered super-profits and meteoric growth for European capitalism and its colonies in the Americas, while resulting in the underdevelopment of African economies and thus ongoing vulnerability to exploitation and dispossession in the centuries to follow.[10] Slave revolts were capitalism's prisoners of war fighting back. They were also what precipitated the making of whiteness. Yet in the critical study of whiteness, scholars have centered a singular white settler revolt as the pivotal moment in the making of whiteness. In *The Invention of the White Race*, historian and labor organizer Theodore Allen famously argues that the constitutive event in the construction of whiteness and racial slavery was Bacon's rebellion of 1676. Nathaniel Bacon was a settler and an enslaver and a member of the Virginia colony's ruling elite. He owned a plantation at the western edge of the colony. Aggrieved that the Susquehannock and other Indigenous nations had defended their lands from illegal settler encroachments and thus impeded his pursuit of wealth, Bacon and fellow settlers provoked a war to displace them. Bacon proceeded to perpetrate several massacres against the Susquehannock. He also kidnapped and sold into slavery Indigenous women and children. Bacon had taken such actions without permission from the colony's governor, Sir William Berkeley, creating a schism among the ruling class that erupted into a civil war. Bacon represented a settler populism that sought to violently seize Indigenous lands to distribute them among land-hungry colonists.[11] Governor Berkeley represented a different faction of the colony's ruling class whose interest was in curbing intra-planter competition by limiting land access to new settler planters. Facing punishment by the colonial government, Bacon waged a campaign to overthrow Governor Berkeley's authority so he could pursue the policy of unrestricted enclosure of Indigenous lands.

Many European and African workers joined Bacon's revolt against Governor Berkeley. Allen argues that it was the class unity between European and African workers coalescing through the revolt that alarmed British enslavers. Allen's study is unclear whether European and African workers joined Bacon to fight for their freedom independent of his settler campaign or if the promise of land through conquest was the incentive for enlisting. Allen only highlights that Bacon granted freedom to all bond laborers who fought for him. Regardless, in the following years, to dissolve any budding unity between European and African workers and the power it gave the Virginia colony's working class to revolt, enslavers invented the "white race" as a privileged racial status to elevate European workers over African workers.

This elevation through conferring privileges on European bond laborers divided and thus weakened the working class's rebellion against early capitalism. White skin privileges—which promised immunity from the forms of violence to which Africans were subjected—bought the loyalty and therefore the consent to be ruled by capital among English workers of the early British settler colonies. In this way, the invention of the white race functioned to control European workers by preventing their rebellion against capital. Allen describes white racial pride as a safety valve, similar to workers accessing cheap or free land in the settler colonies, that released the pressure of class conflict and thereby liquidated European workers' desire to challenge their exploitation. The colony's planter class sought to create a "social control stratum" or group of free persons that could be a buffer between enslavers and the enslaved, like what was practiced in the British colonization of Ireland and Caribbean slavery of Jamaica. This group became exclusively

English workers deemed "white" rather than all free persons as in these other contexts due to the specter of European and African unity among bond laborers of Bacon's rebellion. Allen contends that racial oppression did not exist before Bacon's rebellion. It was strictly class oppression of Europeans and Africans who shared a similar class position as bond laborers. The introduction of racial oppression was opposed to "normal capitalism" that operated only by class oppression.[12]

However, the work of Cedric Robinson, and more recently Ruth Wilson Gilmore, suggests that "normal capitalism" has always been racial capitalism.[13] Slavery and colonialism were primary engines of capital accumulation legitimated through the racialization of the enslaved and colonized. As Sylvia Wynter argues, Africans and Indigenous people were deemed unfree persons, against which Europe defined its new bourgeois humanity. This process of defining the enslaved and colonized as the antithesis of European humanity was well underway before Bacon's rebellion. This is to say that slave revolt was much more of a principal motor force in the history of early capitalism's development than what Allen identifies in Bacon's rebellion as a European and African bond labor unity. In fact, the epicenter of early capitalism was Caribbean sugar production, performed primarily by African labor. It was not small-scale tobacco production of British settler colonies, which in the seventeenth century were minor outposts in North America compared to the booming colonies of the Caribbean. As Horne has noted, British settler colonies were importing practices from places in the Caribbean like Barbados on how to control enslaved Africans.[14] It is the history of slave revolt—the moments when Black abolition war went on the offensive—to which we should look for locating what has shaped the construction of whiteness in relation to capitalism's modes of repression. While there were hundreds of major slave revolts in North America from the sixteenth to nineteenth centuries, I want to examine two that were perhaps the most influential in terms of the development of prison guard whiteness as a tactic of white alliance policing. These were the Stono rebellion of 1739 and Nat Turner's insurrection of 1831.

THE STONO REBELLION

On the morning of September 9, 1739, around twenty enslaved Africans met near the Stono River twenty miles from Charleston in the plantation colony of South Carolina. They convened to review one last time their strategy and tactics for waging an insurrection and a mass escape that they would carry out in the hours to follow that shook the foundations of early slavery in North America.[15] Their goal was to break out of the British plantation colony and fight their way to Spanish Florida, where they had been promised freedom. Spanish authorities had offered freedom to enslaved Africans of the British colonies to deprive the English of laborers and recruit soldiers for potential invasion in a strategy of weakening a competing empire in the Americas.[16] The rebels first raided a local store, where they secured weapons and supplies in preparation for the inevitable battles that awaited them in their trek toward Spanish Florida. They killed the store owners and left their decapitated heads on the store's steps in a dialectical reversal of a common form of punishment enslavers used against rebellious enslaved Africans. Displaying the discarded heads as the footprints of the insurrection was a tactic meant to spread an arresting panic among enslavers, stalling their efforts to repress the rebellion. From there, the rebels visited plantation after plantation with fire and death, razing buildings, equipment, and crops. They killed any combatant whites who crossed their path. The insurrection gathered strength and confidence with each destroyed plantation.

Recruits joined the insurrection as the party marched south, chanting slogans of "Liberty" to the beat of drums and a raised flag. The rebels totaled anywhere from sixty to one hundred. After marching ten miles, they reached the Edisto River and rested in a nearby field.

Historians believe the rebels paused to allow for more recruits to augment their ranks to fortify their newly mobilized army.[17] With such numbers, arms, and organization, they were a match for any of the white militias that would come for them. Unfortunately, the choice to pause was a tactical mistake. In a tragic coincidence, Lieutenant Governor William Bull of the colony was traveling the same road that day en route to Charlestown for the upcoming legislative session. Bull spotted the rebellion from a distance and fled to sound the alarm for local militias to mobilize.[18] The rebels attempted to pursue Bull but gave up the chase. They did not know it was the lieutenant governor and allowed him to escape.[19] By the afternoon, white militias had caught up with the rebels near the Edisto River. A battle ensued in which dozens were killed and the remaining freedom seekers scattered. What was a troop of upward of one hundred splintered into small groups of maroons who would be hunted, captured, or killed in the following weeks, months, and years. While the insurrection had the potential to withstand defeat, it was contained, and the social order of slavery was once again stabilized.

Though the rebels fell short of escaping to Spanish Florida, they succeeded in their aim of terrorizing enslavers. In the aftermath of the Stono rebellion, enslavers went to work fashioning a more effective white alliance policing that could perform the counterrevolutionary prison guard labor necessary to prevent potential future revolts. The South Carolina General Assembly held discussions on how to prevent future slave revolts. These discussions led to the passing of the "Act for the Better Ordering and Governing of Negroes and Other Slaves," also known as the "Negro Act," in May 1740.[20] It granted authority to all white persons to stop and verify the passes of the enslaved who might be traveling between plantations. "If any slave who shall be out of the house or plantation . . . shall refuse to submit to or undergo the examination of any white person, it shall be lawful for any such white person to pursue, apprehend, and moderately correct such slave."[21] With this authority, all whites became prison guards of the plantation colony, tasked with regulating the movements of the enslaved. Furthermore, whites were expected to punish the enslaved who did not submit to prison guard whiteness. The act made Black self-defense punishable by death. Whites were granted the authority to "lawfully kill" any enslaved African who used physical force to defend against whippings, beatings, and other forms of violent punishments.[22]

The act also sanctioned all free persons to be slave catchers. For those deemed fugitives for escaping and seeking refuge in Spanish Florida, the General Assembly offered cash rewards for either their capture or death, in the form of scalp bounties ranging from thirty to fifty pounds for "every scalp of a grown negro slave, with the two ears."[23] Additionally, the act required that enslavers permanently reside on their plantations or have someone reside in their place to ensure potentially unoccupied plantations did not harbor fugitives. "That no person or persons hereafter shall keep any slaves on any plantation or settlement, without having a white person on such plantation or settlement."[24] This augmented the number of whites available to perform both prison guard and slave catcher labor. It also worked in tandem with efforts to recruit more European laborers as a policing force, while decreasing the number of imported enslaved Africans. The population of the enslaved far outweighed that of the free, and the assembly sought to remedy this quantitative imbalance in a way that in other contexts, like Haiti, enslavers did not, which had undermined their power to repress mass revolt. Following the Stono rebellion, enslavers thought carefully about their long-term class interest rather than immediate profits, by balancing in their favor the ratio of whites as police to the enslaved.

These responses to insurrection found in the "Negro Act" reveal calculated choices to fashion white alliance policing. The act enshrined white alliance policing as the principal tool of repression protecting slavery in the colony. From the landless to the propertied, every white was made a de facto slave patroller with the duty to perform prison guard work. This duty would be further developed in the years to come. Furthermore, whether whites worked formally as paid patrollers or informally as volunteers, white patrolling functioned as an anticipatory counterrevolution to prevent revolt. As historian Sally Hadden argues, "Patrols were originally designed to prevent or respond to the worst scenarios slave owners could imagine: slaves free to murder their masters or to run away without impediment."[25] Hadden also documents how from the late seventeenth to the eighteenth centuries a transformation took place in how patrolling was perceived and practiced. In response to slave revolts like the Stono rebellion, what was an expectation to volunteer became a required duty, leading later to the institutionalization of paid patrollers throughout the South by the nineteenth century as the beginnings of modern-day US police departments. "The shift," writes Hadden, "from voluntary effort to mandated duty effectively turned the entire white population into a community police force."[26]

The requirement for enslavers to permanently reside on their plantations, along with the effort to import European laborers as a police force, demonstrates how slave revolt compelled the enslaver ruling class to consolidate the nonenslaved across class and difference into counterrevolutionary communities.[27] European workers were positioned as prison guards and slave catchers first and laborers second. Enslavers were mandated to be on the front lines of enforcing slavery rather than seasonally visiting and administrating from a distance. From enslaver to poor white, it became the duty of every free person to patrol in times of "social peace," with both formal and informal slave patrolling as anticipatory counterrevolutionary forces, and to mobilize as a collective force at a moment's notice in times of emergency to contain Black revolt. The solidification of prison guard whiteness in the aftermath of the Stono rebellion thus shows how to be white was to fulfill the collective duty to carry out anticipatory and reactionary counterrevolution.

Figure 1. *Nat Turner & His Confederates in Conference.* Woodcut. New York: James D. Torrey, 1863. Schomburg Center for Research in Black Culture, Manuscripts, Archives and Rare Books Division, The New York Public Library, New York City. b15262566.

NAT TURNER'S INSURRECTION

Despite white print culture characterizing Nat Turner as a religious fanatic for leading an insurrection that momentarily destabilized slavery in Southampton County, Virginia, Turner was a clear-sighted military leader who had developed a sensible plan for deploying insurrection as a tactic for initiating a protracted military campaign to destroy slavery. He was explicit about this plan and its military objectives. As he shared later, his aim was to "conquer Southampton County as the white men did in the Revolution, and then retreat, if necessary, to the Dismal Swamp."[28] Turner sought to defeat local enslaver power and turn Southampton into a liberated zone or maroon camp. If this was not possible, he would join and reinforce others who had already won such a space in the autonomous maroon communities of the Great Dismal

Swamp. Winning a liberated zone would allow the enslaved to have a revolutionary base area from which to launch further attacks against slavery and sponsor more revolts, and it would serve as a maroon camp to receive those escaping from nearby plantations. This was a strategy for transforming revolt into Black revolution. It was not spontaneous revenge or even rebellion for the freedom of only a few of its participants. Turner is purported to have proclaimed, "Remember that ours is not war for robbery nor to satisfy our passions. It is a struggle for freedom. Ours must be deeds and not words."[29] It was an insurrection to kick-start a guerrilla offensive whose trajectory was the overthrow of slavery. Radical abolitionists like Henry Highland Garnet, William Lloyd Garrison, Harriet Tubman, and John Brown, not to mention the masses of enslaved African rebels, understood it as such.[30]

While they refused to admit it, enslavers also understood the revolutionary character and trajectory of Turner's insurrection. It was in response to it and what it portended that enslavers accelerated the development of white alliance policing to provide the necessary prison guard labor to protect anti-Black capital accumulation. These developments not only extended and consolidated previous forms of white alliance policing like those fashioned after the Stono rebellion less than a hundred years before, but also added new features. In the wake of Turner's insurrection and after the tide of retaliatory white violence subsided, the question of how to respond was debated in newspapers, legislative sessions, and local enslaver communities. While some proposed gradual emancipation to avoid future catastrophe, the more dominant and wealthier enslavers dismissed gradual abolition as fanatical.[31] They would never voluntarily emancipate the very class of laborers on whom their entire economic system rested. It would be class suicide or the end of anti-Black capital accumulation, the primary source of their wealth and existence.

Instead, enslavers called for a series of actions that fortified white alliance policing. Many of the measures taken after the Stono rebellion were repeated after Turner's insurrection. Enslavers demanded the strengthening of state militias, an increase in volunteer militias, greater access to firearms for all whites with the building of more arsenals, better organized and more pervasive slave patrols, and the overall imperative for the white community to unify around the task of mobilizing as the prison guard force to stop insurrection in times of emergency.[32] It became critical that not only must militias and patrols fulfill their purpose of anticipatory counterrevolutionary prison guard forces to prevent revolt, but the white community at large must develop stronger unity and greater discipline to crush revolt where preventative policing might have failed. This way white alliance policing was both preventative and reactive violence through the objective of counterrevolution.

The enslavers also took actions to prevent potential alliances between the enslaved and the free following the insurrection. While there is no evidence that poor whites directly assisted or participated in Turner's rebellion, he famously spared local poor whites from death because, in his experience, they were not as invested in white supremacy as enslavers.[33] It can only be speculated that this was the case because the poor whites he spared might have been closer to the insurrection than Turner or others were willing to divulge. Regardless, enslavers expected increased discipline and commitment from poor whites in their duty to help with prison guard labor following the insurrection. In March 1832, the General Assembly also passed laws that removed free persons of color from the area, writing that "it satisfactorily appears that it is absolutely necessary, not only to the correct government of their slaves, but also to the peace and safety of their society, that the free people of colour should be promptly removed from that country."[34] The assembly borrowed $15,000 to fund the forced removal and deportation of free persons of color to Liberia. White citizens agreed to be taxed to pay back the debt.[35] Enslavers sought to fashion the racialized class structure of slavery according to a social order that Frantz Fanon would later describe as a Manichean world in which there are

Figure 2. *Horrid Massacre in Virginia.* Woodcut frontispiece in *Authentic and Impartial Narrative of the Tragical Scene Which Was Witnessed in Southampton County (Virginia).* New York: Printed for Warner & West, 1831. Library of Congress Rare Book and Special Collections Division, Washington, DC. LC-USZ62-38902.

only two camps, a zone of being and nonbeing, the human and its antithesis, which in the case of slavery in the US context was the position of whiteness and that of the enslaved racialized as Black.[36] Efforts to solidify a Manichean world in Virginia following Turner's insurrection reveal how enslavers imagined the ideal composition and objectives of the white community. A Manichean class structure would serve as a more effective vehicle through which to organize the white community for counterrevolution. It isolated the enslaved from potential allies, which weakened their power to revolt. It also conscripted all free persons for prison guard work as a requirement for being a member of the white community. Virginia would be a community organized around white counterrevolution through the mass policing of the enslaved, in which if one was not organized and committed to these objectives, they would be removed or punished.

FUGITIVITY, ANTI-ABOLITION MOBS, AND SLAVE CATCHER WHITENESS

Nat Turner's revolt also inspired the centralization of the abolition movement in the 1830s, which in turn augmented the growth and reach of the Underground Railroad. These developments galvanized proslavery forces to criminalize and censor abolitionism in the South and awakened violent anti-abolition repression in the North. A flurry of what were called anti-abolition riots broke out in several major Northern industrial cities in the years following Nat Turner's insurrection. These were mobs of white supremacist vigilantes who mobilized to attack abolition organizing and Northern free Black communities. Some of the major anti-abolition mob attacks erupted in New York City (1834), Utica, New York (1835), Cincinnati, Ohio (1835, 1841), Boston (1835), and Alton, Illinois (1837). Historians have interpreted anti-abolition riots in terms of Northern white racism and the backlash against "amalgamation" or the incorporation of free Black communities in Northern white civil society.[37] However, I situate them in the history of white alliance policing, in which anti-abolition mobs were organic mobilizations seeking to destabilize abolition organizing and destroy Northern rear bases of the Underground Railroad to police Black fugitivity and its role in abolition war. They were, I suggest, rehearsals for later anti-abolition slave catcher invasions in the 1850s that served a similar counterrevolutionary function.

In the 1830s the formal antislavery movement was not guided by a revolutionary abolitionism embodied by Nat Turner. Pacifist Garrisonian abolition was its most radical strand. However, the antislavery movement began to take on a national character in its organizing efforts that sent shock waves through the proslavery South and anti-abolition North. Hundreds of antislavery organizations bloomed, and abolition propaganda began to proliferate in the press. The abolitionist pamphlet campaign of 1835 printed and distributed over a million pieces of abolition literature throughout the nation. These included woodcuts visually depicting the violence and cruelty of slavery. The newly invented steam press magnified the capacity for abolition publishing. This in turn increased the consolidation and centralization of the antislavery movement as a political force, even as, at the time, it remained largely a reform rather than revolutionary project. Nonetheless, the movement's enemies considered it radical and thus dangerous. What they feared was the antislavery movement's newly developed centralizing trajectory. They perceived that such centralization gave abolitionist organizers the power to mobilize masses of people to undermine slavery.

These dynamics manifested in the Cincinnati anti-abolition riot of 1841. From the evening of Friday, September 3, to the early morning hours of Sunday, September 5, white anti-abolition mobs attacked the Black community of Cincinnati. Whites assaulted Black residents, destroyed homes and businesses, looted valuables, and helped police and militias arrest over five hundred Black men. The mob attack resulted in dozens of injuries, several deaths, and the expulsion of hundreds of Black residents from the city. What precipitated the riot was the perception that abolitionist organizing was transforming Cincinnati into a city harboring a base of operations for the Underground Railroad. Earlier that summer, a member of the Cincinnati Anti-Slavery Society named Cornelius Burnett and his three sons had attempted to block the kidnapping of a fugitive slave. They had housed a fugitive slave, refusing to turn him over to the authorities. They fought the constables seeking to place the fugitive slave in custody. For this, Burnett and his sons were jailed, and a mob formed in retaliation for such open defiance of slave catching. While the mob was dispersed, it signaled what was to come later that September.[38]

In the weeks before the riot, tensions mounted between whites and the Black community in a series of incidents in which whites provoked Black residents, who in turn acted in self-defense to repel these aggressions. On September 2, a group of whites threw gravel at a Black couple taking a walk. Black residents confronted the harassers, and a fight broke out in which it was alleged two whites were stabbed, possibly fatally. This ignited a powder keg of anti-abolition fury. By the evening of the following day, Friday, September 3, a white mob had formed of up to fifteen hundred people. Their target was the neighborhood that was home to the city's free Black residents, which was the hub for abolition activity and power that was sponsoring fugitivity in the Underground Railroad.[39] Armed with clubs, axes, picks, and other weapons, the white mob launched an attack; much to its participants' surprise, they were met by armed Black residents shooting back. Anticipating a mob attack, the Black community had prepared an armed defense of their neighborhood. They were led by a formerly enslaved leader, Major James Wilkerson, who saw the necessity of fighting mob violence with muskets and rifles. For several hours the white mob was repeatedly pushed back by gunfire. Later they retrieved a cannon and shot scrap metal and boiler punchings indiscriminately at Black homes and businesses. Black residents continued to fire back, keeping the mob at bay. Not until county militias arrived later in the night and surrounded the Black neighborhood to form an open-air prison did the clashes temporarily pause.[40]

On Saturday the mayor held a city-wide meeting in the hopes of quelling the mob and restoring order. The meeting did none of this. Instead, city leaders capitulated to the mob's demands to enforce the defunct Black Codes of 1807, which required Black residents to pay a $500 bond to live in the city. The mob pressured city leaders to pass several resolutions, including the disarming of the Black community and the formation of white patrols tasked with policing the residency status of Black residents.[41] These resolutions emboldened the white mob to reignite their attack against the Black community on Saturday, including carrying out mass arrests with the aid of police and militias of Black residents. More than five hundred Black men were detained and taken to the newly created open-air prison area established by county militias. Their residency and free statuses were interrogated. If Black residents could not prove they had paid or could pay the $500 bond, they were at risk of removal from the city.[42]

With the Black community surrounded by county militias and hundreds of Black men having been arrested, authorities disarmed Black residents. This disarmament allowed white vigilantes to arrest more Black residents and greenlighted the mass looting of Black homes and businesses. This continued into Saturday night; the authorities did not disperse the mob until it threatened to burn down the Anti-Slavery Book Depository, which would have led to the destruction of nearby white-owned businesses and homes.[43] In the aftermath of the riot, whites were shocked that Black residents used armed self-defense to successfully repel the white mob when it was at its worst. In the weeks that followed, mob leaders also held a meeting to form their own anti-abolitionist society. They proclaimed that their objectives were to protect the economic interests of white families: "Abolitionists are practically destroying not only the peace and safety of society but endangering the means of subsistence upon which our wives and children depend. . . . Experience shows that the two races cannot live together on terms of equality—and while we protect the black man from inhumanity we shall firmly and steadily endeavor to fix him in his proper place. . . . [W]e war against Abolitionists—*white men*—who, disregarding the misery of the whites, make a parade of their kindly feelings towards the blacks."[44] While their stated aims might suggest that it was economic competition that motivated the mob attacks, mob leaders were "gentlem[en] of property and standing," as historian

Leonard Richards highlights. They led such attacks not because they feared job competition but rather to stop free Black communities and white abolitionists from organizing bases of refuge, support, and defense in the North as the infrastructure of the Underground Railroad's attack on slavery in the South. In this way, the anti-abolition riot was the rehearsal or precursor to what became a more organized and federalized strategy of slave catcher raids in the 1850s with the passing of the Fugitive Slave Law.[45]

EXPANDING FUGITIVITY
AND SLAVE CATCHER WHITENESS

Du Bois characterized antebellum fugitivity as a pressure release valve that offered another avenue for winning freedom beyond revolt.[46] It is estimated that from 1830 to 1860 more than fifty thousand enslaved Africans per year escaped to territories where slavery was abolished.[47] Fugitivity was a blow to the wealth of enslavers. Such numbers of people escaping each year was a tremendous loss of capital. Even worse, it was a loss of a lifetime of future profits from the stolen labor of each person who had liberated themselves. The enslaved were not only sources of wealth through their labor power but also served as the collateral against which enslavers could borrow funds to finance their plantation factories.[48]

As historian Manisha Sinh argues, fugitivity also produced the leaders and frontline soldiers of Northern revolutionary abolition, whose tactics of direct action, confrontation, and armed defense would culminate in the program of formal abolition war to end slavery.[49] Rising abolition war's key project was the Underground Railroad. The organization and expansion of the Underground Railroad from the late eighteenth century to the antebellum period was a militant project that directly attacked slavery. It was a sophisticated, clandestine machine that not only ushered the enslaved to freedom but provided defenses against attempts at recapture. As historians have documented, vigilance committees in Northern cities were one of the Underground Railroad's sharpest weapons, aiding fugitives to secure freedom, warning the community of slave catchers, and mobilizing to defend and in many cases rescuing recaptured fugitives.[50] From the loss of capital and future profits to fueling radical abolitionism, whose trajectory was a war to destroy slavery, fugitivity created a crisis for enslavers and their mode of anti-Black accumulation, at the center of racial capitalism.

It was this insurgent power of fugitivity and how it became organized into a militant, guerrilla project of the Underground Railroad that hastened the expansion of the second strategy of white alliance policing, namely the duty for all white persons to be slave catchers. As discussed previously, in the aftermath of the Stono rebellion all free persons were given the authority to pursue and capture fugitives, particularly those escaping to Spanish Florida. With the centralizing of the abolition movement and growth of the Underground Railroad following Turner's insurrection, slave catcher whiteness was federalized, which is to say, centralized for reactionary reasons. We can best see this in the history of the US state's use of the posse comitatus doctrine and the South's push to pass and enforce the fugitive slave laws of 1793 and 1850.[51]

The US Constitution provided enslavers the authority to travel across state lines to remand fugitives. In the years after its ratification, cases emerged in which slave catchers were blocked by free states from remanding fugitives, sparking calls from the South for federal legislation that would enforce the "right" of enslavers to hunt fugitive slaves in free states. Congress passed the Fugitive Slave Act of 1793 to appease enslavers and clarify that the Constitution granted authority to enslavers to retrieve their fugitive "property" across state lines.[52] In the following decades, as the abolition movement gained speed in the North, free states passed personal liberty laws that defied the Fugitive Slave Act of 1793.[53] However, two Supreme Court rulings would undermine the personal liberty laws and uphold the Fugitive Slave Law of 1973. In

Prigg v. Pennsylvania (1837), a slave catcher named Edward Prigg captured a person of African descent named Margaret. Local authorities charged and convicted Prigg with kidnapping for violating the state's personal liberty laws. Prigg appealed the conviction. It was overturned by the US Supreme Court, which upheld the constitutionality of the Fugitive Slave Law of 1793. In *Jones v. Van Zandt* (1846), Van Zandt was sued for helping fugitive slaves escape north. Van Zandt appealed the suit brought against him. When the case reached the Supreme Court, the judges voted not to overturn the suit against Van Zandt, arguing that the Fugitive Slave Law of 1973 was constitutional, and that Van Zandt had acted illegally and was responsible for the damages.[54] Despite the Supreme Court rulings that further sanctioned slave catching, the abolition movement continued to organize northern communities to defy the Fugitive Slave Law of 1793 and defend fugitive slaves against slave catching.

With the rise and growth of vigilance committees, the increasing power of the Underground Railroad, and many northern cities and counties defying orders to enforce slave catching, the South responded by calling for a new policy that would use federal authority to force those in the free states not only to allow but to be compelled to assist in slave catching. This call for stronger legislation culminated in the passing of the Fugitive Slave Act of 1850. The law had many provisions that are worth analyzing in detail for what they reveal about slave catcher whiteness. The law punished those who interfered with, obstructed, or undermined slave catchers' attempts to reclaim fugitive slaves. It criminalized those who aided fugitive slaves avoiding recapture. It also criminalized those who attempted to rescue people who had been recaptured by slave catchers.[55] Furthermore, it effectively deputized state, county, and local policing agencies to aid in slave remanding.[56] The punishment for any of these offenses was a fine of $1,000 and up to six months in prison.

The Fugitive Slave Act also deployed and depended on the doctrine of posse comitatus. This was the practice rooted in English common law in which the "power of the county," such as the sheriff or other state agent, was granted the authority to conscript and deputize citizens to assist in fulfilling policing duties and objectives like apprehending those accused of violating laws and maintaining the peace or social order in the face of rebellion and dissent. Posse comitatus was central to the Fugitive Slave Law of 1850. With the law's passing, the federal government granted US marshals the power to conscript all citizens of free states to be slave catchers. Section 5 states that US marshals or other state agents serving a warrant for the capture of a fugitive slave could "summon and call to their aid the bystanders, or posse comitatus of the proper county, when necessary to ensure a faithful observance of the clause of the Constitution referred to, in conformity with the provisions of this act; and all good citizens are hereby commanded to aid and assist in the prompt and efficient execution of this law." Hunting fugitive slaves thus transformed from expectation to duty to forced conscription. US commissioners, marshals, or other federal agents executing warrants at the direction of enslavers and professional slave catchers were given the power to command local citizens to aid them in recapturing those they pursued. All citizens became part of on-call posses of slave catchers. If a person refused, they could be charged with violating federal law.[57] The inclusion of this provision in the law revealed how enslavers expected to draw on long-standing structures of white alliance policing. It demonstrates how they imagined the citizenry as one collective policing body that could be mobilized to recapture people. In fact, the posse comitatus doctrine was seen by many as the most essential element of the Fugitive Slave Law. Without the power to conscript white citizens to mobilize as on-call slave catchers, enslavers did not expect to have much success in their incursions North.[58] Enslavers expected that the precedent and power of white alliance policing would prepare citizens in free states to embrace posse comitatus more as a duty to fulfill and less as a coerced act of conscription enforced by the threat of penalty and imprisonment.

The South's campaign of slave catching in the North and the passing of the Fugitive Slave Law of 1850 that sanctioned it formed a vehicle for reaccumulating lost capital. It was clear enslavers sought to recoup their losses when trying to recapture fugitive slaves. Fugitivity was bleeding the South of potential profits and inspiring further escape attempts as the Underground Railroad continued to become, as mentioned, more organized and sophisticated in its ability to liberate people. However, the principal reason for the South's slave catching incursions and the passing of the 1850 Fugitive Slave Law was to extend white alliance policing throughout the entire nation as an anticipatory counterrevolution against how fugitivity not only undermined the social control of the enslaved on plantations in the South but fueled the abolition movement in the North. While slave catching was a mission of hunting and recapturing people in the North, it was also about invading and terrorizing abolition-led communities providing refuge and sanctuary for the liberated. The incursions were counterinsurgent assaults on these communities to weaken them in their goal of receiving and protecting fugitive slaves.

The Fugitive Slave Law and its use of posse comitatus also sought to export to and impose on Northern communities the South's slave catcher whiteness as a strategy of white alliance policing, to organize them for anti-abolition counterrevolution. This was done in response to how fugitivity was fueling the abolition movement in the North, which in turn was increasing the effectiveness of the Underground Railroad to strike blows against the South. Exporting and imposing slave catcher whiteness through the Fugitive Slave Act aimed to turn Northern rear bases for abolition into counterrevolutionary outposts for slavery. The Fugitive Slave Act was also an effort by enslavers to wield the centralized power of the state to organize what was a mass-based project of slave catcher whiteness in which everyone was conscripted to participate.

Figure 3. *A Bold Stroke for Freedom*. Woodcut illustration in William Still, *The Underground Railroad* (1872), 125. Library of Congress Rare Book and Special Collections Division, Washington, DC. LC-USZ62-76205.

The Fugitive Slave Law was also a counterrevolutionary reaction to how abolition was organizing people to betray whiteness in their commitment to Black liberation. The conscripting of white citizens to force them to be slave catchers was a direct attack on the abolition movement's ability to organize white citizens in defense of Black fugitivity. Federalizing posse comitatus to command all whites to be slave catchers sought to shore up white alliance policing, which abolition was undermining in revolutionary projects like the Underground Railroad. If the Underground Railroad was organizing whites to aid, assist, and defend freedom seekers at the risk of imprisonment or even death, the enforcement of slave catcher whiteness through posse comitatus of the Fugitive Slave Act in the North was the counterrevolutionary response from enslavers to fortify white alliance policing where abolition was perceived to be unraveling it.

MARTIN DELANY'S *BLAKE*

It was during this period of sharpening class war between abolition and slavery that Black abolitionist Martin Delany emerged as a movement leader, serving as a writer, editor, doctor, and organizer. While Delany is more widely recognized for his commitment to Black emigration, which was the strategy of organizing free Black communities to leave the United States to establish an independent Black nation as a counterpower to European nations, he also published a serialized novel imagining the potential for international Black revolution. Delany's *Blake: or, The Huts of America* (1859, 1861–1862) envisions how enslaved Africans of the United States and Cuba could organize a clandestine movement for international mass insurrection initiating protracted abolition war.[59] Delany first published *Blake* the year following his work with John Brown at the Chatham Convention of May 1858, where radical abolitionists discussed and approved plans to implement Brown's famous "Virginia plan" to raid the South and overthrow slavery through armed resistance.[60]

While Delany declined Brown's invitation to be a leader in what became the Harper's Ferry Raid in October 1859, Delany remained a committed supporter of Brown's abolition war strategy following the Chatham Convention. In August 1858 Delany wrote to John Kagi (Brown's closest adviser and secretary of war in the provisional government) with updates on his work recruiting and organizing men for Brown's plan. Delany shared that he had received a letter from Brown and was surprised that Brown had not initiated his plan, which would have grabbed national headlines: "I have been anxiously looking and expecting to see something of Uncle's [Brown's] movements in the papers."[61] Yet scholars often interpret Delany's 1859 trip to West Africa to advance Black emigration, which was a few months before the Harper's Ferry Raid, as his choice to withdraw support for abolition war in North America. Robert Levine argues that Delany's letter to Kagi was "disingenuous" because while Delany might "have been hopeful for Brown's enterprise . . . he had committed himself to a different cause: establishing an African American colony in Africa."[62] Delany's participation in Brown's abolition war planning and preparations is often considered a footnote to Delany's emigrationism and its aim of establishing an independent Black nation beyond North America.

However, Delany's history of calling for armed struggle and slave revolt, combined with his leadership at the Chatham convention and commitment to recruiting for Brown's campaign, demonstrates that he not only endorsed abolition war but considered it a strategy complementing Black emigration. Brown's campaign promised to scale up many of the tactics that Delany had championed in previous years. Following the passing of the Fugitive Slave Law of 1850, Delany called for armed resistance among the Northern free Black community. In one speech, he promised to shoot to kill any slave catcher or US agent, even the US president, who dared cross the threshold of his house to enforce the law.[63] In his analysis of Cuban annexation, Delany argued that slavery was a mode of capital accumulation with a limitless appetite for imperial expansion. The US campaign to expropriate Cuba could only be defeated, Delany contended, by international slave insurrection.[64] Delany returned to this theme in his only work of fiction, *Blake*, which as mentioned envisions, much like Brown's plan, how the enslaved could foment, as its titular protagonist Henry Blake proclaims, "a general insurrection of the slaves in every state, and the successful overthrow of slavery!"[65] Furthermore, when Delany returned from his West African emigration trip around the onset of the Civil War, he joined fellow abolitionists in pressuring Union leaders to transform their campaign of merely quelling Southern rebellion into full-blown abolition war. Only when the Union shifted to abolition war strategy due to abolitionist' pressure and because it was facing potential defeat did Delany join the effort. He was commissioned a major in the US army and played a pivotal role in recruiting Black soldiers.[66]

Here I rediscover the insurgent Delany to suggest that scholarly attention to Delany's more well-known emigrationism—read as a noninsurgent strategy—has overshadowed in potentially limiting ways how his embedded role in North American abolition war informed his novel *Blake*.[67] I maintain that scholars too readily interpret North American abolition war as a reformist endeavor bound by US nationalism that Delany discarded rather than as a revolutionary insurgency attacking the foundations of US racialized class society in ways that complemented Delany's theory of emigration as the movement to build Black counterpower to US imperial hegemony.[68] I concentrate on Delany's role in North American abolition war to illuminate how *Blake* registers the ways that this insurgent struggle produced critical understandings of slavery and Black resistance that not only were foreclosed among nonviolent strategies but have been overlooked by the dominant scholarly focus on Delany's emigrationism. In *Blake*, Delany explores pressing questions about abolition war under debate at the time among its partisans. I argue that Delany's engagement with these questions—stemming from his participation in abolition war planning—leads him to offer critical representations of white alliance policing and its role in the history of counterrevolutionary repression that maintained US racialized class society. In other words, it is Delany's interest in imagining Black revolution housed in abolition war strategy that gives his story a vantage point from which to map the counterrevolutionary strategies of slavery capitalism. *Blake* sheds light on counterrevolutionary white alliance policing precisely through how it imagines Black revolution's confrontation with slavery. Delany suggests that white alliance policing was a principal mechanism repressing revolt and fugitivity and thus was a force that must be mapped, analyzed, and understood to be overcome, if abolition war was to overturn slavery. I do not suggest that Delany's support for abolition war outweighed his emigrationism insofar as we should not consider emigration an important context for understanding the novel. Rather, I am interested in illuminating how insurgent social movements—of which Delany was a planner and partisan—produce knowledge about the power structures they challenge. As such, I read North American abolition war alongside *Blake* to uncover what this insurgent struggle knew about slavery and resistance precisely through its revolutionary orientation and how *Blake* inscribes this knowledge.

ABOLITION WAR AND BLACK PRINT CULTURE

Delany wrote and published *Blake* during a moment when abolition war transformed into a formal military program with plans to launch an offensive against slavery. In 1856, as discussed in the introduction, John Brown's militia waged an armed campaign to repel proslavery forces in Kansas territory, demonstrating not only the viability but the necessity of abolition war for combating expanding slavery power. By 1858 Brown was agitating, recruiting, and fundraising to escalate this strategy. As examined in chapter 4, the Chatham Convention was the keystone in Brown's preparations for consolidating his Virginia plan. It is most likely that Delany was in the process of drafting *Blake* when he joined Brown in abolition war planning. There is also the possibility that Delany commenced drafting the novel following the Chatham Convention. If so, this would indicate that Brown's proposed Virginia plan could have inspired the novel. While evidence suggests the former, it is nonetheless underappreciated that Delany composed *Blake* alongside serious deliberations on how to wage armed insurgency. Such planning carried grave risks; the Chatham Convention was a clandestine affair with its participants sworn to secrecy. Eight months after the Chatham Convention, Delany initiated the first serialization of *Blake* in Thomas Hamilton's *Anglo African Magazine*. Chapters 1–28 were published from

January to July 1859. These were the same months of Brown's original final preparations for the Harper's Ferry raid, which was first planned, following the counsel of Harriet Tubman (who was also a coplanner of the raid), for July 4, 1859.[69] Delany abruptly suspended the serialization in July before embarking on his trip to West Africa.[70]

Following the Harper's Ferry raid and during the first year of the Civil War, Delany revised and republished *Blake* serially from November 1861 to April 1862 in Thomas Hamilton's newspaper the *Weekly Anglo-African*. In the months preceding *Blake*'s second serialization, the *WAA* had experienced a shakeup in ownership and editorial direction. Facing financial troubles, Thomas Hamilton was forced to sell the newspaper to Scottish American abolitionist James Redpath, who was receiving funding from Haiti to use the *WAA* to promote emigration to the island. Redpath appointed George Lawrence Jr. the new editor and changed the name of the *WAA* to the *Pine and Palm*, which began to feature editorial positions calling for Haitian emigration. As Brigitte Fielder, Cassander Smith, and Derrick R. Spires point out, this undermined Hamilton's previous editorial approach of managing the *WAA* as a forum of debate for its Black readership rather than imposing editorial positions. In response Thomas, and his brother Robert Hamilton, with funding from Black abolitionist James McCune Smith (who had also worked closely with John Brown) and Delany, revived the *WAA* to combat Redpath's wielding of the *Pine and Palm* to promote Haitian emigration.[71] Benjamin Fagan reveals that the new *WAA*'s reporting on the Civil War encouraged Northern Black militancy in support of Southern slave insurrection over supporting the Union's initial strategy of suppressing the South's rebellion without attacking slavery.

Furthermore, Thomas Hamilton was an advocate of abolition war strategy. In December 1859, the month John Brown was executed, Hamilton honored Brown by republishing Nat Turner's *Confessions*, accompanied by an introductory essay that compared the two. Hamilton argued that Brown was mild in his use of revolutionary violence, speculating that if Turner had been in command of the Harper's Ferry raid, the entire South would be drenched in blood.[72] In November 1861, the first month of the *WAA*'s return, Hamilton began publishing serially Delany's *Blake* as one of the newspaper's featured stories. Fagan argues that if Delany intended *Blake* to be a pro-emigration narrative, this choice "would have been a radical departure" from Hamilton's and the *WAA*'s pro-abolition war, anti-emigration position.[73] Whether Hamilton published *Blake* as an emigration story to challenge his readership or not, as Fagan also speculates, is less important than the fact that this publication history shows how Delany continued to work with and fund abolition war thinkers like Hamilton, evincing how Delany was entrenched in this movement despite his ongoing support for emigration. In other words, Delany's emigrationism did not extract him from abolition war's insurgent contexts. This publication history also reveals that *Blake* was in direct dialogue with abolition war theory, which Hamilton's *WAA* was incubating through its revived platform.

A few years earlier, on October 25, 1859, just over a week after the Harper's Ferry raid, a story ran in the *Chatham Tri-Weekly Planet* reporting that Delany, referred to as the innocuous local "physician amongst the coloured people" was "implicated in the [Harper's Ferry] uprising" and that the "doctor is upon pretty good understanding with those who knew well what was going on."[74] The story indicates that Delany's letter to John Kagi promising support for Brown's plan had been recovered among Brown's belongings following the raid. Later, the Senate congressional hearing investigating the raid interrogated one of Brown's soldiers, Richard Realf (not present at Harper's Ferry), about the Chatham Convention. Realf implicated Delany as a coconspirator with Brown, testifying that "the whole tenor of Dr. Delany's speeches was to convey the idea to John Brown that he might rely upon all the colored people in Canada to assist him."[75] After the Civil War and after gaining national notoriety as the first Black major in the Union army, Delany commissioned Francis Rollin to write a biography in which Delany denied participating in any insurgent activity related to the Harper's Ferry raid. Delany claimed that while he fully supported Brown, it was with the understanding that Brown's plan was to establish in Kansas territory a new terminus of the Underground Railroad where an independent abolition state could be formed beyond the reach of US sovereignty.[76] While Brown and Delany most likely did discuss during their time together in Chatham potential plans for an abolition state in Kansas, other attendees at the Chatham convention remembered that Brown had revealed his plan to attack the South through armed insurgency. Historians demonstrate that Brown discussed his Virginia plan at Chatham and in personal meetings and interviews with its leaders preceding the convention.[77]

Whether or not Delany's account of Chatham is true is less important than what to make of his effort to disavow his relationship to Brown's insurgency. It certainly embodies Paul Gilroy's contention that Delany's contradictory "political trajectory . . . dissolves any simple attempts to fix him as consistently either conservative or radical."[78] While Delany may have disavowed his proximity to the insurgent currents of abolition war, I am more interested in reading how this insurgent struggle as a social movement—of which Delany was a participant—speaks through his novel. I reground *Blake* in its context of insurgency to spotlight how this mode of struggle enabled forms of thought and imagination about slavery and resistance that find expression in the novel, even if Delany moved away from or did not take them up elsewhere in his writings. I am interested in how *Blake* allows readers to see what abolition war strategy knew about slavery and resistance through the vantage point of its insurgent orientation.

WHITE ALLIANCE POLICING IN *BLAKE*

Blake is widely recognized for its hemispheric representation of enslaved Africans organizing to foment mass insurrection from the US South to

Cuba. In part 1 the novel follows the actions of its titular character, Henry Blake, who after learning that his wife Maggie has been sold and sent to Cuba, escapes from a Mississippi plantation and travels through the US South organizing rebel slaves in preparation for revolt. He returns to his former plantation to free his son and close friends, ushering them to freedom in Canada. In part 2, Blake journeys to Cuba to rescue Maggie, where after liberating her, Blake organizes the beginnings of an abolition army composed of the island's enslaved and free persons of color. This provisional army prepares for an impending revolt that will spark mass insurrection in the United States.

When read alongside Delay's abolition war planning, this representation also evinces a concern for mapping the obstacles to slave insurrection. The novel identifies these obstacles to imagine how they could be overcome. As a planner of abolition war, Delany engaged in debates about the hurdles this strategy faced. I am interested in examining the novel's narrative strategy for imagining resolutions to the obstacles of abolition war. I suggest that the narrative strategy for resolving these obstacles crystallizes an understanding of slavery's strategies of counterrevolutionary repression that secured its power. This becomes visible when we compare the novel's narrative strategies for resolving obstacles to abolition war across the two national contexts of the United States and Cuba.

In the US context, the novel identifies two obstacles besetting the organizing of insurrection. One is characterized as the false promise of freedom for African-descended people in US society. For instance, when Blake arrives in Kentucky to recruit leaders and spread the plan for insurrection, he observes how the promises of emancipation from enslavers have liquidated potential for insurgency among the enslaved. "There seemed to be a universal desire for freedom, there were few who were willing to strike. To run away, with them, seemed to be the highest conceived idea of their right to liberty . . . but their right to freedom by self-resistance, to them was forbidden by the Word of God.

Their hopes were based on the long-talked-of promised emancipation in the state."[79] Here and elsewhere in the novel Delany criticizes how enslavers use religion to deradicalize the enslaved from revolting. The solution to such proslavery propaganda becomes Blake's work of political agitation among the enslaved, or as he says, "to make them sensible that liberty was legitimately and essentially theirs."[80]

What is less recognized in scholarship is the novel's attention to policing as an obstacle besetting the organizing of insurrection. The novel emphasizes how slave patrols are a pervasive force confronting Blake at every turn in his trek across the South. When Blake travels to Arkansas, he visits the hut of an Aunt Rachel and Uncle Jerry, where they discuss the problem of local white patrols: "'You are closely watched in this state, I should think, Uncle.' 'Yes, chile, de patrollers da all de time out an' gwine in de quahtehs an' huntin' up black folks.'"[81] In this same scene, white patrollers arrive, invade, and occupy Aunt Rachel and Uncle Jerry's hut, stealing their dinner while interrogating Blake. The patrol then visits a nearby tavern, where auctioneers are hosting a raffle whose prizes include a "fine horse and buggy of Colonel Sprout, a mare and colt, a little negro girl ten years of age, and a trail of four of the finest negro-dogs in the state."[82] The patrol functions not only to control the enslaved but also as a social activity cohering the white community. The narrator observes: "The patrol this evening were composed of the better class of persons, principally men, two of whom being lawyers who went out that evening for a mere 'frolic among the negroes.'"[83] Patrolling is a recreational event offering pleasure and comradery among whites.

Additionally, the scene emphasizes how policing the enslaved was both a cross-class and mass-based project. The raffle leader, Colonel Sprout, offers a demonstration of the tracking capabilities of the bloodhounds "to test their quality previous to the raffle." A patroller asks how the handlers command the dogs to ensure they pursue intended targets of 'strange negroes?'" Sprout responds, "'O, the command of any white man is sufficient to call 'em off, an' they's plenty o' them all 'as wherever you find [enslaved Africans].'"[84] Sprout's assumption that all whites by nature of their whiteness can command bloodhounds pursuing rebel slaves is a metaphor for how whiteness carries the duty to police Black resistance. It suggests that to be counted as white, Europeans are expected to police the enslaved and that, as a community effort, this expectation supersedes class conflicts. Sprout's remarks also spotlight how policing the enslaved is understood as a mass project in which whites live embedded in the spaces of slavery as an informal anti-Black occupying police force.[85] A patroller responds to Sprout, asking, "We're to understand you to mean, that white men can't live without [enslaved Africans]?" Sprout clarifies, "'I'll be hanged, gentlemen, if it don't seem so, for wherever you find one you'll all 'as find tother.'"[86] In this scene, the novel demonstrates how this collective, cross-class, mass-based policing—what in this chapter I have theorized as white alliance policing—extends and supplements the state's policing power, embodied in the formal slave patrols, in guarding against revolt or fugitivity.

Delany also highlights how white alliance policing is not exclusively performed by people of European descent. All people claiming free or nonenslaved status are organized into police in the US context. In South Carolina, Blake confronts the "Brown society," an "organization formed through the instrumentality of the whites to keep the blacks and mulattos at variance. To such an extent is the error carried, that the members of the association, rather than their freedom would prefer to see the blacks remain in bondage."[87] Due to this, South Carolina is depicted as the state most effective at policing the enslaved.[88] Blake remarks that "for every night of sojourn in the state he had a gathering, not one of which was within a hut, so closely were the slaves watched by patrol, and sometimes by mulatto and black overseers. These gatherings were always held in the forest."[89] The novel's portrayal of free persons of color policing the enslaved suggests that individual freedom in the United States is entangled with reproducing the unfreedom of enslavement. In the US context, the nonenslaved are allied across both class and race to repress Black resistance.[90]

To resolve the problem of white alliance policing, Delany deploys the speculative mode to offer the image of supernatural fugitivity as a resolution. Blake is the figure for this supernatural fugitivity. The speed and distance of his movement across the United States to sow the seeds of insurrection exceed individual human capacities.[91] The narrator describes this superhuman movement as apocalyptic: "From plantation to plantation did he go, sowing the seeds of future devastation and ruin to the master and redemption to the slave, an antecedent more terrible in its anticipation, than the warning voice of the destroying Angel, in commanding the slaughter of the first born of Egypt."[92] Blake is also immune to harm and danger. On several occasions, he easily defends himself against slave catchers, overseers, and patrollers: "Proceeding on in the direction of the Red River country, he met with no obstruction, except in one instance, when he left his assailant quietly upon the earth. A few days later after an inquest was held upon the body of a deceased overseer—verdict of the Jury, 'By hands unknown.'"[93] Blake's supernatural power of flight and defense exceeds the threat of white alliance policing. This speculative representation of fugitivity in the US context stands out from the mode of realism that McGann suggests Delany uses to narrate part I.[94] Brit Rusert has characterized Blake's fugitivity as cosmic in a way that defies the boundaries of liberal personhood: "Blake bears more resemblance to the vibrating stars, comets, and meteors that he observes from the Mississippi steamboat than to a properly developed character."[95] Rusert argues that *Blake* likely unnerved critics because of the rejection of traditional categories of personhood, and of the human itself, as the horizon of political, and no doubt, artistic activity."[96] Building on Rusert's reading, I see this cosmic fugitivity functioning in the novel as a resolution to what is characterized as a totalizing white alliance policing. Delany's supernatural fugitivity makes him unpoliceable. The organizing of the insurrection becomes possible precisely due to this supernatural power of flight and defense.[97]

In part 2, when the plot turns to Cuba, the novel remains concerned with white alliance policing in the US context. Delany suggests that the US annexation movement intends to import this US strategy of counterrevolution to the island to secure slavery in the face of potential revolt. Unlike the realism of the US context, Cuba functions as a speculative world in relation to the US context. It is not only speculative as alternate history fiction through its anachronist representation of the Cuba slave conspiracy known as the Conspiracy of the Ladder, or La Escalera (1843–1844), as many have noted.[98] It is also speculative in how Fred Jameson conceptualizes speculative fiction as a form of utopian thinking that imagines alternative worlds whose ideal character or very alterity embodies resolutions to unsolvable or nonreformable social contradictions of the author's world.[99] In this way, Cuba becomes a speculative space onto which Delany projects solutions to contradictions of the US context that are felt as irresolvable. While scholars have cited the US annexation movement, Caribbean slave revolt, and the transnational character of slavery as contexts explaining Delany's interest in Cuba, I maintain he approached the island as a utopian location to portray what was impossible to imagine in the US context, namely free workers plotting with rather than policing the enslaved in the aim of abolition war. I am interested in the relationship between this image of free worker and enslaved unity in speculative Cuba and the speculative depiction of Blake's cosmic fugitivity in the US context.

Before the relationship between the two can be examined, however, we must first grasp how Delany fashions the image of free workers transforming into rebels and unifying with the enslaved in speculative Cuba. Initially, divisions between the enslaved and free workers in Cuba are shown to beset the organizing of the insurrection: "The political relations of the colony were peculiar, and singularly mischievous and detrimental to the best interests of this class of inhabitants [the enslaved]. The four great divisions of society were white, Black, free and slave; and these were again subdivided into many other classes, as rich, poor, and such like. The free and slaves among the Blacks did not associate, nor the high and low among the free of the same race. And there was among them even another general division—Black and colored—which met with little favor from the intelligent."[100]

However, these divisions turn into unity in the face of racist repression carried out by US nationals who increasingly arrive in Cuba as part of a larger annexation movement. As historian Gerald Horne details, US enslavers considered Cuba a place of potential Black insurgency that could spread to the US mainland because of what they perceived was the inability of Spain to control the enslaved and free Black workers in Cuba.[101] When speaking with Colonel Franks and other fellow enslavers about Cuba, Judge Ballard expresses this anxiety: "The idea of meeting negroes and mulatoes at the levees of the Captain General is intolerable! It will never do to permit this state of things so near our shores."[102] US enslavers feared Cuba could become another Haiti. To prevent this, they sought to annex Cuba. Many moved their holdings to Cuba to precipitate filibustering missions that could win annexation.[103]

The novel spotlights how such US nationals in concert with Spanish planters supportive of annexation attempt to impose in Cuba a white alliance policing targeting free persons of color regardless of class in public spaces the same as the enslaved. For example, Plácido, the movement's poet and coleader with Blake, is publicly beaten by a US national bookshop owner, and Ambrosina, the daughter of one of the wealthier families of free persons of color, is publicly whipped by a white shop owner, enforcing this increased repression of free persons of color. Plácido tells Blake: "'Ah, cousin, though you consider us here free—those I mean who are not the slaves of white man—I do assure you that my soul as much as your pants for a draft from the fountain of liberty! We are not free, but merely exist by sufferance—a miserable life for intelligent people, to be sure!'"[104] This repressive policing of the free persons of color dialectically leads them to forge unity with enslaved Africans that did not exist before.

This budding unity is shown to develop in the blind spots of Spanish authorities. During the celebrations of Gala Day in "honor of the Infanta Sovereign of Spain," the narrator describes how the free and enslaved classes are forging unity and plot their preparations for insurrection under the veil of the festival's activities: "Never before had the African race been so united as on that occasion, the free Negroes and mixed free people being in unison and sympathy with each other. . . . There was a greater tendency to segregation instead of a seeming desire to mingle as formerly among the whites, as masses of the Negroes, mulattoes and quadroons, Indians, and even Chinamen, could be seen together, to all appearance absorbed in conversation on matters disconnected entirely from the occasion of the day."[105] In speculative Cuba, white alliance policing cannot take root when free workers are radicalized to join the enslaved in abolition war struggle. Free workers in Delany's Cuba become fighters in a multiethnic abolition war army in contrast to the US context in which free workers enter alliances with capital across class and race to police Black rebellion.

When looking across the two national contexts, we see that Delany repeatedly turns to the speculative mode in the novel's narrative strategy for managing white alliance policing. That is, Delany uses realism to narrate the plot of the US context but introduces the speculative mode to fashion the image of Blake's supernatural fugitivity as a resolution to white alliance policing. It is only in speculative Cuba that Delany presents the reader with the image of free worker and enslaved unity, a solidarity that not only unravels white alliance policing but serves as the linchpin for the creation of an actual abolition war army. I contend that this repeated dependence on the speculative mode to manage white alliance policing inscribes how the novel understands white alliance policing as slavery's principal repressive force—its most effective counterrevolutionary strategy—for combating Black rebellion and abolition war. That the speculative mode is the only language through which Delany envisions solutions to white alliance policing crystallizes how white alliance policing is felt as insuperable in North America—not in a defeatist but rather in a structural way. It registers how white alliance policing serves as slavery's principal tool of counterrevolution, securing its power and reproduction. It is not a standing army or a strong centralized state but rather the mass-based, cross-class alliances between free workers and capital to police Black rebellion that the novel sees as the force upholding slavery. In its narrative strategy for contemplating obstacles to abolition war, the novel inscribes the feeling that if abolition war is to win in North America, it must determine a strategy for overcoming slavery's counterrevolutionary machinery of white alliance policing.

It is from Delany's embedded position in abolition war with its insurgent orientation that his novel captures this understanding of white counterrevolution enacted through white alliance policing. It is an early and unique literary representation of whiteness and its role in the history of counterrevolution. The novel also illuminates the theme this chapter has tracked of how Black rebellion and its power to destabilize US racialized class society called into existence white alliance policing in the first place. To protect slavery's relations of production from Black rebellion, those with anything to lose from the abolition of enslavement and the class society it upheld were compelled to unify around the objective of anti-Black counterrevolution.[106] The novel's theory of white alliance policing demonstrates how Black revolution (here housed in abolition war) has served as the motor force for shaping the structures of repression upholding US racialized class society.

ABOLITION WAR AND TREASON TO WHITENESS

From its understanding of white alliance policing, Delany's *Blake* reflects on how abolition war led by the insurgent aims of the enslaved could function as a vanguard force in directing white workers to betray white alliances. In one passing scene in part I, Delany dramatizes an interaction between a white ferryman and a party of fugitive slaves led by Blake, who is conducting them north to Canada. The interaction allegorizes the potential for abolition war to compel white workers to renounce their policing duties. The scene is less a resolution to white alliance policing, like Blake's cosmic fugitivity we saw earlier, than a reflection on how abolition war held the potential to confront white workers in ways that moved them to support rather than repress Black resistance. After Blake has traveled the US South spreading the secret plan for insurrection, he returns to Colonel Frank's plantation to help his son and close friends escape north to Canada. Early in their journey, the fugitive group pass through southern Missouri, where they must cross the Mississippi River above its confluence with the Ohio River. A posse of slave catchers is close behind in pursuit. The group must use a ferry to cross the river.

When they ask a white ferryman for assistance, he questions whether they are fugitives or free. "'Am yers free?' enquired the ferryman." One member of Blake's group retorts: "'Am I free! are you free?' rejoined Eli. 'Yes, I be's a white man!' replied the boatman." Carrying out his duty of white alliance policing, the ferryman explains that the fugitive slave law requires him to police all people of African descent who request his ferry services. "'I be 'sponsible for 'em 'cording to the new law, called, I 'bleve the Nebrasky Complimize Fugintive Slave Act, made down at Californy, last year,' apologized and explained the somewhat confused ferryman." Blake points out that their status should not concern the ferryman since his job is to transport customers, not police them: "I thought you were here to carry people across the river." The ferryman explains that "this are a law made by the Newnited States of Ameriky, an' I be 'bliged to fulfill it by ketchin' every fugintive that goes to cross this way, or I mus' pay a thousand dollars, and go to jail till the black folks is got, if that be's never." His remarks highlight that it is the threat of punishment over any promises of reward that underpins white alliance policing.

Blake responds by naming the class contradiction that white alliances conceal, inviting the ferryman to betray his obedience to the duty expected of him: "'Are you willing to make yourself a watch-dog for slaveholders, and do for them that which they would not do for themselves, catch runaway slaves? Don't you know that this is the work which they boast on having the poor white men at the North do for them? Have you not yet learned to attend to your own interests instead of theirs?—Here are our free papers,' holding his open hand, in which lay five half-eagle pieces." With the offer of gold, the ferryman gives up his policing post and agrees to ferry the fugitives. "'Jump aboard!' cried the ferryman." There are a few insights to draw from this exchange. First, Delany represents the ferryman's choice to aid the fugitives as a question of class interest rather than a moral problem. Jeffory Clymer, building on John Ernest, contends that this scene ironically participates in the same market logics underpinning slavery. It "demonstrates that in capitalist America money, and evidently only money, can trump political ideology and individuals' racist beliefs." However, I suggest that Blake pays the ferryman an amount that outprices the benefits of consenting to white alliance policing. Blake's offer of gold symbolizes how whiteness as the duty to perform counterrevolutionary policing is not necessarily reciprocated with the "pay" it might promise, pointing up how whiteness clashes with the ferryman's class interest of securing his material needs.

Second, the scene intimates that on their own as a class, antebellum white workers were not positioned to break from the white alliances protecting slavery. It required the insurgent position of a slave vanguard in command to compel white workers to break from white alliances. When the slave catchers arrive at the boat landing, they demand the ferryman assist them in capturing the fugitives. Blake tells the ferryman he can take the money and be of assistance to Black freedom; if not, Blake will shoot him: "Your cause is a just one, and your reward is sure; take this money, proceed and you are safe—refuse, and you instantly die!" With a gun to his head, the ferryman chooses to assist, "'Then I be's to do right,' declared the boatman; 'if I die by it,' when applying the whip to the horses, in a few moments landed on the Illinois shore." In this way, the scene exhibits how abolition war with a slave vanguard has the potential to compel white workers to confront their role in counterrevolution and how this relates to their own exploitation by capitalism. This is what Blake's threat to shoot the ferryman is a metaphor for: if the white worker is not under the command of abolition war to betray white alliances, whiteness will already have them organized to police Black resistance.

At a time when antebellum white worker movements (explored in chapter 3) attempted to leverage white alliances to shield themselves from increasing capitalist domination, further distancing themselves from unity with a worker internationalism, Delany contemplates how abolition war with slave vanguardism in command could compel white workers to defy their duty to enforce capitalism to create the opportunity to join with other oppressed people organizing for revolutionary change. Where whiteness organizes (and depends on) white workers to do the counterrevolutionary policing for capitalism, abolition war led by a slave vanguard confronts this alliance and invites a refusal. While abolition war prompted white alliance policing as a necessary measure to protect accumulation, it also held the power to precipitate refusals of whiteness. This is the character of the class struggle between abolition war and slavery that Delany illuminates. Resistance intensifies the struggle, increasingly leaving no room for neutrality. The options become to police insurgency or join it.

In this way, the novel's view of abolition war working to dislodge white workers from their alliance with capital was in dialogue with questions about proletarian internationalism that Karl Marx and Frederich Engels, who were contemporaries of Delany, were also contemplating. In the *Communist Manifesto* (1848), Marx and Engels famously argue that the proletariat is the revolutionary vanguard of the anti-capitalist movement to overturn bourgeois power.[107] Marx and Engels analyze capitalism from the vantage point of its development in Europe, arguing that the European working class is this vanguard class with the historical mission of conquering bourgeois power and winning a workers' state to facilitate the transition to a classless and stateless society of communism.[108] In his writings on the Civil War, Marx agitates for European workers to support the abolition movement in the United States. Slavery's abolition would allow Black workers, Marx reasons, to become fellow wage workers of the European proletariat.[109] At this newly shared class position of wage labor, European and Black workers could unify in ways that the presence of slavery had prevented. This is what Marx means when he writes in *Capital*: "In the United States of America, every independent workers' movement was paralysed as long as slavery disfigured a part of the republic. Labour in a white skin cannot emancipate itself where it is branded in a Black skin."[110] In this way, Marx theorizes that proletarian internationalism flows from the struggle led by a European industrial proletariat as its vanguard force.[111] Where Marx, from his embedded position in European worker struggles, sees abolition as what enables enslaved workers to join the European industrial proletariat at the same structural location in capitalism of the "free" wage worker, Delany, from his participation in abolition war planning with Brown, sees the inverse. *Blake* sees an alternative proletarian internationalism developing through a slave vanguard of abolition war. *Blake*'s fugitive party confronting the white ferryman rehearses how abolition war is the catalyst for white workers to betray white alliance policing, allowing them to be available and ready to join the enslaved in the struggle to overthrow racial capitalism. We also see this in speculative Cuba, where the free workers of many different ethnicities and nationalities make themselves *politically* into the image of the insurgent enslaved to unify with their struggle of abolition war. The joint celebration of important marriages between free persons of color and the enslaved symbolizes this. The enslaved Africans Gofer Gondolier and Abyssa Soudan and free persons General Juan Montego and Madame Cordora elect to hold their wedding ceremonies "at the same sacred hymeneal altar," a decision that "was received with great favor among the high and low classes, especially the slave portion of the Black inhabitants, and their social relation was now regarded as a mutually fixed reality."[112] While we have already observed how free persons of color are policed like the enslaved, compelling them to unify with the enslaved, we also see how the slave's insurgent strategy is what prompts free workers of Cuba to fight for revolution that on their own as a class they would not have.

ABOLITION WAR'S ENDINGS

The novel also contemplates the trajectory of abolition war. It does this through its perplexing nonending. For as much as Delany focuses on the story of insurrection, his novel ends without a representation of it. That is, *Blake* ends without a depiction of the insurrection that its plot has anticipated. The incompleteness is less a question of lost chapters, as many believe is the case, than a feature of the novel's narrative strategy.[113] While many see the nonending as a shortcoming of the novel, I read it as a formal feature of the novel's narrative structure that embodies the trajectory of abolition struggle. What is this nonending? Delany concludes the novel with a series of scenes in which the provisional army that Blake has organized in Cuba, composed of the enslaved and free workers of color, is ready to revolt but the right moment to do so is always deferred. The insurrection is treated as always yet to come. This is repeated in the closing pages, where the enslaved and free workers call for revolutionary violence to both defend themselves in response to their most recent brutal treatment at the hands of US nationals and to overthrow the Spanish authorities. Ambrosina calls for the burning of the city: "I wish I was a man, I'd lay the city in ashes this night, so I would."[114] The enslaved cook Gondolier proclaims that "as they shed the blood of our brother [Plácido] two days ago by dashing him on the pavement, and the blood of our sister here today by a horsewhip, I would like to shed theirs with a knife."[115] While Madame Montego and Madame Barbosa argue for nonviolence as a response to avoid intensifying the conflict, the novel gives Gondolier the last say on the matter: "Thank you, Madame, for the advice. . . . But we have a race of devils to deal with that would make an angel swear. Educated devils that's capable of everything hellish under the name of religion, law, politics, social regulations, and the higher civilization; so that the helpless victim be of the Black race. Curse them! I hate 'em! Let me into the streets and give me but half a chance and I'll unjoin them faster than ever I did a roast a pig for the palace dinner table."[116] Ambrosina and Gondolier's position wins the debate over what is the best course of action following the attack on Ambrosina. The novel famously ends with Gondolier leaving the meeting to share a call to action: "He left the room to spread among the blacks an authentic statement of the outrage: 'Woe be unto those devils of whites, I say!'"[117] No representation follows of the insurrection.

I join Susan Gillman and Alex Moskowitz in reading the nonending as productive rather than limiting.[118] It withholds the representation of the novel's stated object of representation, namely a slave uprising that initiates abolition war. In doing so, the nonending disrupts the narrative closure that would provide coherence to the novel's representation of Black resistance. In this way, it expresses what the trajectory of abolition war means for a world premised on slavery. The nonrepresentation of insurrection in a plot that unravels without it crystallizes the novel's affirmation of what abolition war portends for a world premised on anti-Black accumulation: such a world's destruction. It articulates how abolition war's victory would be the death knell for European nations like the United States with a foundation of anti-Black exploitation and dispossession. For Moskowitz, the nonending "challenges us to read what is insensible in the world of nineteenth-century transatlantic slavery: Black freedom and the abolition of slavery as the abolition of capital itself."[119] The refusal to provide narrative closure that would envision Black liberation coexisting with the modern world rehearses at the level of form how Black liberation won through insurgent revolutionary struggle cannot be reconciled with the modern world, whose premise is capital accumulation by anti-Black subjugation.

It is in this way that the novel sees abolition war as the movement that satisfies Marx's early definition of communism, found in *German Ideology*: "Communism is for us not a *state of affairs* which is to be established, an *ideal* to which reality [will] have to adjust itself. We call communism the *real* movement which abolishes the present state of things. The conditions of this movement result from the premises now in existence."[120] *Blake* sees abolition war to be the movement whose success, following Fred Moten's formulation, would be the end of the world of racial capitalism as the birth of a new one.[121] We see in *Blake* not only a way of understanding how whiteness is a counterrevolutionary strategy to save capitalism from Black revolution, but also a theory of abolition war as an alternative form of anti-capitalist struggle than what was taking shape and conceptualized in the labor struggles of the European proletariat at the time. In chapter 4 I explore how abolition war partisans on the front lines confronting slavery capitalism, like John Brown, Osborne Anderson, and Harriet Tubman, with whom Delany worked directly, put into practice what Delany envisions in his novel about abolition as an alternative form of revolutionary anti-capitalist struggle.

2

ANTICOLONIAL WAR AND
SETTLER MASS MILITARISM

IN THEIR SOCIAL HISTORY of the class struggles of early capitalism, Peter Linebaugh and Marcus Rediker note that the
first English settlers who invaded the lands of the Powhatan
Confederacy to establish the Virginia colony at Jamestown
encountered Indigenous governance and political economy
as radical alternatives to Europe's class society. Funded and
managed by the Virginia company, the colony was established to generate profits through tobacco production. One
of the settlers, John Smith, a former mercenary, would later
publish maps and writings on the New World to promote
further settler colonization of North America. In contrast
to the Virginia Company's rigid, hierarchical, and milita-
rized labor regime, in which torture and execution were
used to extract labor from the colony's workers, "the classless, stateless, egalitarian societies of [Indigenous] America,"
write Linebaugh and Rediker, "were powerful examples of
alternative ways of life."[1] Almost immediately the investors

and leaders of the Virginia colony confronted the problem of their workforce deserting to join the Powhatan Confederacy. Linebaugh and Rediker detail how "in search of food and a way of life that many apparently found congenial, a steady stream of English settlers opted to become 'white Indians,' 'red Englishmen,' or—since racial categories were as yet unformed—Anglo-Powhatans."[2] Colony leaders began to adopt harsher policies criminalizing such desertion. They introduced the Laws Divine, Moral and Martial, a set of rules to govern the colony modeled on a Dutch military manual. Linebaugh and Rediker argue that "one of the main purposes of the laws was to keep English settlers and Native Americans apart."[3] If the choice was between the unfreedom, terror, and subjection of the Virginia colony's class society of early capitalism and the Powhatan's system of cooperative economics and political egalitarianism, it is easy to see why English indentured servants took the risk to desert the colony and seek incorporation under Indigenous governance.

While it could be argued that criminalizing desertion was done mostly to prevent the loss of labor, colony leaders were troubled by the deserters' inclusion in "enemy" Indigenous societies. The laws punished workers not only for refusing their labor but also, perhaps more importantly, for demonstrating how Indigenous societies were preferable political economies to early capitalism. In other words, the criminalization of English indentured servants' desertion of class society to join Indigenous societies suggests that North American settler colonialism emerged as a project that—together with the goal of seizing Indigenous territory through the logics of elimination—presented Indigenous societies as alternative political systems undermining the legitimacy of class society. Settlers feared the presence of Indigenous societies not only because they governed the lands settlers sought to occupy but also because they modeled viable alternatives to class society. If settler colonialism is a structure of capital accumulation by dispossession, it also aims to destroy competing noncapitalist societies or societies whose development could produce classless futures in its presence, which Indigenous nations have always embodied in relation to settler colonialism's imposition of European racial capitalism in North America. In this way, the defense of Indigenous forms of governance and political economy against settler colonialism's imposition of class society has always been a revolutionary struggle to maintain the development of alternatives to capitalism.

In recent years, scholars of Indigenous studies and Marxism such as Iyko Day, Roxanne Dunbar-Ortiz, Nick Estes, Glen Coulthard, Joanne Barker, and Manu Karuka, have productively examined the relationship between Indigenous critiques of settler colonialism and Marx's theory of capitalism. Scholars highlight the ways Indigenous social relations, governance, and anticolonial struggle embody a revolutionary anti-capitalism that is sometimes overlooked in Western Marxism's understandings of proletarian struggle.[4] Contributing to these conversations, I explore in this chapter how Indigenous anticolonialism—and its revolutionary character of upholding noncapitalist Indigenous social relations—has been a motor force for shaping the development and workings of settler society. I ask what we see differently about US settler colonialism when we not only foreground Indigenous anticolonialism but also understand this struggle as one of revolutionary anti-capitalism in its aim of decolonization. I argue that in response to Indigenous anticolonialism's revolutionary character, US settler society devised what I call settler mass militarism as a method for waging anti-Indian counterrevolutionary war to maintain and expand settler colonization. Settler mass militarism is the decentralized project of settler-citizens unifying across internal divisions or hierarchies of class society to act as combatants in conducting anti-Indian counterrevolution to advance settler colonization.

How I understand settler mass militarism builds on Indigenous studies scholars Estes, Yazzie, Denetdale, and Correia and their understanding of "anti-Indian common sense" as a structuring force of settler society. They write that "settler citizens and vigilantes are conscripted into anti-Indian common sense to carry out the sacred duty of land dispossession and capitalist accumulation. And they are typically not coerced or forced but see their everyday obligation to carry out the project of Native elimination as a part of their identity as settler citizens."[5] Looking back to chapter 1, I conceptualize settler mass militarism working in tandem with white alliance policing to form the larger structure of white counterrevolution. The aim of this chapter is to study how the revolutionary threat to class society of Indigenous anticolonialism called into existence settler mass militarism. In this way, I explore how settler mass militarism was developed, how it has worked to uphold settler class society, and what its relationship has been with centralized state power in the objective of anti-Indian counterrevolution.

I turn to two flashpoints in the history of Indigenous anticolonialism and settler colonization in the antebellum nineteenth century that shed light on settler mass militarism. I investigate the Second Seminole War of Florida (1836–1842) and the US settler colonization of Indigenous California after 1848. These two flashpoints serve as counterpoints in the history of settler mass militarism's historical development during this conjuncture. The Second Seminole War witnessed the Seminoles wage a protracted anticolonial war to defend their autonomy in the face of threats to be "relocated" to lands west of the Mississippi under the directives of Andrew Jackson's Indian removal policies. This was a war of both Indigenous anticolonialism and Black abolition. The Seminole leadership forged a united front among Seminoles, Black Seminoles, and Black maroons to win liberated zones from Florida's settler plantation order. I study the role, or the troubling lack thereof for many US leaders, that settler mass militarism played in the US state's response to Seminole insurgency. From there I study post-1848 California, a moment when settler mass militarism was the vanguard force for advancing US settler colonization of the Indigenous territories that became

California following the annexation of Mexico's northern territories. I conclude the chapter with a reading of Cherokee writer John Rollin Ridge's novel *Joaquín Murieta* (1854). Ridge's life and novel bridge the two flashpoints of Florida and California. The same campaign of Indian removal targeting the Seminoles also displaced the Cherokee and led to a series of events that pushed Ridge to take up residence in gold rush California. There he penned and published *Joaquín Murieta*, which represents the titular character and historical figure's anticolonial insurgency against the US settler invasion of California. While Ridge's novel dramatizes anticolonial resistance, it is also recognized for its many ideological and formal contradictions. However, I contend that these very contradictions are what make legible the dialectic of revolutionary anticolonialism and the rise of settler mass militarism, a relationship that in dominant narratives both then and now is often disavowed. The novel's contradictions also crystallize the autonomous character of settler mass militarism in relation to state power, even as the state depends on settler mass militarism to conduct anti-Indian counterrevolution. Ridge explores how this autonomous character of settler mass militarism often defies the oversight or control of the centralized state, creating the potential for crippling instability within the settler colonial project.

ORIGINS OF SETTLER MASS MILITARISM

During the period of British settler colonization of North America, English settlers developed and refined what scholars of military science today call *irregular warfare* in their campaigns to seize Indigenous lands to expand colonial territories. The principal difference between traditional and irregular warfare is the relationship between the opposing forces. Traditional warfare is a military conflict between nation-states. Irregular warfare is defined as the conflict between a nation-state and nonstate actors, or when nation-state forces seek to defeat or control civilian populations of a given territory. Historian Roxanne Dunbar Ortiz highlights this history of British and later US settlers deploying irregular warfare to target all members of Indigenous nations as enemy combatants to control or eliminate. "Anglo settlers organized irregular units," writes Dunbar Ortiz, "to brutally attack and destroy unarmed Indigenous women, children, and old people using unlimited violence in unrelenting attacks. . . . [W]hile large regular armies fought over geopolitical goals in Europe, Anglo settlers in North America waged deadly irregular warfare against the Indigenous communities."[6] Dunbar Ortiz draws on the work of the military historian John Grenier, who conceptualizes this history as US society's "first way of war." Grenier argues that the "first way of war" was a period of anti-Indian irregular warfare from the first British colonies of the sixteenth century to the emergence of US settler society of the early nineteenth century. It was during this time that settlers learned, cultivated, and refined anti-Indian irregular warfare as the foundation for modern-day US military's strategies of asymmetric warfare marked by special operations forces, which continue to play a central role in global US military strategy.

Grenier notes that anti-Indian irregular warfare was carried out through three principal tactics: "extirpative war making, the creation of specialized units for Indian fighting (rangers), and the use of scalp hunters to motivate privatized, commercialized campaigns through the issuance of scalp bounties."[7] Extirpative war making had the goal of the total destruction of the infrastructure underlying the life of Indigenous societies, beyond merely the defeat of their military forces. This meant the razing of food production and housing and the wanton killing or kidnapping of noncombatants, particularly women and children, to undermine the social reproduction of Indigenous societies. Ranging was the practice of small militia units carrying out proactive and mobile exploratory missions into Indigenous territories to search for, engage, and destroy Indigenous combatants. Emerging around the

same time as ranging, scalp bounties were issued by colonial governments, which paid high prices for settlers to murder Indigenous people.
Ranging and scalp bounties fueled extirpative war with their specific
targeting of civilian populations. These practices kick-started settler
mass militarism. They surfaced in response to the Indigenous anticolonialism that encumbered the expansion and thus viability of the early
British settler colonies.

Ranging and scalp bounties were devised to counteract the success of
Indigenous nations in destabilizing the advance of English settlements
in some of the first major wars of the seventeenth century, particularly
Metacomet's Pan-Indian war of 1675 (also known as King Philip's War).
During this war, the Wampanoag and Narragansett tribes unleashed a
wave of defensive attacks on English settlements that destroyed twelve
hundred of the twelve thousand settler houses, made one-tenth of the
settler male population casualties, and incurred £150,000 in damage.[8]
Many settlers felt that the British settler colonial project was close to
collapsing due to these losses. British settlers were only able to defeat
Metacomet's insurgency by manipulating existing conflicts among Indigenous nations. They secured the help of allied Indigenous tribes to
harness the forces necessary to subdue Wampanoag and Narragansett
resistance. However, during these same years and in the period that
followed, settler leaders also devised the tactics of ranging and scalp
bounties to expand their colonies' capacity for extirpative war.[9] The
turn to these tactics was a symptom of the revolutionary potential of
Indigenous anticolonialism to destabilize or possibly even destroy, settler colonialism in North America. The answer to this concern became,
in part, to make all settlers into soldiers conducting anti-Indian counterrevolution. The threats of both a viable alternative to class society
and formidable Indigenous resistance destabilizing British settlements
required an all-hands-on-deck approach to uphold settler colonialism.
Ranging and scalp bounties did the work of incentivizing and recruiting civilian settlers to be at the same time anti-Indian soldiers.

Ranging was mostly performed by volunteer or private militias made up of citizen-soldiers. It also principally recruited these citizen-soldiers with the promise of securing scalp bounties, showing how the two practices were intertwined. Grenier points out that through the issuance of scalp bounties "the colonial governments had discovered the means to motivate untold numbers of men to take to the field and range against the Indians. In the process, they established the large-scale privatization of war within American frontier communities."[10] For example, only a few decades later these practices were consolidated to give greater military power to English settlers in the Tuscarora War of 1711. With a more advanced mass base of anti-Indian citizen-soldiers "seasoned" in the practices of ranging and scalp bounties, English settler forces displaced, kidnapped into slavery, or murdered thousands of Tuscarora people. Tuscarora refugees who survived were driven to New York.[11] Settler mass militarism proved to be an effective strategy for routing the Tuscarora from their lands. It became a strategy that would be repeated and expanded in successive anti-Indian wars as British settler colonization advanced west toward the trans-Appalachian region.

The later formation of the US settler state with a regular army would centralize the strategy of anti-Indian counterrevolutionary war. However, a tension emerged between the push to centralize and the pull of an ongoing decentralized, informal settler mass militarism. Unlike in Europe, where the emerging bourgeoisie wrested the state away from a landed aristocracy, settler capitalists constructed their own state to serve their class interests of upholding settler colonialism and slavery. Gerald Horne argues that American settler and enslaver capitalists revolted from the British empire to form their own centralized nation-state that could guard against both Indigenous anticolonialism and Black abolition.[12] The desire for unfettered access to Indigenous lands, the destruction of their societies as alternatives to class society, the fear of British-sponsored slave revolt, and British authorities signaling their intention to abolish slavery in their colonies precipitated patriot settlers

Figure 4. *Massacre of the Whites by the Indians and Blacks in Florida.* Woodcut frontispiece in *An Authentic Narrative of the Seminole War; and of the Miraculous Escape of Mrs. Mary Godfrey, and Her Four Female Children: Annexed Is a Minute Detail of the Horrid Massacres of the Whites, by the Indians and Negroes, in Florida, in the Months of December, January and February.* New York: Printed for D. F. Blanchard and others, 1836. Rare Book Division, The New York Public Library, New York City. b14115936.

taking up arms to constitute a government that could maintain settler colonialism and slavery in the face of such developments.

The US state was crafted as a weapon for better organizing and consolidating the strategies of advancing settler colonialism and slavery. The ongoing foundation of this centralization of anti-Indian counterrevolution embodied by the US state continued to be settler mass militarism. The settler state and mass militarism functioned together, but this combination was not without contradiction. The decentralization and self-directed character of the origins of settler mass militarism shaped it into a force that functioned autonomously or beyond state authority in the shared objective of anti-Indian counterrevolutionary war. The tension between state centralization and mass militarism decentralization figured centrally in the history of antebellum anti-Indian counterrevolutionary war. To understand how settler mass militarism continued to be consolidated in response to the revolutionary challenge of Indigenous anticolonialism, how this process related to the rise of centralized state power, and how settler colonialism intersected with slavery's imperial expansion, I analyze the Second Seminole War (1836–1842) of Florida and the US conquest of Indigenous California post-1848 as key flashpoints in this history.

"THE FLORIDA WAR"

The Second Seminole War of Florida was one of the most powerful anticolonial insurgencies against settler colonialism and slavery in the history of the United States. By examining Seminole anticolonialism and US settler colonialism's response, I show how this moment registers key insights for understanding settler mass militarism. As scholarship on the Second Seminole War often highlights, it was one of the most disastrous and costliest US military campaigns in the history of the "Indian Wars." The federal government spent a total of $40 million to fund the war, and fifteen hundred US soldiers perished. Thousands of settlers, many of whom were enslavers who owned sugar plantations, were displaced and their property either destroyed or expropriated.[13] An uncounted number of settlers were killed. The failure of the US military to win the war drew national criticism and disfavor among the public. Historian and Indigenous activist Winona LaDuke notes that "fifty thousand federal soldiers served in the Second Seminole War, and there were never fewer than 3,800 soldiers in the field at any one time. The Seminoles, by contrast, had no more than 1,500 warriors total."[14] As historian C. S. Monaco states, the Seminole war was a "setback to national esteem."[15] The inability to defeat the Seminoles undermined the national myths of settler dominance and white supremacy. More dangerously than undermining US military power, Seminole anticolonialism evinced a capacity to thwart settler colonization and maintain political and economic autonomy, which is to say, to assert Indigenous governance over territories that settlers expected to seize. The Seminoles also granted membership to formerly enslaved Africans that ranged from forms of indentured servitude to full equality and coleadership under Indigenous governance. The Seminoles cooperated and allied with independent Black maroon communities. Seminole anticolonialism sponsored Black revolt, fugitivity, and marronage against enslavers of Florida. Through these factors, Seminole governance posed a revolutionary alternative to the class society of settler colonialism and slavery of Florida. As US leaders confronted the reality that Seminole anticolonialism could not be so easily subdued, they worried that, as Monaco argues, "failure risked dismantling the mask of invulnerability and white privilege; as a result, the entire social and economic order might collapse like a house of cards. A pan-Indian rebellion would surely end in unthinkable horrors and . . . open the door for slave revolt."[16] In other words, Seminole anticolonialism panicked settler society for what it portended: a larger pan-Indian revolutionary movement with capacity to overturn settler colonialism and slavery.

The Seminoles initiated their defensive insurgency against the US state and Florida settlers in response to the threat of forced removal stemming from Jackson's Indian Removal Act of 1830. In May 1832, US officials fraudulently coerced and manipulated several Seminole leaders into signing the Treaty of Fort Payne, which mandated that in three years the Seminoles would relinquish their lands in Florida and be removed to lands west of the Mississippi.[17] When the time arrived to enforce the coerced agreement, the Seminole war council determined to refuse the mandate to give up their lands and relocate. Andrew Jackson—who a decade earlier in the First Seminole War (1817–1821) had illegally invaded what was at the time Spanish Florida to attack Seminole villages and Black maroon settlements—sent a communiqué to the Seminole war council castigating them for their decision and promising that Seminole land would be surveyed, sold, and occupied by US settlers; this process would be backed by armed force if necessary.[18] Undeterred by these threats, the Seminole war council prepared to defend their lands against the promise of impending illegal settler incursions. In December 1835 the Seminole unleashed a series of well-planned and coordinated attacks on US military forces. The Seminoles first routed hundreds of settler planters in the Alachua region, burning their plantations and destroying property.[19] This was followed by Seminole leader Osceola leading an attack on a Florida volunteer militia guarding a supply train sent to the embattled Micanopy settlement, which resulted in the Seminoles expropriating enemy supplies and leaving several settler rangers dead or wounded. A few weeks later, on December 28, Seminole forces led by Halpatter Tustenuggee (Alligator) and Ote Emathla (Jumper) ambushed a military caravan commanded by Major Francis Dade composed of two companies traveling from Fort Brooke to Fort King. Only three soldiers survived the ambush. Seminole forces retreated only when they believed that they had either killed or dispersed every soldier from the two companies. On the same day, Osceola led his group of fighters in an attack on the agent in command of Seminole removal, Wiley Thompson, and other leaders at Fort King. Seminole fighters specifically assassinated Thompson and fellow government administrators for their leadership role in carrying out the removal policy.[20]

In coordination with these events, Seminole leaders Emathla (King Philip) and Coacoochee (Wildcat) launched a weeks-long campaign on the east coast targeting sugar plantations from St. Augustine to New Smyrna. As in the attacks in the Alachua region, Seminole fighters burned plantations and extracted hundreds of enslaved workers. Monaco describes the impact of the east coast campaign: "All sugar mills, cotton gins, plantation houses, slave quarters, crops, and an unknown number of settler homesteads were eventually burned and left in ruins. Although the fledgling sugar industry in Florida represented a small fraction of sugar production compared to Louisiana, for instance, these losses created an economic cataclysm in the territory as many mills, outfitted with the latest steam-powered technology, were heavily mortgaged and also employed hundreds of people."[21] Along with economic ruin, of great concern to settler planters was seeing John Caesar, a Black Seminole, lead his own war party within this campaign to destroy east coast sugar plantations. One of the targets that Caesar's group razed was the conspicuous New Smyrna mansion and plantation of the prominent citizen Judge David R. Dunham.[22] During the weekslong campaign, Caesar destroyed dozens of plantations and freed around three hundred enslaved Africans, who joined the Seminoles.[23]

In the days following the attack on Dade and the assassination of Thompson, Clinch's regular army forces and Florida militia volunteers mobilized to mount a counterattack against the Seminoles to put down what they perceived as a momentary uprising. What became known as the Battle of Withlacoochee ended in another disastrous loss for settler forces. Clinch had led his troops to an area referred to as the "Cove" near the Withlacoochee River, believed to be a stronghold for Seminole forces. The Seminoles, under the leadership of Osceola, anticipated Clinch and had prepared to launch an ambush attack. At the moment when Clinch's forces began to cross the Withlacoochee River using only a single dugout canoe with a portion of the soldiers still waiting to cross, the Seminoles attacked, wounding fifty-nine US forces and killing four. Clinch's army was compelled to flee, in a shock to their confidence that they could quickly repress the Seminole rebellion.[24] News of the Seminoles' effective offensive against US forces in December through January, which resulted in millions of dollars in damage, the death of dozens of soldiers and settler planters, and the liberation of hundreds of enslaved Africans, was received by Florida settlers and the nation as apocalyptic. Reports of the war filled the headlines of the nation's leading newspapers and gripped the public.

While it is beyond the scope of this chapter to provide a detailed account of the ensuing actions in the following years of the war, I do want to examine how US settler society responded to Seminole armed resistance to forced removal. The response contained a tension between two differing strategies on how to conduct anti-Indian counterrevolution.

One strategy was to fund a large regular army as the principal tool for defeating the Seminoles. The second strategy was to draw more heavily on the strength of settler mass militarism through the increased use of volunteer militias and the resettlement of settler planters as permanent armed occupiers. US leaders chose the first strategy, and it proved to be a failure. In the next years, the US spent millions of dollars to fund and equip a large regular army in its fight to defeat the Seminoles. Several generals were appointed and fired over the course of the war due to their inability to attain victory. For example, Major General Winfield Scott, in the summer of 1836, led a counteroffensive campaign of five thousand soldiers, one of the largest of the war, but failed to quell Seminole resistance. The guerrilla warfare tactics of ambush and retreat, combined with knowledge of their own terrain, helped the Seminoles persist despite the asymmetrical relationship between their forces and the United States. Their protracted uprising also exhausted US forces. In one of the months of Scott's campaign, it cost $1.5 million. News of Scott's failures caused the public to lose confidence in the war effort, and many of the garrison forts in central Florida were abandoned in a retreat of US forces.[25]

A few years later, when Major General Thomas Jesup was appointed and, like his predecessors, could not force the Seminoles to surrender, he proposed to offer a major concession of no longer enforcing the order for forced removal and granting the Seminoles the territory of South Florida, encompassing the Everglades. Although federal leaders rejected this proposal and later fired Jesup, replacing him with Colonel Zachary Taylor, Jesup's proposal became the blueprint for the later Macomb Treaty of 1839, which stipulated that the Seminoles could remain in Florida below the Peace River if they agreed to cease hostilities.[26] While US leaders expected the Macomb Treaty to be temporary—they secretly had planned to return at a later point to remove the Seminoles—it nonetheless marked the power of Seminole resistance to force the US government to rescind removal orders and allow the Seminole to remain in Florida. It was a concession that could never have been won through negotiation or diplomacy; it was won through protracted armed resistance. Furthermore, Seminole leaders like Abiaka and others refused to sign the Macomb Treaty or any agreement with the US government, based on the precedent of US leaders not honoring previous treaties. Abiaka also continued to refuse offers to receive payments in exchange for removing west. Abiaka-led Seminoles used armed resistance to defend their land bases in the areas where they remained rather than appealing to the Macomb Treaty. It is from these groups led by Abiaka, who fought to remain and refused removal by never signing a peace treaty, that the Seminole Tribe of Florida and the Independent Traditional Seminole Nation trace their origins.[27]

Throughout the US military's unsuccessful campaign to subdue the Seminoles, there were demands from some US leaders to turn away from the strategy of traditional war with the use of a regular army and instead adopt the practices of settler mass militarism. Those who made these demands believed that deploying more volunteer militias from Florida and other states and facilitating white settlers returning to occupy the areas surrounding Seminole lands would give US forces the advantage over the Seminoles. For example, when General Taylor assumed command, he called for settlers to return and rebuild their plantations in the areas where they had been routed by Seminole attacks. He promised the US Army would provide security in these areas, with the expectation that returning settlers would be armed and ready to fight alongside the regular army to subdue the Seminole. Monaco writes that Taylor "urged the formation of military/settler 'colonies,' especially since the application of brute military force, which included the latest technology in cannons and rocketry, had failed. . . . Taylor differed markedly from Jesup by the latter's distrust and disdain of Florida settlers, an attitude that also permeated much of the army. Instead, Taylor followed a pattern long established in his native Kentucky as well as other 'frontier' (Indigenous) regions in the Old Southwest and concluded that pioneer farmers and ranchers, while formerly a missing component in the army's plans, were vital to success."[28]

Cultural historian Laurel Shire has studied these efforts to aid white settlers in the reoccupation of Florida to help in the war effort against the Seminoles. Shire argues that gender played a key role in this process, which she calls "expansionist domesticity," in which settler women were expected to play active roles in the labor of homemaking that legitimized the settler family's occupation of Seminole lands.[29] Shire notes that many white settlers fled to settler towns in 1836 and 1837 seeking rations and housing after their plantations had been razed by the Seminoles. The image of the victimized settler family was mobilized to demand resources be allocated to support the displaced settlers. In response, Congress passed the Aid the Suffering and Indigent Inhabitants of Florida Act in 1836 to provide welfare for routed settlers. While the act guaranteed food rations and other essential supplies, it required that settlers reoccupy Seminole lands as a condition for receiving ongoing aid. This welfare policy for routed settlers aimed to prevent them from fleeing Florida and sponsored their return to playing the role of occupiers essential for buttressing the fight against Seminole resistance.[30] Shire observes that through this state welfare, recolonization parties, whose goal was to "resettle" those who had been drive out by the Seminoles, occupied nineteen sites in Florida by August 1841. By June 1842 there were over one thousand settlers, the majority of whom were women and children, receiving rations from the army in exchange for resettlement. These settler planter families had not only reoccupied areas near Seminole lands but also brought with them their captives of 394 enslaved Africans.[31] This policy paid settler families to enter a war zone and become counterrevolutionary combatants for settler colonization.

In addition to government aid, US leaders also proposed to offer free land to any settlers willing to establish homesteads in buffer zones between Seminole lands and major settler towns. Thomas Hart Benton, the Missouri senator, spearheaded these proposals in Congress in response to witnessing the failure of the regular army to subdue Seminole forces. Benton wanted to give large tracts of lands to settlers who promised to serve as permanent armed occupiers of the lands on which they established homesteads. The requirement to bear arms with the expectation to target insurgent Seminole forces was essential to receiving land for free. After a few unsuccessful attempts to pass such legislation, Benton succeeded in 1842 with the Armed Occupation Act. The law stipulated that any head of household could receive 160 acres of free land in exchange for a minimum of five years of armed occupation and land improvements.[32] In chapter 3 I discuss in further detail Benton's vision of the armed occupier within the context of the aspiration for white equality and homesteading. For now, it's worth noting that Benton saw the mass armed occupier as the linchpin in the strategy for conducting anti-Indian white counterrevolution. In the congressional debates on the bill, he argued that populating buffer zones near the Seminole insurgency was crucial for bringing an end to the war and retaining conquered land from any future anticolonial resistance. More importantly, he believed that armed occupiers were the strongest line of defense protecting the settler society from potential catastrophic pan-Indian revolt.[33] Under the Armed Occupation Act, 1,312 settlers filed for permits to receive free land. However, only 459 were granted ownership after five years.[34] Both the aid to routed settlers and the offer of free land to armed occupiers were designed to bolster settler mass militarism in Florida. The aim was to create an army of permanent settler-citizen soldiers as the frontline forces in counterrevolution against Seminole insurgency. Like white alliance policing of Black revolt and fugitivity that made white enslaver communities function as carceral social bodies, settlers serving as armed occupiers consolidated their communities into anti-Indian military units in which everyone was a soldier for settler colonialism. Calls for this strategy stemmed from witnessing the failure of regular armies to wage successful anti-Indian counterrevolution. The centralized state was insufficient. Settler mass militarism was viewed as the strategy to rescue Florida from Indigenous anticolonialism.

The Seminoles had a sophisticated analysis of their enemy and understood, I suggest, this very role of settler mass militarism in helping to uphold settler colonization. We can see this in how they sought to decimate the construction of settler mass militarism in Florida in the first place. As mentioned, their first targets were settler plantations and homesteads functioning as buffer zones between Seminole lands and major settler towns. These attacks also weakened the base from which volunteer militias recruited and resourced themselves. While the Armed Occupation Act and settler welfare policies sponsored the return of many settler plantations and homesteads, the Seminoles continued to rout these armed occupiers. In Benton County (named in honor of Senator Benton for his role in the passage of free land policy), settler families that occupied free lands or recolonized areas where they had been previously displaced were run off by Seminoles in 1842. This chilled further participation in such policies going forward.[35] With settler mass militarism weakened, the Seminoles could continue to thwart the US regular army through guerrilla tactics. The Seminoles' strategic attacks on settler mass militarism, combined with the inability of US leaders to establish a strong chain of settler occupiers, produced a disavowed dread among Florida settlers.

A widely circulated account of the Seminole War that, I maintain, registers the anxiety about the underdevelopment and thus weakness of settler mass militarism in Florida was a pamphlet published by Daniel Blanchard in the spring of 1836, titled *Authentic Narrative of the Seminole War; and of the Miraculous Escape of Mrs. Mary Godfrey, and Her Four Female Children.*[36] The Blanchard pamphlet offered a sensationalized, proslavery, settler colonial depiction of the Seminoles' initial uprising in the winter of 1835–1836, or as the caption to its title-page woodcut states, "Horrid Massacres of the Whites, by the Indians and Negroes, in Florida, in the months of December, January, and February." The pamphlet also included a folding-plate frontispiece with a woodcut of a massacre scene vilifying Indigenous and African forces, depicted as mercilessly attacking victimized white settler families, most notably women and children. In an interesting print culture connection to Nat Turner, the literary scholar Alexander Mazzaferro shows how the folding-plate frontispiece of the Blanchard pamphlet duplicated sections of the folding-plate frontispiece "Horrid Massacre in Virginia" from Samuel Warner's pamphlet on the Nat Turner insurrection.[37] The Blanchard pamphlet also reused portions of another woodcut already in circulation, "Massacre of Baldwin's Family by the Savages," from the pamphlet *Narrative of the Massacre, by the Savages, of the Wife & Children of Thomas Baldwin* (1836).[38] Mazzaferro suggests that because all three pamphlets were published in New York City, they might have shared the same printer, who recycled woodcuts.[39] Kathryn Walkiewicz notes that regardless of the reason for repurposing the woodcuts, their presentation in the Blanchard pamphlet "shaped readers' perceptions of Florida and Afro-Native collectivity, given the pamphlet's popularity."[40] Like the ideological work of the woodcut "Horrid Massacre in Virginia," which demonized the resistance of the unfree, the anonymous author of the Blanchard pamphlet states that the narrative's purpose is to document for the public the Seminoles' recent attacks on the "defenceless inhabitants (male and female) of the Floridas" who had "fallen victims to the tomahawk and scalping knife!" The Seminoles' actions are characterized as a "war of extermination, as they appear disposed neither to give or take quarter."[41] In a well-worn trope of inverting revolutionary and reactionary violence, the images and language of the pamphlet cast white settler enslavers of Florida as innocent victims of unjustified aggression by Seminoles and Black maroons.

The featured story of the pamphlet is the captivity narrative of Mary Godfrey. While the story of Godfrey is presented as factual, historians agree that it was a fictionalized account assembled from the general experiences of routed Florida settlers.[42] The author narrates how the Seminoles' campaign of razing East Coast sugar plantations near St. Augustine forces Godfrey and her four children to flee from their home to the nearby woods to hide from their assailants. While in hiding, they are exposed to the elements and lack food. After a few days, when they are close to succumbing to their conditions, a formerly enslaved African who has joined the Seminoles discovers Godfrey and her children. Instead of kidnapping or murdering them, as the pamphlet leads the reader to assume are his intentions, the Black Seminole sympathizes with their plight and helps them find safe passage back to guarded white settlements. He does so because, as he reasons, "he had two children who were held in bondage by the whites . . . to enjoy his own liberty he had left them to their fate, and something now seemed to whisper to him, that if he should destroy the lives of her innocent children, God would be angry, and might doom his little ones to a similar face by the hands of the white men in whose power they were!"[43] Those who have studied the Blanchard pamphlet have taken notice of its contradictory representation of Blackness. The vilification of Black Seminoles and Black maroons as murderous rebels was typical of proslavery literature. Yet the figure of the sympathetic African, whom Godfrey refers to as the "humane African (our deliverer)," and the comparison between his children held in bondage and the plight of Godfrey and her children, could be read as an abolitionist critique of slavery.[44] Mazzaferro argues that the "Blanchard text's repurposing of the Warner and Baldwin woodcuts recasts the encounter between an emancipated Black man and a white family as the site not of brutality but of tenderness toward innocents and so advances an argument for abolition rooted not in a self-serving fear of reprisal but in a more capacious sense of human equality," and that the recycling of woodcuts depicting Black revolt also undermines the "proslavery argument for insurrectionary singularity and nonrecurrence."[45] Cultural historian Michele Navakas argues that the Blanchard pamphlet is not an abolitionist text, but rather reinscribes proslavery ideology precisely through the figure of the sympathetic African who symbolizes, for enslavers, the potential for Black maroons to become "recoverable property." Navakas also suggests alternatively that the sympathetic African figure could have served as a warning to enslavers to increase their protection of slavery from fugitive slaves joining alternate communities of the Florida swamps, posing a challenge to slavery.[46] Beyond whether the pamphlet was proslavery or antislavery, I argue that the Blanchard text not only encodes a white settler-enslaver anxiety related to the failure of settler mass militarism to take root in Florida, but also the Seminoles' understanding of settler mass militarism as a fulcrum of settler colonialism and slavery in Florida to target, weaken, and destroy.[47]

Before the Blanchard text relates the Godfrey story, it describes how Seminole forces attacked the plantation of Mr. William Cooley, "an old and respected inhabitant of New River." The narrator explains that Cooley is away from the plantation at the time of the attack but upon his return discovers that "his wife, three children, and Mr. Joseph Flinton, a teacher in the family" have been killed. The text highlights Cooley's surprise that he was a target of attack when he had previously enjoyed good relations with the Seminoles. "Cooley had always been on the most intimate terms with the Indians; his wife was taken captive by them several years since, and was as such retained by them a sufficient length of time to become acquainted with their language, customs, &c. and has ever since been considered a favorite with them; his son was a particular pet of theirs." The pamphlet suggests that none of this matters to the Seminoles, who indiscriminately attack all white settler plantations and homesteads, including the Cooley family. The Seminoles "commenced an attack on the plantations of the whites in the interior, and upon their settlements at New River and Cape Florida, and plundered, destroyed and laid waste every thing of value that came in their way." The text notes that "one of the negroes belonging to Cooley," who had fled the attack and returned safely, remarks "that the outrage was committed by Indians well known to him and the other inhabitants of that part of the peninsula." When read in relation to Mary Godfrey's story, in which her husband, Mr. Godfrey, is absent serving as a volunteer in the Florida militia, the pamphlet's attention to what is suggested as Cooley's naïve and misguided friendship with the Seminoles marks the breakdown in settler mass militarism. The Seminoles are shown as never losing sight of treating the Cooley family as enemy combatants. Yet Cooley, the pamphlet implies, has forgotten his duty as a mass armed occupier to see the Seminoles in this same light as insurgents to guard against, a shortcoming for which he has paid a great price. "If any family could rely on past friendship for present forbearance from the savage foe, it was this—but all calculations of this sort were horribly disappointed by the awful result."[48] The Cooley family, it is implied, should have remembered their primary role was to serve as armed occupiers.

Unlike other captivity narratives, most famously Mary Rowlandson's *A Narrative of the Captivity and Restoration of Mrs. Mary Rowlandson* (1682), or the white victimization ideology of slave revolt accounts, the Blanchard pamphlet does not represent white families as helpless victims overtaken by monstrous Indigenous and Black rebellion.[49] In fact, as Mazzaferro points out, the pamphlet's narrative seems not to adhere to the ideology of its fold-out and title page woodcuts depicting such scenes of Native and Black rebellion targeting defenseless white settlers. Unlike Mazzaferro, who reads the pamphlet as abolitionist, I suggest that the pamphlet is more concerned with representing white settlers as forgetful, lax, or disorganized in their purpose as soldier-colonizers in enemy territory, making them susceptible to defeat in the face of Indigenous insurgency. The lack of discipline to maintain their role as anti-Indian soldiers leaves them with only one recourse: flight. "Families widely separated from one another, had no other means of safety than flight afforded them." Instead of armed occupiers creating refugees, white settlers were made refugees by Seminole resistance:

"500 families were thus driven from their homes, and in almost a state of starvation, sought protection under the walls of St. Augustine and other fortified places." This language crystallizes the trepidation concerning the lack of mass militarism among Florida white settlers and how such a breakdown produced a vulnerability in settler society that the Seminoles identified and attacked to their advantage. The Blanchard pamphlet served as a reminder to its readers that settlers could not expect to live as civilians in the project of anti-Indian counterrevolution. They were to be anti-Indian soldiers before they were anything else, as settler mass militarism demanded. In this way, the Blanchard pamphlet also intimates that where settler mass militarism breaks down, so too does white alliance policing of Black revolt and fugitivity. Rebellious slaves, like the figure of the "humane African," sharing thoughts of abolition and combining with Indigenous forces, move about freely when settler mass militarism is absent. In fact, the "humane African" has replaced the white male settler head of household in the role of protector of white women and children in such conditions. It is noted that the Black Seminole promised to escort Godfrery to "within view of [settler militias], which the friendly negro did, although at the risk of his own life!"[50] While settler men are absent, as in the Godfrey family, or too trusting of Indigenous enemies, like Mr. Cooley, Black Seminoles play the role of protectors of white settler women and children, dangerously undermining the racial and gender hierarchies of white settler order. The breakdown in settler mass militarism has allowed both Indigenous anticolonialism and Black abolition war to enter and destabilize the white settlement. In other words, it is suggested that for settler-citizens to falter in the role of anti-Indian soldiers was a major crack in the defenses against Indigenous anticolonialism (and its catalyzing of slave revolt and fugitivity) and thus invited the collapse of settler society itself.

But more than expressing the dread of settler mass militarism's breakdown, the Blanchard pamphlet also allegorizes how Seminole

Figure 5. Seminole fighters lay siege to a US military blockhouse on the Withlacoochee River to fight forced removal. *Attack of the Seminoles on the Block House.* Lithograph. Charleston, SC: T. F. Gray and James, 1837. Library of Congress Prints and Photographs Division, Washington, DC. LC-DIG-ppmsca-19924.

and Black maroon resistance has produced a potentially insurmountable fear among white settlers about resettling as armed occupiers. Walkie-wicz argues that the pamphlet's "inconsistent relationship between text and image" and other contradictions remind readers of the irrepress-ible resistance of the Seminoles.[51] Instead of a call to arms to reinforce settler mass militarism, as might be expected, the pamphlet ends with the pessimistic and defeatist image of Florida's terrain as not conquer-able, or "un-occupiable." "The face of the country, interspersed with hammocks, cyprus swamps and marshes, almost impenetrable to the white man, presents serious obstacles to the prosecution of a campaign in Florida; and while these fastnesses constitute the natural defense of the Indians, they present difficulties almost insurmountable to their pursuers."[52] The recognition that Seminole insurgency has targeted and weakened settler mass militarism, destabilizing settler colonialism's capacity to wage anti-Indian counterrevolution, is displaced onto Florida's terrain, characterized as naturally inhospitable to white settler society and therefore not colonizable. Despite the national context of Manifest Destiny and other visions of limitless settler expansion, Seminole anti-colonialism had engendered a settler pessimism or despondency that dampened dreams of colonizing Florida. Surfacing in the very pamphlet meant to do the work of championing settler invincibility and white supremacy was the awareness that settler colonization was a tenuous project when its weak points were exposed and attacked.

COLONIZATION OF INDIGENOUS CALIFORNIA

Only a few years after the official withdrawal of the US military from Florida in 1842, the United States instigated its expansionist war against Mexico, which would result in the seizure of territories that became the Southwest, including the present-day states of California, New Mexico, Utah, and Nevada; large portions of Arizona and Colorado; and areas of Oklahoma, Kansas, and Wyoming.[53] The Treaty of Guadalupe Hidalgo (1848) officially ended the war and opened the newly seized territories to US settlers for occupation. Sparked by the discovery of gold in 1848 and 1849 and the desire to seize land as wealth, US settlers spilled into what became the state of California in 1850. Arriving by sea or overland travel, US settlers, many of whom had previous experience engaging in anti-Indian violence as volunteers in state militias or private farmers displacing Indigenous people, functioned as the shock troops in campaigns to expropriate Indigenous territories for mining, ranching, and farming.[54] Before this invasion, the Indigenous population was estimated at 150,000 people. After only a few decades, this number would plummet to just over 16,000 by 1880.[55] Put simply, the post-1848 gold rush period was a destructive and targeted genocide of the Indigenous peoples of California. Historians have noted that the

US settler colonization of Indigenous California was not principally carried out by a centralized state with a regular army but rather informally by European settlers acting privately or as citizen volunteers in ranger militias. That is, if settler mass militarism was considered weak and ineffectual in Florida, it was the vanguard force of settler colonialism in post-1848 California. I want to examine how it functioned in this role in California to understand how settler mass militarism was both the fulcrum of anti-Indian counterrevolution/colonization and an autonomous force that worked beyond the US settler state. What did it mean that the very strategy on which the US state depended was also autonomous from its control in its decentralized, mass character? In what follows in this section, I suggest that one of the factors that constituted this contradiction was the often overlooked Indigenous anticolonialism of post-1848 California.

Before US settler colonization, centuries of Spanish colonization had subjugated the Indigenous peoples of California. Spanish colonizers had imposed and maintained a ranching economy premised on unfree Indigenous labor. After achieving independence from Spain in 1825, Mexico continued to use and depend on Indigenous slavery in California. When US settlers invaded, they took over the reins of this system to maintain a pool of unpaid Indigenous labor for their new settlements. While some "free-soil" US settlers objected to Indigenous slavery in California for the same reasons they opposed Black slavery—it advantaged, they argued, wealthy slaveholders over independent white settler miners or farmers—the majority supported it as an important source of wealth for early US California. US settlers relied on Indigenous workers, both paid and unfree, to perform the arduous work of mining. Historians Damon Akins and William Bauer Jr. point out that in 1848, around "half of the four thousand miners in the mining districts" were Indigenous workers.[56] Indigenous labor was also the backbone of the major industries of early California's economy, which included cattle ranching, wine grape production, farming, and domestic work.[57] US settler leaders passed a series of policies sanctioning Indigenous slavery. The infamous 1850 Act for the Government and Protection of Indians authorized the indenturing of Indigenous children to whites; prohibited Indigenous people from testifying against whites; criminalized "vagrancy" among Indigenous people to punish the unemployed and prevent public assembly; and outlawed Indigenous stewardship practices of performing prescribed fires and cultural burning, which prevented severe forest fires.[58] Los Angeles passed a law that allowed Indigenous people arrested for vagrancy to be sold at public auction to bidders who paid the bail or fines of the incarcerated in exchange for forced indentured servitude. Such laws and other practices not only delivered for US settlers a pool of easily exploitable Indigenous labor, but they also fueled the kidnapping and sex trafficking of Indigenous women and children, which further targeted the social reproduction of Indigenous tribes.[59]

As US settlers arrived in waves, staking out mining claims, occupying lands for farming and ranching, and seizing control of Indigenous labor, their imprint immediately impacted Indigenous food systems and economic activity. Cattle grazing destroyed roots and other plants that Indigenous people cultivated and foraged as vital sources of food. Settler overhunting of wild game depleted rabbit, deer, bear, elk, and other animal populations. Mining damaged river fisheries, and the overfelling of trees ruined pine nut harvest yields.[60] The destruction of food systems, the interruption of economic activity, and enslavement were conditions that also made Indigenous peoples vulnerable to disease and illness. These factors all greatly undermined Indigenous communities' capacity to challenge settler invasion. However, despite these attacks, Indigenous people of California resisted and fought to defend their lands, water, and governance against settler colonization. One of the most common and effective forms of resistance was expropriating livestock from settler ranches and farms. Similar to the activities of Black maroons, who would raid plantations to take goods that would support their communities while also forcing their enemies to suffer losses in capital, Indigenous raids to seize cattle and other livestock to resell or feed their communities was a formidable problem for California settler economies premised on beef production. In fact, Akins and Bauer argue that one of the reasons US settlers already living in what later became California supported the US war against Mexico was the grievance that Mexican governance could not properly stop Indian raids on cattle. These settlers believed that installing US leadership would provide better protection of their property. After US forces took control of California, they commissioned military campaigns to hunt and capture Indigenous groups who were successful at expropriating cattle. These campaigns failed in their mission, and the raiding continued.[61] Indigenous workers who faced abuse, assault, and overworking resisted settler bosses. In some cases, Indigenous workers killed settler bosses to hold them accountable for anti-Indian violence. While this sometimes led to violent reprisals, this resistance incurred a cost to settlers who abused their Indigenous workers.[62] Indigenous tribes also waged yearslong campaigns to defend territories from settler incursions. The Hupa people of Northwest California engaged in protracted defensive attacks against trespassing miners and other settlers in the Hoopa Valley region. This led to the US state granting a concession of promising to respect the rights of the Hupa people to hunt, fish, and gather on their lands without settler interference.[63]

Indigenous people also organized and carried out armed insurgencies to eject settlers from their lands. One of the most impactful was the pan-Indian revolt known as Garra's uprising of 1851.[64] Antonio Garra was a leader of the Cupeño people who collaborated with several Indigenous tribes, including the Cahuilla, Cocopahs, Kumeyaay, Luiseño, and Quechan, to coordinate and execute an insurrection to drive out all settlers from Southern California. Garra led pan-Indian forces in attacks on several settler ranches and settlements, stealing thousands of head of sheep, burning homes and other buildings, and killing some of those who fought back. Garra targeted settlers known for anti-Indian abuse and violence. The insurrection terrified settlers and embodied their worst fears of "Indian war" that would upend settler colonialism in California. The major general of the state militia, Joshua Bean, who was called to lead forces to repress Garra's revolt, wrote of the event in a letter to a colleague: "All these things demonstrate the fact that an Indian war is upon us. The citizens sensible of this fact are taking the most energetic steps to meet the crisis."[65]

As Bean's letter indicated, US settlers waged retributive campaigns to subdue Indigenous resistance. As historians have highlighted, these campaigns were punitive and pedagogical. Their aim was to retaliate against those who rebelled and terrorize entire Indigenous communities to "teach" them that submission to colonization was preferable to counterrevolutionary violence. Historian Benjamin Madley writes that "for many whites, Indians defending their homelands against conquest and colonization were intolerable. When California Indians resisted incursions, defended themselves, or took livestock to survive, newcomers often responded with indiscriminate, disproportionate attacks. In classic blame-the-victim style, some claimed that California Indians fully deserved these attacks, and insisted that Indians had brought the attacks upon themselves by daring to resist. This created local cycles of largely one-sided violence in which whites—carrying out what became an unwritten doctrine of collective, mass reprisal—killed large numbers of California Indians."[66] These campaigns to neutralize Indigenous resistance were carried out through the strategy of settler mass militarism. Beyond only focusing on the violence, it is important to analyze the constitutive elements of settler mass militarism to understand how it worked to facilitate anti-Indian counterrevolution in California. It was in this context that its inner workings were more prominent due to its vanguard and principal role in settler colonization. I suggest that these constitutive elements of settler mass militarism were the practices of solidarity and democracy among settlers across class, religion, ethnicity, and other differences in the shared goal of anti-Indian war. Settler mass militarism was also "grassroots" in character, or self-directed and decentralized, operating beyond the oversight of the state even as it served the shared objective of anti-Indian counterrevolution.[67]

The widespread mobilization of volunteer ranger militias best embodied how settler-citizens cultivated democratic and grassroots practices to wage anti-Indian counterrevolution in California. In April 1850 the state of California passed militia acts that codified what was already an informal practice underway of settlers organizing vigilante militias to conduct retributive violence against Indigenous people. It was the vigilantism that prompted the state to sanction and sponsor settlers raising their own militias. Through these militia acts, the state authorized settler-citizen volunteers to form their own "independent companies" to wage counterinsurgency campaigns against local Indigenous communities. Madley writes: "The 'Act concerning Volunteer or Independent Companies' gave rise to over 303 militia units in which more than 35,000 Californians served between 1851 and 1866. This act allowed citizens to organize a volunteer company by following procedures that included advertising an enlistment location, electing officers, and reporting the unit's name and members. . . . Once the company had been organized and uniformed, its commander could petition the governor for weapons and supplies, as long as he sent along a bond certified by his county judge. The governor could then order California's quartermaster general to provide arms and supplies."[68]

This was settler democracy in action. Citizens came together to petition their government leaders to enact their interests. In return, volunteer militias enacted and extended state power. They also at times worked in tandem with the US Army. For this, the state funded volunteer militias even though they were expensive endeavors. The cost of supplies, munitions, weapons, and wages of members for the duration of a monthslong campaign was significant. "In the 1850s and the 1860s,"

Akins and Bauer write, "the United States paid more than $1 million to California to fund these militias. Politicians praised their actions as 'pedagogic killing,' claiming that murdering Indigenous People taught the survivors a lesson."[69] The state was willing to fund volunteer militias because they did the work of anti-Indian counterrevolution, but without the need to use what would have been a more expensive project of deploying a large regular army, as was the case in Florida during the Seminole Wars.

However, where the state was slow to fund or sometimes could not promise financial backing, settlers organized grassroots fundraisers to pay for their own vigilante militias. Lindsay points out that in some locations, settlers created subscriptions to finance vigilante militias.[70] Brendan Lindsay also explains that "taxes and subscriptions such as these were inherently democratic, in the view of some Californians. They represented the recourse that any community might turn to in the absence of what they deemed effective government responses at higher levels."[71] Anti-Indian counterrevolution was the driving force in cultivating popular democracy among settlers.[72]

Despite intra-settler conflicts in competing for land, resources, and jobs, not to mention class, ethnic, and religious differences, settlers closed ranks to defend each other in the face of Indigenous resistance. It was solidarity in the settler position that was key to settler mass militarism. For example, it was common and well-known that settlers refused to testify against fellow settlers in the rare cases when they were charged with crimes against Indigenous people. While it was not expected for all settlers to directly participate in anti-Indian violence, it was expected to express solidarity for those who did by refusing to participate in the prosecution of settler crimes. As mentioned earlier, this settler solidarity occurred alongside laws that prohibited colonized and enslaved people from testifying against whites in a court of law.[73] The result was the assumption that any settler could commit violence against Indigenous people with impunity.

One infamous example of settlers demonstrating solidarity for the settler position in the face of anticolonial resistance was the volunteer militia mobilization to avenge US settler John Joel Glanton and his fellow soldiers of fortune, who were killed by Quechan resistance along the Colorado River in Southern California in 1850.[74] Glanton was a former Texas ranger who fought in the settler revolt against Mexico or the Texas revolution (1835–1836). He later served as a mounted volunteer for the regular army in the US-Mexican War. With this experience and after a failed gold-seeking expedition to California, Glanton assembled a team of for-hire Indian killers. State governments of northern Mexico contracted Glanton's gang through scalp bounties to hunt and murder Apache communities. After several campaigns targeting the Apache, Glanton also began to murder Mexico's own citizens, passing off their scalps as Apache in return for payment. Once this deception was discovered, Mexico placed a scalp bounty on Glanton, which caused him to flee to the United States. Glanton continued his crimes, seizing control of a ferry on the Colorado River at the intersection of the Gila trail where overland travelers would pass from Mexico en route to California. While operating the ferry at extortionate rates, Glanton's gang began to rob, kill, and rape US settlers and Mexican citizens. To monopolize their ferry service, Glanton's gang also destroyed a nearby competing ferry operated by the Quechan.

After attempting to negotiate a compromise, only to be met by Glanton assaulting Quechan negotiators, the Quechan answered with an uprising in which Glanton and several of his men were killed. In response, settler solidarity motivated US settler-citizens of nearby San Diego and Los Angeles to petition for permission to raise a volunteer militia to wage counterinsurgency against the Quechan in retaliation for ending Glanton's violence. Lindsay points out that "the brutal actions of John Glanton and his men not only failed to show Angelinos that their own countrymen were more of a threat than Indians, but also inflamed citizens against the Quechans."[75] Furthermore, Glanton and his men, who had committed such heinous acts of violence against fellow settlers, not to mention the theft and destruction of settler property, were honored as martyrs for being attacked by the Quechan.[76] Settler solidarity easily overcame any effects of intra-settler conflict, no matter the degree, that involved Glanton. In the summer of 1850, the governor of California responded to citizen petitions and dispatched a ranger militia of over one hundred volunteers with mass support from surrounding settlements to the Colorado River Basin to subdue the Quechan, at a cost of $120,000 (close to the purchasing power of $4.6 million today). The campaign was a failure. For months the Quechan evaded the militia's movements while launching costly counterattacks, until it was clear they would not be subdued. The militia was disbanded after only a few months in the field.

While the militia acts and forms of state approval authorized settler mass militarism in the form of proliferating volunteer militias, they also, in turn, spurred further escalating vigilante violence beyond the control of the state.[77] What emerged was a contradiction between centralization and decentralization in the strategy of anti-Indian counterrevolution in California. The state's dependence on self-directed citizen-soldiers was a deal with the devil, so to speak. Instead of deploying a much costlier regular army, the state was amenable to outsourcing anti-Indian war to local settler-citizen communities, but this also meant greenlighting a type of anarchy of anti-Indian counterinsurgency in which settlers acted to achieve the same objectives but independently, leading to untrammeled anti-Indian violence. This is not to say that the state was a counterweight to the anti-Indian violence of settler mass militarism through its more centralized strategy. Rather, the state's sponsoring of settler mass militarism as its vanguard force unleashed a force that the state could not simply oversee or command if or when it ever decided to curb anti-Indian violence. Put simply, the violence of settler mass militarism could not be turned off once it was unleashed. This is a contradiction that continues to haunt settler colonialism in today's context, as I will further examine in the conclusion. It was also a contradiction that concerned Cherokee author John Rollin Ridge.

JOHN ROLLIN RIDGE'S *JOAQUÍN MURIETA*

A few years after arriving in California, Ridge wrote and published his only novel, *The Life and Adventures of Joaquín Murieta* (1854).[78] The novel tells the story of Mexican social bandits led by the titular character waging an armed anticolonial insurgency against US occupation in post-1848 California. *Joaquín Murieta* (*JM*) was the first novel written by an Indigenous author and the first novel written in English published in California. It is also a narrative situated in the history of both Southeast Indian removal and the settler colonization of California. It was a precursor to the western dime novel and the inspiration for both the figure of Zorro and Batman comics.[79]

While most notably recognized for its attention to anticolonial resistance, the novel also reflects on settler mass militarism. It gives special attention to the role of settler-citizens in conducting counterrevolutionary violence to repress Murieta's campaign. At a pivotal moment in the novel, when Murieta's organization appears close to overtaking US settler rule, the narrator describes how settler mass militarism is mobilized. "A large meeting was held . . . at which it was resolved that *everybody* should turn out in search of the villain Joaquín. . . . Thus was the whole country alive with armed parties." Ridge describes this mobilization as a frenzied counterinsurgency exceeding the novel's capacity to depict it: "Arrests were continually being made; popular tribunals established in the woods, Judge Lynch installed upon the bench; criminals arraigned, tried, and executed upon the limb of a tree; pursuits, flights, skirmishes, and a topsy-turvy, hurley-burly mass of events that set narration at defiance."[80] These forms of unchecked settler mass militarism that Ridge observed in California and that he novelizes in *JM* were present as the vanguard of colonization in the Southeast that forcibly removed the Cherokee nation to lands west of the Mississippi. It was this violent history of Cherokee removal that precipitated the events that led Ridge to go to California in the first place.

In 1850 Ridge fled the Cherokee nation for the goldfields of California to escape potential prosecution for allegedly killing a person whom Ridge believed was responsible for the murder of his family members, stemming from a political conflict among the Cherokee over the choice to cede ancestral lands to the United States. Before this, in 1839, Ridge's father John Ridge, grandfather Major Ridge, and cousin Elias Boudinot had been assassinated by members of the Ross faction for their role in signing the New Echota Treaty of 1835, which had ceded Cherokee territories in the Southeast for lands west of the Mississippi. Like with the Seminoles, Andrew Jackson's genocidal policy of Indian removal had targeted the Cherokee and other Indigenous nations of the Southeast to open their territories for settler occupation. In 1828 the discovery of gold in Georgia had intensified US settlers' demand for Cherokee removal. This was a catalyst for Jackson's campaign to seize Indigenous territories of the Southeast. The Ridge family were members of the Cherokee nation's minority faction of enslavers who had come to adopt the plantation economy model of the United States. Most of the Cherokee nation opposed the model and the decision to cede ancestral lands. Led by principal chief John Ross, they refused to recognize the New Echota Treaty as legitimate.[81] In 1838 those who rejected the treaty and chose to remain on ancestral lands were forcibly removed to Tennessee at bayonet point and interned in stockades by state militias under the command of Major General Winfield Scott (following his failed campaign in the Seminole War), before being marched to "Indian Territory," or what later became Oklahoma and Arkansas. During this forced removal, known as the Trail of Tears, the loss of life among the Cherokee was by some estimates a staggering and catastrophic 40–50 percent.[82]

In California, after trying his hand as a miner without much success, Ridge became a journalist, writing for a few local newspapers.

With the goal of publishing a bestseller, Ridge decided to write a popular novel dramatizing the historical events surrounding Joaquín Murieta, a Mexican social bandit who had led a series of attacks against US settlers.[83] Stories and notices circulated in California newspapers from 1850 to 1853, reporting the actions of a Mexican "outlaw" named Joaquín, wanted for committing numerous thefts from and murders of US settlers in several counties. Reports indicated that there were five people bearing the name of Joaquín who were suspected of leading these actions.[84] The *San Joaquín Republican* of Stockton published a notice that expressed Joaquín's threat to settler order: "It is well known that during the winter months a band of Mexican marauders have infested Calaveras County, and weekly we receive details of dreadful murders and outrages committed in the lonely gulches and solitary outposts of that region. The farmers lost their cattle and horses, the trader's tent was pillaged, and the life of every traveler was insecure. . . . The band is led by a robber, named Joaquín, a very desperate man, who was concerned in the murder of four Americans, sometime ago, at Turnerville."[85]

In the summer of 1853 newspapers reported that California's governor John Bigler had commissioned Harry Love to lead a ranger militia to repress Murieta's rebellion. Sensationalized news reports narrated Love's pursuit, capture, and murder of Murieta and several of his men. The mounted rangers gruesomely decapitated Murieta's head and severed the hand of his comrade Manuel Garcia or Three-Fingered Jack, as evidence of their deaths and war trophies of counterinsurgency.[86] The head of Murieta was paraded around surrounding settlements for the entertainment of US settlers.[87] Later it was preserved in a jar of alcohol and permanently displayed in San Francisco by a quack doctor at the The Pacific Museum of Anatomy and Science alongside wax models, Egyptian mummies, and other looted curiosities of empire. Murieta's head remained on display until 1906, when an earthquake and subsequent fire, it is believed, destroyed it or caused it to be lost.[88]

Unlike US newspaper accounts characterizing Murieta as an enemy of the state deemed murderable, Ridge novelizes Murieta's campaign as a revolt against the violence and racism of US settler colonization. Critic Hsuan Hsu argues that Ridge's novel is a "classic American story of antiracist insurrection."[89] Louis Owens's foundational reading suggests that Murieta's anti-American campaign allegorizes Cherokee resistance to US occupation. At the same time, Owens and subsequent scholars have noted the novel's many ideological and formal contradictions.[90] While *JM* champions Murieta's anticolonial resistance to US occupation, it also at times puzzlingly endorses settler colonial logics directed at other oppressed groups like Chinese laborers and Indigenous peoples of California. This has led to debates about the novel's politics regarding the question of resistance or assimilation.[91] *JM* also exhibits tension among its modes of narration. As Shelby Streeby argues, Ridge intended to write a historical romance that "transcends wild romance and cheap sensationalism."[92] Ridge writes that his novel is "not for the purpose of ministering to any depraved taste . . . but rather to contribute my mite to those materials out of which the early history of California shall one day be composed."[93] Yet Ridge uses sensationalism excessively in ways that clash with his literary aspirations of writing a historical romance. This tension produces dissonant aesthetic experiences for readers within the representations of Murieta and his campaign. Many scholars have characterized the novel's contradictions as shortcomings or have avoided them altogether. Like with the narrative contradictions of Martin Delany's *Blake* examined in chapter 1, I consider *JM*'s ideological and formal contradictions to be productive rather than limiting. They inscribe *JM*'s understanding of settler mass militarism, demonstrating that it is both the fulcrum for state power in carrying out anti-Indian counterrevolution and a force operating beyond the direction of the state in ways that can potentially destabilize the reproduction of settler colonial capital accumulation and delegitimize its political and ideological superstructure.[94]

Ridge's Murieta does not begin as an anticolonial fighter leading a collective rebellion to liquidate US occupation. He is first a settler from Mexico seeking to accumulate a fortune, like fellow settlers descending upon California at the time. How the novel narrates Murieta's transformation from a settler to an anticolonial figure articulates a critique of the internal contradictions of settler colonialism that lead to the potential breakdown of its mass militarism. *JM* registers a similar concern with the limits of settler mass militarism that we encountered in the Blanchard pamphlet in the Seminole insurgency context. The narrator introduces Murieta to readers as a citizen of Mexico of Spanish descent from the state of Sonora. Murieta joins the rushes on gold and land alongside US settlers in the emigration to California following 1848.[95] He becomes "tired of the uncertain state of affairs in his own country, the usurpations and revolutions which were of common occurrence, and resolve[s] to try his fortunes among the American people, of whom he had formed the most favorable opinion."[96] Murieta espouses US ideologies of Anglo supremacy over Mexican citizens. "Disgusted with the conduct of his degenerate countrymen and fired with enthusiastic admiration of the American character, the youthful Joaquín left his home with a buoyant heart and full of the exhilarating spirit of adventure."[97] Upon arriving in California, Murieta acquires a lucrative mining claim and becomes a fellow property owner among US settlers, gaining the "confidence and respect of the whole community around him."[98]

This is short-lived, and Anglo settlers soon target Murieta because he is a Mexican national. Their violent removal and dispossession of Murieta is a racializing action:

> The country was then full of lawless and desperate men, who bore the name of Americans but failed to support the honor and dignity of that title. A feeling was prevalent among this class of contempt for any and all Mexicans, whom they looked upon as no better than conquered subjects of the United States, having no rights which could stand before a haughtier and

superior race. They made no exceptions. If the proud blood of the Castilians mounted to the cheek of a partial descendant of the Mexiques, showing that he had inherited the old chivalrous spirit of his Spanish ancestry, they looked upon it as a saucy presumption in one so inferior to them.[99]

Anglo settlers reject Murieta's appeal to whiteness through Spanish colonialism and racialize him as a rightless colonized subject.[100] They beat Murieta, sexually assault his wife, Rosita, and oust him from his mining claim. Following this, Murieta travels north and claims a plot of land that he turns into a successful farm. Once again US settlers violently attack and dispossess him. "A company of unprincipled Americans—shame that there should be such bearing the name!—saw his retreat, coveted his little home surrounded by its fertile tract of land, and drove him from it, with no other excuse than that he was 'an infernal Mexican intruder!'"[101] Shortly afterward, Murieta visits his half brother in Calaveras County, where they are falsely accused of horse theft. A vigilante mob forms to punish the Murieta brothers. "They listened to no explanation, but bound him to a tree, and publicly disgraced him with the lash. They then proceeded to the house of his half-brother and hung him without judge or jury."[102] Anglo settlers commit gratuitous violence against Murieta in ways similar to the colonization of Indigenous peoples of California.

In response to such acts of dispossession and terror, Murieta pledges to become a social bandit. "It was then that the character of Joaquín changed, suddenly and irrevocably."[103] He vows to avenge the wrongs committed against him by stealing the wealth and ending the lives of invading US settlers. He quickly tracks and kills the members of the vigilante mob who had whipped him and lynched his half brother, catalyzing a larger commitment to wage an anticolonial war against US occupation: "He had contracted a hatred to the whole American race, and was determined to shed their blood, whenever and wherever an opportunity occurred."[104] The novel then follows the story of the many movements, actions, scenes, and episodes of Murieta's campaign of expropriating and terrorizing US settlers until he is captured and killed by Love.

Scholars read Murieta's conversion to anticolonial revenge as Ridge's condemnation of US settlers not upholding US liberal bourgeois values of individual rights.[105] The narrator instructs readers to interpret the wrongs committed against Murieta in such a way: "He also leaves behind him the important lesson that there is nothing so dangerous in its consequences as *injustices to individuals*—whether it arise from prejudice of color or from any other source; that a wrong done to one man is a wrong to society and the world."[106] If Anglo settlers only would have respected Murieta's liberal individual rights to pursue wealth as a fellow settler, it is implied, his destructive campaign against settler order could have been avoided.[107] Murieta's transformation from wronged settler to anticolonial insurgent exposes how settler solidarity required for mass militarism is not a given but must be forged across class and ethnic differences. In direct violation of the intra-settler solidarity necessary for settler mass militarism, Anglo settlers have dispossessed Murieta. This violation has provided the opening for anticolonialism to deal death and destruction to US settler colonialism. To uphold the settler project, Anglo settlers must learn to prioritize intra-settler solidarity over national and ethnic differences. That they have failed to do so suggests there remains a tension between the imperative to cultivate settler solidarity and the forces of bourgeois individualism and competition inflaming differences that produces costly vulnerabilities in settler mass militarism and cause it to break down as a strategy of counterrevolution.

Murieta's anticolonial campaign wreaks havoc. It destabilizes US settler order. "The scenes of murder and robbery shifted with the rapidity of lightning. At one time, the northern countries would be suffering slaughters and depredations, at another the southern, and, before one would have imagined it possible, the east and the west, and every point of the compass would be in trouble."[108] For settler colonialism, the danger of Murieta's rebellion is much more than the loss of life and property. It threatens to interrupt the very stability necessary for the reproduction of settler society and capital accumulation. The narrator describes the rebellion as an uncontainable mass insurgency that produces settler anxiety about impending structural breakdown: "Around San Andreas, Calaveritas, and Yackee Camp, numerous thefts and robberies had been committed for several weeks past. Property was missed, but no one knew whither it was gone. Men were murdered, and the bloody hand remained unseen. Yet every one knew that thieves and murderers walked unknown in the midst of the community. A strange dread hung over every face and gave vigilance to every eye. The fearful shrunk back from a danger which they could *feel* but not see."[109] By describing how mayhem follows US settlers unjustly attacking Murieta, the novel intimates that settlers who do not uphold solidarity for the settler position across national, racial, and ethnic difference, like those who targeted Murieta, risk jeopardizing the integrity of the entire settler project itself. Settler colonialism cannot benefit all settlers if it is under threat of liquidation by anticolonial rebellion that a faltering in settler solidarity has dangerously permitted to emerge.

The Blanchard pamphlet in the Seminole insurgency context had suggested that a breakdown in settler mass militarism exposed settler society to Indigenous insurgency as well. It did so in order to call for the reinforcement of settler mass militarism. It was a warning about the danger of a weak mass militarism unable to rally settlers when Seminole insurgency was demoralizing them. Yet Ridge's representation of a similar breakdown in settler mass militarism is ambiguous. Is the representation a warning for settlers to uphold settler solidarity to avoid provoking anticolonial insurgencies, or does it expose the breakdown of settler mass militarism stemming from the internal contradictions of settler society to emphasize its fragility in ways that inspire further anticolonial revolt? This ambiguity is productive. It crystallizes the dialectical movement between settlers' efforts to forge solidarity across difference to fortify anti-Indian counterrevolution and anticolonialism's constant reading, exposure, and targeting of these very points of weakness of settler colonialism. The ambiguity encodes the dance between opposing forces in which settler society desperately seeks to fortify its vulnerabilities, which insurgent anticolonialism uncovers, exposes, and exploits in its resistance to occupation.

Related to the transformation from settler to anticolonial insurgent is the perplexing ideological contradiction at the center of the novel, in which Murieta's campaign is both revolutionary and reactionary. Murieta wages a progressive insurgency to overturn US settler colonialism while also engaging in reactionary attacks on Chinese workers and Indigenous nations of California. These reactionary attacks do the same work of bolstering the US occupation that Murieta's insurgency seeks to upend. For example, Murieta proclaims the objective of his rebellion is anticolonial war for the defense of colonized nations:

> I am at the head of an organization . . . of two thousand men whose ramifications are in Sonora, Lower California, and in this State. I have money in abundance deposited in a safe place. I intend to arm and equip fifteen hundred or two thousand men and make a clean sweep of the southern counties. I intend to kill the Americans by "wholesale" burn their ranchos, and run off their property at one single swoop so rapidly that they will not have to collect an opposing force before I will have finished the work and found safety in the mountains of Sonora. When I do this, I shall wind up my career. My brothers, we will then be revenged for our wrongs, and some little, too, for the wrongs of our poor bleeding country.

Through anticolonial war, Murieta aims to win a future based on communalism and cooperation in which peace will be won after colonialism is defeated: "We will divide our substance and spend the rest of our days in peace."[110] In fact, one of the principal tactics of Murieta's anticolonial war is the expropriation of horses and cattle from US settlers. As mentioned previously, historically this was the same tactic that Indigenous peoples of California used in their land defense campaigns against invading US settlers. Early in the rebellion, Murieta's organization joins with Indigenous nations in stealing settler horses: "They induced the Indians to aid them in this *laudable* purpose" (emphasis in original).[111] As the campaign advances, however, Murieta and his men begin to carry out massacres against Chinese workers and Indigenous people.[112] Murieta's second-in-command, Manuel Garcia or "Three-Fingered Jack," leads in this killing of other colonized peoples. Referring to Chinese workers, he tells Murieta, "I can't help it. . . . [I]t's such easy work to kill them. It's kind of a luxury to cut their throats."[113] Later the narrator observes the impact of Murieta's campaign on Chinese workers: "The miserable Chinamen were mostly the sufferers, and they lay along the highways like so many sheep with their throats cut by the wolves. It was a political stroke . . . to kill Chinamen in preference to Americans, for no one cared for so alien a class, and they were left to shift for themselves."[114] These reactionary attacks on other colonized people align with the same objectives of US settlers who mobilize en masse to crush all forms of anticolonial rebellion in California.

The narrator also inexplicably praises and endorses Captain Harry Love and his mounted rangers, whom the governor, after receiving a grassroots petition from settler citizens, commissions as a volunteer militia to hunt down and murder Murieta. "A leader was now in the field and armed with the authority of the State whose experience was a part of the stormiest histories of the frontier settlements, the civil commotions of Texas, and the Mexican War, whose soul was as rugged and severe as the discipline through which it had passed."[115] The very leader of the ranger militia tasked with assassinating Murieta becomes a hero for doing so in the same narrative that has characterized Murieta as a hero for rebelling against US settler power. The lines between revolutionary and reactionary violence become blurred, with the narrator praising both at the same time. Additionally, Murieta also contradictorily displays a shared "honor" with US settlers amid his organization's campaign to rid the area of them. In one scene, Murieta spares the lives of a hunting party of US settlers who have accidentally stumbled into Murieta's camp. He does so only because one of the hunters, an Anglo settler from Arkansas, indicates a commitment to this shared settler honor.[116] In another scene, Murieta is also shown to be greatly troubled that he must rob and kill a US settler traveling overland by wagon: "Joaquín's conscience smote him for this deed, and he regretted the necessity of killing so honest and hard-working a man as Ruddle seemed to be."[117] This theme of honor embodies the settler solidarity that US settlers violated when they dispossessed Murieta. In a paradox, then, it is Murieta who is more dedicated to the ideal of settler solidarity than US settlers, or as Jesse Alemán argues, "Joaquín Murieta espouses the very ideals Anglo-Americans lack in the narrative, creating what is perhaps the most criminal aspect of Joaquín Murieta—he is more ideally American than Anglo-Americans are. . . . [H]e earnestly attempts to live up to the country's social ideals, even after he realizes most Anglos fall short of them."[118]

Alemán compellingly interprets the contradiction between the revolutionary and reactionary Murieta as evidence of Ridge's narrative strategy for exposing the pitfalls of the colonized adopting US ideologies. Alemán contends that Ridge has Murieta, as a colonized subject, perform prosettler reactionary violence to demonstrate how the colonized appealing to or adopting US ideologies liquidates the radical character of colonized peoples' struggle for justice. "The larger point of Rollin Ridge's narrative is thus not to espouse America's cultural myths but to expose their shortcomings by having the Mexican racialized body politic perform them."[119] Extending this interpretation in the context of settler mass militarism, Ridge portrays Murieta conducting reactionary settler violence while simultaneously waging armed insurgency against US occupation to dramatize and thus make legible for readers the co-constitutive relationship between anticolonial war and settler mass militarism that in dominant narratives is disavowed. Ridge's revolutionary and reactionary Murieta is the literary figure articulating what this chapter has theorized: that anticolonial war and settler mass militarism are the opposing strategies in a protracted struggle between Indigenous governance and settler colonialism, in which the promise of revolution from the former prompts the development of reactionary unity, solidarity, and democracy among the members of the latter to execute the counterrevolutionary violence necessary to protect capital accumulation by settler colonization. Where in dominant colonial narratives settler colonialism is narrated as "civilization" overtaking "savagery," or in today's terms Western democracy defeating "terrorism," Ridge's revolutionary and reactionary Murieta inscribes how the United States as a settler colonial society has only ever been democratic precisely through its waging of anti-Indian counterrevolution.

Depicting Murieta's campaign as simultaneously revolutionary and reactionary also undermines dominant narratives of settler self-defense that justified counterrevolutionary violence against the colonized. Murieta's performance of settler violence defamiliarizes for readers assumptions about such violence. It reveals that the duty of a settler to uphold mass militarism is to be a combatant in conducting or supporting reactionary colonial violence. Murieta performs how to be a settler-citizen combatant when his campaign slips into committing vigilante violence against colonized populations. In these moments, Murieta's organization allegorizes US settler colonialism's targeting of colonized populations. By having Murieta perform or be the figure for waging this violence, Ridge exposes its content and form as counterrevolutionary rather than defensive. In this way, Murieta's performance of settler violence showcases its illegitimacy as purely reactionary rather than defensive, thus challenging narratives of settler self-defense that suggested settlers were the victims of illegitimate anticolonial resistance.

JM also theorizes the relationship between settler mass militarism and centralized state power in the work of white counterrevolution. Such a perspective registers through the formal contradiction between Ridge's aspiration to write in the mode of historical romance and the novel's over-the-top use of sensationalism to depict scenes of violence. The excessive sensationalized representations of violence interrupt or unravel the novel's mode of historical romance in ways that embody the interdependent but also tenuous relationship between settler mass militarism and centralized state power. The figure of this excessive sensationalized violence in the novel is Garcia or Three-Fingered Jack. He is characterized as a fiendish killer who murders not for any righteous cause but for the sake of it. It is worth quoting at length one of the narrator's descriptions of Garcia:

> His delight was in murder for its own diabolical sake, and he gloated over the agonies of his unoffending victims. He would sacrifice policy, the safety and interests of the band for the mere gratification of this murderous propensity, and it required all Joaquín's firmness and determination to hold him in check. The history of this monster was well known before he joined Joaquín. He was known to be the same man, who, in 1846, surrounded with this party two Americans, young men by the name of Cowie and Fowler, as they were traveling on the road between Sonoma and Bodega, stripped them entirely naked, and, binding them each to a tree, slowly tortured them to death. He began by throwing knives at their bodies, as if he were practicing at a target; he then cut out their tongues, punched out their eyes with his knife, gashed their bodies in numerous places, and, finally flaying them alive, left them to die. A thousand cruelties like these had he been guilty of, and, long before Joaquín knew him, he was a hardened experienced, and detestable monster.[120]

In some ways, this representation does the same ideological work as the woodcuts depicting Black and Native revolt in the pamphlets on Nat Turner's insurrection and the Second Seminole War. The novel echoes the language of US newspapers that demonized Garcia, as a pivotal member of Murieta's anticolonial insurgency, to justify violent settler reprisal. However, as this description and other passages in the novel indicate, Garcia's violence is also characterized as indiscriminate and gratuitous, targeting all populations, not just settlers.

As such, Garcia's anticolonial violence slips into a reactionary form more closely resembling the wanton "total war" violence that settler mass militarism indiscriminately unleashed on Indigenous peoples of California. There is a parallel between the unchecked and uncontrollable settler mass violence targeting Indigenous people that unfolded during this period and Murieta's inability to manage the excessive violence of Garcia. When it is advantageous for the campaign, Murieta depends on the unhinged violence of Garcia. "When it was necessary for the young chief to commit some peculiarly horrible and cold-blooded murder . . . he deputed this man to do it." Yet there is a price to pay for the effectiveness of its excess, in which Garcia "would sacrifice policy, the safety and interests of the band for the mere gratification of this murderous propensity, and it required all Joaquín's firmness and determination to hold him in check."[121] Murieta depends on Garcia's violence to advance the anticolonial insurgency and defend their organization, even as Murieta fails to adequately direct such violence toward these objectives. Just as excessive sensationalized violence undermines the novel's conventions of historical romance at the level of form, so too, at the level of content, Garcia's violence exceeds the directives of Murieta's campaign. While this unchecked violence gives power to the campaign, it also threatens to destabilize it. This formal contradiction and the relationship between Murieta's authority and Garcia's uncontrollable violence perform the contradiction between the settler state and the decentralized character of settler mass militarism.

As this chapter has examined, the state depends on the masses of settlers to wage counterrevolution to crush Indigenous anticolonialism, yet it is this very mass character that exceeds the authority or command of the state. The state depends on a force that exists always beyond its control. Murieta's organization and campaign are represented as centralized projects. In fact, this is where their power derives from: the centralization of the organization and campaign across region and borders. At the peak of his campaign, Murieta promises to mobilize men, resources, and violence from Sonora to California to overturn US occupation.[122] While his organization is a powerful anticolonial fighting machine, it also becomes a figure for the centralized settler state when it conducts reactionary violence. As such, the reactionary Garcia is both crucial to this centralized strategy but also its potentially destabilizing force through his inability to be under the command of its directives. The novel displaces the excessive, uncontrollable violence of settler mass militarism onto the figure of Three-Fingered Jack to illuminate precisely what US settler society wished to disavow, namely, how settler mass militarism is the monster set loose to conduct counterrevolution without a way to put it in check.

While the settler state depends on settler mass militarism to protect and thus expand settler colonial capital accumulation, it knows no bounds and is not accountable to the state. Like Garcia's reactionary violence, unhinged settler mass militarism threatens to delegitimize and destabilize settler colonialism even as it is pivotal to its reproduction. If in Florida settler society worried there was not enough mass militarism to guard against Seminole insurgency and autonomy, the disavowed concern in California—which Ridge's novel brings to the surface—was that there might be too much settler mass militarism in ways that threatened to destabilize the reproduction of settler colonialism and undermine its veneer of a civilizing democratic project that provided cover for its crimes.

3

WHITE INSURGENCY

Industrializing Capital and Counterrevolution

IN APRIL 1865 Union armies forced the surrender of pro-slavery Confederates, bringing a formal end to the US Civil War. Following their defeat, it was unclear how the rebellious Confederates would relate to the US state going forward. When Union Republicans won sweeping majorities in the congressional elections of 1866, they answered this question by passing a flurry of policies that initiated the era of Radical Reconstruction. Compelled by the strategy of abolition war, the state was used to dismantle the political power of former confederates, while extending rights and resources to freedmen. These policies included the Thirteenth, Fourteenth, and Fifteenth Amendments; the Reconstructions Acts; and the establishment of the Freedman's Bureau. W. E. B. Du Bois characterized these developments as approaching a dictatorship of Black labor over Southern capital.[1] In this same moment, Union Republicans approved amendments to the Homestead Act that had been passed in 1862. The Homestead Act provided settlers the chance to own 160 acres of public lands to establish small farms where the landless could become independent producers.

A Republican congressional committee report published in 1868, *Homes for the Homeless: What the Republican Party Has Done for the Poor Man*, showcased the amendments and how they expanded the benefits of the Homestead Bill.[2] The report's authors highlighted that homesteads were available to all workers, even former Confederates who had rebelled against the US state. The original Homestead Act had prohibited those who took up arms against the government to fight for slavery from accessing its benefits. The prohibition ensured that antislavery settlers would conquer western lands to choke off the expansion of slavery. The authors argued that this change from the prohibition to the inclusion of former Confederate workers was done to oppose the class inequality of the South's former plantation economy in which, they suggested, land monopoly had cruelly dominated the landless Confederate laborer turned conscripted soldier. The lifting of the prohibition against former Confederates was also aimed at rebuilding unity with the former white insurgents through settler colonization and capitalist development of Indigenous lands.

The report also claimed that "the United States owns about 900,000,000 of acres of unsurveyed land, all of which will be free to the Homestead settler as fast as the lines of public surveys are extended over it." The authors confidently predicted that over thirty-one million people or "a number nearly equal to the entire population of the United States" at the time would come to occupy homesteads, boasting that "it may with truth be said, the Government, through the benign policy of the Republican party, offers homes to all its people."[3] While the Homestead Act would not live up to such high hopes as anticipated in this report, 270 million acres of land, or 10 percent of the continental United States was settled by over two million claimants.[4] I refer to the report's vision of every settler accessing a small farm to be freed of poverty as *homestead utopianism*. With a homestead, the proletarianized land-less laborer could become the propertied small farmer. It was imagined that the distribution of public lands could resolve the class contradictions between labor and capital.

Yet while the amended Homestead Act officially provided lands to any US citizen (and European migrants wishing to become citizens) regardless of race, its aim of turning the landless laborer into a small farmer had been the objective of a decades-long struggle by white labor from the South to the North to win access to public lands to achieve an exclusively white equality.[5] Homestead utopianism best embodied this aspiration for white equality in which European workers demanded that expropriated Indigenous lands be distributed among them to temper, and, ultimately, overcome the antagonism between white labor and capital. Including former white Confederate insurgents in the Homestead Act was thus not an exceptional decision by Union Republicans. Rather, it was a return to realizing an earlier and long-standing dream of white equality among free labor that had always spanned the conflict between Northern and Southern capital.

While scholars have studied Jacksonian democracy and free labor republicanism of this period as ideologies uniting free labor and capital in the goal of providing workers equality of opportunity or social mobility, there has been less attention given to this specific aspiration for white equality that maneuvered within and through these larger trends. White equality was the demand of white labor to be corulers with capital in the project of racial capitalism.[6] I see this as slightly distinct from the broader aims of Jacksonian democracy and later free labor republicanism, which sought to cultivate a harmonious coexistence or mutually beneficial relationship between white labor and capital despite the class conflict between the two.[7] The demand for white equality was a utopian aspiration to resolve the class conflict altogether, with white labor sharing power with white owners. This chapter examines the history of European workers' demand for white equality during the antebellum period to illuminate the relationship between white counterrevolution and white labor's response to expanding capitalist exploitation.

Previous chapters examined how the imperative to repress abolition and anticolonial wars compelled enslaver and settler ruling classes to fashion cross-class alliances with European workers to enlist them in the conducting of white counterrevolution, securing capital accumulation. Relatedly, there is the question of how these cross-class alliances for counterrevolution in turn shaped European labor's relationship to capital's accelerating domination of wage labor, which began in the 1850s. This chapter examines how the movement for white equality indexed a contradiction between white counterrevolution and capitalism's internal dynamics. White counterrevolution united free labor and capital to secure the forms of primary accumulation of settler colonialism and slavery from Black and Native rebellion. Yet this protection also ensured the further maturation of capital, leading to its expanded exploitation of free labor. I argue that the alliances between free labor and capital forged in white counterrevolution recursively engendered the aspiration for white equality as the solution to capital's intensifying exploitation of wage labor, which emerged during this conjuncture. The project of white equality, however, was no solution at all, but rather a reactionary confrontation with capital's logic of the subordination and increased absorption of wage labor. White equality would erupt as a reactionary insurgency against the state's enforcing of these developments of industrializing capital that sought to subordinate greater portions of European workers to the discipline of wage labor exploitation, placing pressure on the cross-class alliances between free labor and capital of white counterrevolution. In this way, the alliances of white counterrevolution that formed out of the necessity to repress abolition and anticolonial wars also gave rise to an insurgent white equality utopianism by the mid-nineteenth century.

In his classic study *The Wages of Whiteness*, David Roediger demonstrates how European workers responded to an increased dependency on the wage by fashioning their laboring position as "white" defined against the racialized enslaved. Crafting whiteness to be an immunity from the unfreedom of the enslaved position enabled European workers to demand relative privileges and protections. Roediger describes free labor's appeal to whiteness as a herrenvolk republicanism or what Joel Olson characterized as "white democracy," in which the shared racial position of whiteness promised political equality between labor and capital.[8] These studies highlight the role of anti-Black subjugation in providing the image of Black enslaveability against which free labor defined itself as the white or un-enslaveable worker. This chapter asks how we can expand our understanding of free labor's relation to exploitation when attention is also given to Black struggle, not merely Black suffering, in the study of how slavery shaped the European worker's relation to changes in capital taking place in the antebellum period. It was the uniting of free labor and capital to repress abolition and anticolonial wars in the first place that enabled free labor to demand white equality as the solution to increasing exploitation. Seeing the role of white counterrevolution in structuring how free labor related to capital illuminates how European workers demanded that the cross-class alliances between them and capital did more than solely provide immunity from disposability and symbolic compensation. They called on the alliances of white counterrevolution to end their exploitation and deliver to them the reactionary dream of full equality with capital within the projects of settler colonialism and slavery. White counterrevolution to stop abolition and anticolonial war was the underlying motor force for producing such demands for white equality.

This chapter also seeks to better understand the history of white insurgency in racial capitalism. We often recognize white insurgency during Reconstruction and later moments when white power movements have challenged the state following periods when they perceive it has conceded demands or gains to abolition or anticolonial struggle. However, in what follows I show that white insurgency has an earlier history related to the maturing of industrial capitalism and this ongoing dynamic's relation to white counterrevolution. This longue durée view helps us see that white insurgency is not exceptional, but rather the result of internal contradictions of racial capitalism in which the logic of wage labor exploitation clashes with the infrastructures of white counterrevolution.

WAGE LABOR IN THE SETTLER COLONIES

Eric Foner's famous study on free labor ideology details how free labor came to be defined in the antebellum period as labor owned and controlled by the worker. Those with the power to determine how to use their labor and its product considered themselves free laborers. Free labor was also considered labor that produced a use value for the economy, a product or service that satisfied a need, rather than abstracted or commodified labor, whose purpose was to produce surplus value.[9] Of course these definitions of free labor were not constructed in isolation from enslaved African labor or Indigenous dispossession. To own one's labor and its products was precisely what was denied to the unfree African worker or colonized Indigenous person. As mentioned, Du Bois and later Roediger and others have shown how free labor was defined as un-enslaveable labor in which enslavement was racialized as Black.[10] Free labor thus became white labor in relation to enslavement. Free labor also united workers and small capitalists under the banner of producers. A small farmer whose labor mixed with the land to produce cash crops was considered of the same class of free laborer as a tradesperson who did not own land or property but produced concretely useful products or services for the economy.

The expanding exploitation of wage labor posed a problem to such definitions of free labor. By the 1850s larger manufacturers emerged, and skilled tradesmen and artisan workers began increasingly to be-come dependent on wage work. Wage laborers became a permanent working class in the United States; 60 percent of laborers were waged.[11] The growth of wage labor corresponded to decades of punctuated eco-nomic crisis known as "panics." Major panics of 1819, 1837, and 1857 prepared the way for the emergence of the centralization of capital while proletarianizing large swaths of small farmers, shopkeepers, and skilled workers. Wage labor was considered "hireling" labor and seen as beneath the station of the free worker as the independent producer. Roediger explains how Northern free labor initially compared wage labor with slavery to decry capital's violation of the whiteness of Eu-ropean workers, who were seen as being treated the same or worse than unfree Africans. Wage labor was characterized as "white slavery." In fact, many Northern labor reformers claimed that capital treated wage workers worse than the enslaved Africans. The plight of "white slaves" was considered a priority over that of enslaved Africans. In this way, free labor was expected to be protected from proletarianization through appeals to whiteness.[12]

In *Capital*, Karl Marx studied the role of European labor in settler colonies to understand this question of proletarianization in the devel-opment of capitalism. Marx argued that one of the conditions for the emergence of capitalism was the privatization of the peasant commons in Europe, which produced a new class of landless workers forced to sell their labor power to private owners in exchange for subsistence wages.[13] In the settler colonies, this process of proletarianization took a different path. The settler colonial expropriation of Indigenous lands gave Europe's landless proletariat access to land, depleting the pool of proletarianized wage workers for capital to exploit to accumulate surplus value. For Marx, the settler colonization of Indigenous lands accumulated land as capital but in turn stunted the development of capitalism's higher forms of wage labor accumulation. "The essence of a free colony," writes Marx, "consists in this, that the bulk of the soil is still public property, and every settler on it can therefore turn part of it into his private property and his individual means of production, without preventing later settlers from performing the same operation. This is the secret both of the prosperity of the colonies and of their cancerous affliction—their resistance to the establishment of capital."[14] Marx unearths a contradiction between settler colonialism as a mode of primitive accumulation and wage labor capitalism. The very process by which proletarianized workers became settler farmers through the ownership of expropriated Indigenous lands stalled the development of capital accumulation through the exploitation of wage labor. While free workers acquiring ownership of "public lands" was understood as a "safety valve," alleviating growing discontent against capitalist owners, this process, more importantly, both expanded settler colonialism and led to the depletion of capital's exploitable wage labor pool.[15] If European workers were pushed into wage labor, they were pulled into settler colonialism to serve as its frontline agents of conquest and counterrevolutionary combatants, as explored in chapter 2. They were needed as both vanguard settlers and wage workers, a contradiction that leads to the impasse that Marx unpacks, in which the landless are provided access to land, both growing and stunting capital accumulation.

To manage this contradiction, Marx highlighted, the state would need to sell public land to the landless at a price high enough to maintain a sufficient pool of wage labor. The greatest source of revenue for the US government in its first decades was the sale of public lands to settlers and speculators.[16] The price or cost of access to the land became a battle between capital and free labor. For free labor, this contradiction between the pull of settler colonialism and the push of capitalism came to a head in the 1850s. Free labor expected access to land, to escape from increasing proletarianization. Yet northern capital had whetted its appetite for wage labor to extract surplus value. For European workers, it appeared that the movement of this contradiction was veering toward the expanded exploitation of wage labor to develop higher forms of capital accumulation. The demand for white equality became the solution. I explore the emergence and development of this demand for white equality through three moments of the antebellum period.

SQUATTER VANGUARD

George Washington was one of the wealthiest land speculators in US history. He bought up western lands on the assumption that the British settler colonies would expand and land prices would soar. He was a frontline leader of the American revolution to help the colonies become a nation that could ensure not only that slavery as a mode of production would be upheld, but also that settler colonization would continue to expand westward. Washington engaged in a treasonous rebellion to win conditions in which he could cash in on his speculative investments in land. He embodied how wealthy settler planters perceived the "public domain" or the expropriated Indigenous commons. Land was a speculative investment to generate wealth. Similarly, as previously mentioned, the early US government considered its public lands a principal source of revenue. The state, as Marx pointed out, would set a price on lands to manage the contradiction of maintaining wage labor in the settler colonies, while generating revenue for its operations. Thomas Jefferson embodied a different approach to settler colonialism than Washington. He saw the Indigenous commons as a resource for facilitating equality of opportunity to European settlers. Jefferson envisioned that public lands could be distributed among settler citizens to cultivate a democracy of small farmer capitalists. The equal distribution of land was key to building his vision of an "empire of liberty."[17] Washington's and Jefferson's differing visions reveal how in the first decades of the US nation a division arose between how settler capital would distribute seized Indigenous lands. The division indexed the contradiction between capital's need for European settlers to serve as armed occupiers or wage workers.

When the price of land was too high, many European workers simply became squatters. Without title or authorization, they seized and occupied lands to claim ownership through their labor of "improvement" and "cultivation." US Whig senator and enslaver Henry Clay, who represented the interests of eastern manufacturers and speculators, notoriously called squatters "lawless rabble."[18] European workers claiming ownership of land without paying for title set a precedent that undermined the power of capital over wage workers. However, squatters saw themselves as the vanguard of settler colonization, ushering capitalism into new lands. Squatters advocated for the doctrine of preemption. Without the funds to purchase the land, the squatter would occupy and take possession of a land plot and develop it for agricultural production. In exchange for this development, squatters could later receive the land for free or purchase it at cheap rates, being given priority over those with wealth, who could easily purchase public land sold at auction. Preemption doctrine enabled and incentivized squatters to appropriate lands before the speculators could do so. Squatters challenged the potential wealth accumulation of speculators and eastern capital. They also undermined the state's ability to maximize revenue through the sale of lands at the highest prices.[19] In this way, squatterism embodied one of the first forms of the demand for white equality. Whereas the state priced land as a lever to ensure a favorable pool of wage labor for eastern capital or speculator capitalists drove up the price of land to augment their wealth, the squatter directly seized the land to realize white equality.

Jacksonian democracy came to embrace and support the squatters' demand for white equality. Leaders of Jacksonian democracy looked at squatters as agents of expropriation and anti-Indigenous counterrevolution, for which their interests aligned with capital's imperial expansion.[20] Roxanne Dunbar Ortiz writes that Andrew Jackson sought to align landless European workers with enslavers. Jackson rose to prominence as a celebrated Indian killer. He led massacres against Indigenous people.[21] When Jackson was elected president in 1828, he used the federal government to extend his mission of Indigenous genocide to enclose lands for slavery. Through fraud, coercion, and violence, Jackson's administration negotiated several treaties that relocated Indigenous nations to lands west of the Mississippi in exchange for large land concessions that became the states of Georgia, Alabama, and Mississippi.[22] These coerced agreements were codified in the Indian Removal Act, passed on May 28, 1830. The expropriation of Indigenous lands was related to Jackson's support for squatters as the vanguard of occupation. The very next day Jackson signed into law the Preemption Act, which answered the call from squatter-settlers for the government to sponsor, not stifle, their seizure of Indigenous lands to develop them for US capitalism.[23]

Historian John Suval has highlighted a moment in the years after Jackson's signing of the Indian Removal and Preemption Acts that best embodied Jacksonian enslaver capitalists' decisions to sponsor and collaborate with squatters in the expropriation of Indigenous lands. In the fall of 1833, a government auction of public lands was held in Chocchuma, Mississippi. The land office was selling recently seized lands from the Choctaw nation to the highest bidding settlers. While squatting on these lands was strictly prohibited, squatters had already invaded, hoping to appeal to the doctrine of preemption. The lands they occupied were set to be carved up and sold to speculators and large enslaver landowners, who could easily outbid them. One speculator, Robert J. Walker, intervened to assist the squatters, proposing a plan whereby if squatters united with him and fellow speculators, his investment company would buy a large portion of the lands and then resell them to squatters at a price similar to the government rate of $1.25 per acre. Squatters were asked to withhold their bids to drive down overall prices. The proposed pact between Walker and the squatters resulted in benefits to both parties. Squatters received land at cheap prices, and with the elimination of competing bids at the auction, Walker and fellow speculators bought up thousands of acres for much less than they had expected. While it might be easy to say Walker cut this deal with squatters to manipulate auction prices, he believed it was his duty to help fellow settlers share in the bounty of empire. He considered all settlers, rich or poor, landed or landless, as squatters in their role of invading, occupying, and transforming Indigenous lands into capital for the development of US capitalism. Following the auction, squatters held a celebratory dinner for Walker. Only a few years later, in 1836, Walker was elected US senator to represent Mississippi. He was buoyed by his mass support among landless workers, who saw in him a champion of white equality through equitable land distribution.[24]

What is important to note here is that the squatter demand for white equality emerged in the first place from the alliances of white counterrevolution. One squatter in Southwest Michigan, Moses Finch, claimed that his labor erected infrastructure that benefited the public and, more importantly, he served as a soldier of counterinsurgency against Indigenous resistance. As a squatter, he was a bulwark against the "dangerous Indian aggression and the expense of protection to frontier settlements."[25] Jacksonian democrats embraced squatters because they saw them as useful counterrevolutionary forces for preventing Indigenous attack and disruption. Missouri senator Thomas Hart Benton, who had once scuffled in a gun and knife fight with Andrew Jackson in an interpersonal conflict, later became perhaps the most influential political leader of Jacksonian democracy, advocating for squatters and their role as frontline counterrevolutionary forces in curbing Indigenous insurgency.[26] In his advocacy for squatters, Benton contended that "the government gets a body of cultivators whose labor gives value to the surrounding public lands, and whose courage and patriotism volunteers for the public defence whenever it is necessary."[27] Benton was a fierce advocate for preemption laws to incentivize squatter occupation.

He also sponsored several Donation Acts, which offered free land to settlers in exchange for their armed invasion and occupation of Oregon and Florida territories to suppress Indigenous anticolonialism, which was threatening capital's expansion into these areas.

While a senator representing Missouri, Benton made it his cause to advocate for squatters in Florida territory. His interest in Floridian squatters was counterrevolution to protect imperial expansion of capitalism. As detailed in chapter 2, Florida became a US territory (through the Treaty of Adams-Onis in 1819), after Jackson's illegal incursion into Spanish Florida to suppress Indigenous resistance. In the following decades, the Seminoles waged an effective protracted insurgency to expel invading US settlers. The insurgency was very costly for the United States to combat. When the second Seminole War of 1835 to 1842 ended in the defeat and withdrawal of the US military, Benton called for the state to reinforce its long-standing tactic of sponsoring squatters to occupy territories as counterinsurgent forces. At the height of the Seminole insurgency in 1839, Benton introduced "A Bill for the Armed Occupation and Settlement of that Part of the Territory of Florida Overrun by Hostile Bands of Marauding Indians," which promised to supply food, clothing, arms, ammunition, and free land to settlers in exchange for their permanent settlement in Florida territory, where they would serve as a line of counterrevolutionary forces repressing Seminole Indigenous and African resistance. Benton's bill would later be signed into law, with some modifications, in 1842 as the Armed Occupation Act. It made available two hundred thousand acres of land, mostly south of present-day Gainesville. Any head of household or single man at least eighteen years old who could bear arms qualified to receive a permit for 160 acres, and 1,312 permits were issued, with most of the acres being distributed.[28] Congress had previously passed the Donation Act of 1824, which promised settlers of Florida territory up to 640 acres in exchange for permanent settlement, to build a base of small farmers to act as counterrevolutionary forces.[29] Benton's Armed

Occupation Act extended this promise of free land to squatters to procure a permanent counterrevolutionary force that could protect the recently seized territory from Indigenous insurgency, to ensure the territory's future valorization.

Benton contended that where the US military, as a standing army, had failed to conquer the Seminoles, masses of squatters would succeed in Florida territory. As examined in chapter 2, the Seminole insurgency had proven to be a formidable deterrent to the settlement of Florida territory. The valorization of land as capital and all the future wealth that was to flow from its expropriation and development were impeded by Seminole revolution.[30] For Benton, the squatter was more than a small farmer expanding the market as producer and buyer. The squatter was the "armed cultivator," tasked with counterrevolution. In his speech introducing the Armed Occupation Act, Benton argued,

> We want people to take possession and to keep possession; and the armed cultivator is the man for that. The blockhouse is the first house to be built in Indian country; the stockade is the first fence to be put up. . . . [T]he heart of the Indian sickens when he hears the crowing of the cock, the barking of the dog, the sound of the axe and the crack of the rifle. They are the true evidences of the dominion of the white man; these are the proof that the owner has come, and means to stay; and then they feel it is time for them to go.[31]

One squatter who applied for land in Florida through the act remarked, "I have come from North Carolina with two good guns and several hundred pounds of ammunition. I pitched my tent and started to work to make the land worth defending."[32] Several congressional leaders opposed Benton's bill, arguing that it would only reward the "idle" and "worthless population of our large cities."[33] Florida was vulnerable to attack, Benton countered, not only by Indigenous anticolonial war, but also by Black abolition war potentially erupting from the Caribbean. Benton warned that Great Britain, which had abolished slavery, could muster Black battalions to invade Florida and kick-start mass slave revolt. As such, it was imperative to fortify the recently seized Florida territory to secure its ongoing and future valorization. Armed squatters committed to permanent settlement could provide this security, which a standing army could not. The jobless surplus from the cities could be recruited as the armed cultivators to secure the territory from revolt and insurgency, creating the stability necessary for later higher forms of capital accumulation. In this way, capital sponsored squatters in their pursuit of white equality, but only insofar as squatters fulfilled the role of counterrevolutionary occupiers.

FROM LAND REFORM TO HOMESTEAD UTOPIANISM

In the *Communist Manifesto*, Marx and Engels called for communists of North America to unify with the land reform movement to advance the struggle of wage labor to overthrow capitalism. "In America, where a democratic constitution has already been established, the communists must make the common cause with the party which will turn this constitution against the bourgeoisie and use it in the interests of the proletariat—that is, with the agrarian National Reformers."[34] Marx and Engels perhaps offered this suggestion because they observed from afar that land reformers were a vanguard of the antebellum US free labor reform movement or at least its most active sector in terms of organizing workers. However, the goal of land reform was not revolutionary overthrow or even progressive reform. Rather, it was the reactionary demand to reform how settler colonialism distributed expropriated Indigenous lands. Founded and led by Henry George Evans, the land reform movement formed the National Reform Association in 1844. The NRA united various strata of antebellum labor reformers in the goal of opposing land monopoly to demand the equal distribution of public lands for wage workers. The platform of land reformers entailed three demands: stop the repossession of indebted homesteads, pass legislation to provide free homesteads to the landless, and limit the amount of land one individual could own.[35] Evans argued that landless workers coerced to sell their labor to capital for poverty wages could liberate themselves from such conditions if public lands were only made accessible and land monopoly destroyed.

But public lands were Indigenous lands. The land reform movement, spearheaded by the NRA, was at its core a settler movement that sought to use expropriated Indigenous lands to generate not merely opportunity but equality among Europeans. At one of their mass meetings in New York in the spring of 1844, NRA members unfurled a display banner with the slogan, "Free Land." The party's ladies' auxiliary carried a banner declaring, "The Only Effective Remedy for Hard Times is to Make the Public Lands Free to Actual Settlers."[36] Land reformers also frequently distributed at meetings and published in their newspapers the agitational circular titled, "Vote Yourself a Farm." It expressed land reform's political ideology of converting Indigenous lands into the means for European workers to escape from proletarian life. Engaging in antebellum discourse of "white slavery," the pamphlet asks, "Are you tired of slavery—of drudging for others—of poverty and its attendant miseries? Then, Vote yourself a farm?" Evans frequently argued that the landless European worker had it worse than the enslaved African. It was "slavery" to be made landless, according to land reformers.[37] The pamphlet also articulated a form of producerism thought that later became the cornerstone of free labor ideology of the Republican Party, "Are you a man? Then assert the sacred rights of man—especially your right to stand upon God's earth, and to till it for your own profit. Vote yourself a farm." Free land generated free labor, or labor that the worker owned and benefited from. For land reformers, freeing labor was understood as workers possessing land as private property to become independent producers and thus no longer wage workers.[38]

The circular, more than anything, laid out how the land reform strategy could win white equality in response to the labor-capital antagonism. Land reform was described as the emancipation of white labor from capital: "The antagonism of capital and labor would forever cease. Capital could no longer grasp the largest share of the laborer's earnings, as a reward for not doing him all the injury the laws of the feudal aristocracy authorize, viz.: the denial of all stock to work upon and all place to live in." Anticipating Marx's theory of proletarianization, land reformers pointed out how making people landless or divorced from the means of producing their lives outside of capitalism was a precondition of the wage worker's exploitation. "Free land" could thus resolve the antagonism between capital and labor. "Capital, with its power for good undiminished," the pamphlet declares, "would lose the power to oppress; and a new era would dawn upon the earth, and rejoice the souls of a thousand generations. Therefore forget not to Vote yourself a farm."[39] However, if land reformers anticipated Marx's theory of proletarianization, they greatly differed from his theory of revolutionary change. Land reformers did not believe in the recommoning of land and resources to fight proletarianization. Their vision of white equality through land reform was to become fellow members with the ruling class of maintaining racial capitalism.

The call for "free land" was thus the vanguard demand among both the labor and socialist movements in antebellum United States. Evans and the NRA forged a united front, spanning from utopian socialists like the Owenites, Fourierites, associationists, and radical labor, to some abolitionists, to oppose land monopoly and demand land for the landless.[40] While some historians contend that land reformers were a progressive force insofar as they opposed capitalist exploitation, opposed slavery, and even called for homesteads to be distributed to displaced Indigenous people, they nonetheless were organized around the reactionary aspiration for white equality capitalism.[41] Pivotal to land reform was the ongoing seizure and occupation of Indigenous lands to carve up them up into homesteads where labor could be "free" or owned by the small farmer settler as a "free laborer."

The land reform movement collapsed by the early 1850s. It was absorbed by the emerging free soil republican movement. Free soil republicanism carried forward the demand for public lands to be turned into homesteads. Under free soil republicanism, however, land reform moved away from its wage labor leadership. Land reform now served both the small farmer looking to expand their operations with cheaper and better land to the west and the landless worker of eastern cities. Furthermore, with the introduction of popular sovereignty and the Kansas-Nebraska Act of 1854 opening western territories to the possibilities of slavery, land reform under the banner of the free soil movement took on a much more anti-slavery character. The Republican Party emerged at this intersection of free soil and anti-slavery movements. Yet the anti-slavery aspect of free soil republicanism did not mean solidarity for enslaved Africans. The vanguard position of free soil republicanism was to demand the distribution of public lands to exclusively European settlers to ensure the nation remained a "white man's country."[42] It was homesteads for whites only. White homesteading was paired with the call for African colonization or the deportation of the enslaved and freedmen to Africa. The Republican anti-slavery position was less about ending slavery than about the expansion of a white equality capitalism.

In fact, the Republican Party's founders saw themselves carrying on the Jeffersonian vision of an "empire of liberty" through their homestead platform. Famously, a socialist land reformer was one of the founders of the Republican Party. Alvan Bovay, the former secretary of the NRA, played an instrumental role in cobbling together a united front of political tendencies under the banner of anti-slavery and free land advocacy, which they named the Republican Party. Bovay remarked that he selected the name "Republican" to denote equality.[43] The founding ideals of the Republican Party were entangled with the preceding land reform movement for white equality. This ideal was not possible, as they saw it, if slavery expanded and dominated western lands. Many northern Jacksonian Democrats united with the Republican Party to advance these ideals of white equality. They saw that southern democrats had renounced the previous Jacksonian Democratic vision of supporting the landless receiving land to temper class antagonism. There were also Southern Republicans who similarly condemned what they considered the South's abandonment of the commitment to the landless white worker.[44] As this chapter began, it was this ideal of white equality motivating Republican anti-slaveryism that culminated in Republicans passing the Homestead Act in 1862, which was meant to kill slavery's chances of expanding westward. From squatters to land reformers to the Republican Party, the aspiration for white equality under a homestead utopianism spanned from the South to the North and was a through line during the antebellum period among European workers.

In the debates in Congress on the Homestead Bill, Stephen C. Foster, a representative from Maine, argued that offering homesteads to the landless would also cultivate a garrison force of settlers in western territories to secure the nation from Indigenous anticolonialism. Foster contended that homesteads would distribute an army of counterrevolutionary guards and that this was the value or usefulness of homesteading for which the bill should be passed: "Whoever chooses to reside five years on a quarter section of the public domain will amply repay the Government for it, since he will be a pioneer of civilization and Christianity; he will, to that extant, curtail the area of the savage wilderness, and limit the territory to be defended by the Army. He will become a sentinel on the outposts of civilization, and his compensation will be not more than adequate to the service he will render his country."[45]

Foster's perspective embodied how capital saw the value of homesteaders. As Benton had advocated for squatters in Florida territory, Foster championed the homesteader as an armed occupier to guard against Indigenous insurgency. He was clear-eyed about the power of Indigenous anticolonialism to halt and disrupt capitalism's expansion: "We now have two frontiers exposed to the predatory attacks of savage

Indians. The States on this side of the continent have a western frontier; the States on the Pacific have an eastern frontier. . . . This state of things will become worse and worse, so long as the Territories remain wild and unsettled, and the Indians continue their savage customs."[46] As settler homesteaders labored to turn Indigenous land into capital, they also, perhaps more importantly for Foster, transformed into a counterrevolutionary guard protecting capital accumulation. "The actual settlers are the men who make the new States; it is their labor which confers value upon the lands; they make the marts for the commerce and manufacturers of the older States, and they are entitled to the lands. Pass this bill, and every foot of our Territories will, within twenty years, be as secure against Indian depredations as Ohio or Kentucky is to-day."[47] Providing land for the landless procured the necessary counterrevolutionary forces to defend capitalism from Indigenous anticolonialism. While the vision of white equality found in homestead utopianism longed to dissolve the antagonism of white labor and capital, capital nonetheless sponsored such an aspiration if only to extend the project of counterrevolution to protect the reproduction and expansion of accumulation. As expressed by Foster, capital supported white equality's counterrevolutionary function. It would not, however, tolerate the full realization of white equality. White labor had capital's support for counterrevolution, not for the demand to be a coruler of racial capitalism.

In the South by the 1850s, white equality recursively became the demand to create conditions favorable to hold together the cross-class alliances of counterrevolution to guard against Black revolt. Historian Walter Johnson has examined how sharpening class contradictions between the enslavers and the nonenslavers in the South drove the imperial expansion of slavery.[48] Enslavers had taken notice of the discontent among their policing forces of landless whites. It was feared that this discontent could turn into disloyalty, leaving enslavers exposed to Black revolt. If European workers did not have the prospect of possessing free or cheap land and enslaved labor, their allegiance to protect slavery would be put to the test. Johnson shows how enslavers supported expropriating land in the West and South to distribute to landless Europeans to temper the class contradiction that drove potential disloyalty to police the enslaved.[49] Enslavers also supported the formal reopening of the slave trade to increase the supply of the enslaved to lower their price on the market. With lower prices, landless Europeans could more easily acquire enslaved workers along with land to start their own plantations. Thus, the call for cheaper land and slave labor to deliver white equality was motivated by the need to maintain the loyalty of European workers performing counterrevolutionary policing. Because enslavers depended on the alliances of white counterrevolution to preserve accumulation, they were forced to worry about how to renew these alliances. In this way, the underlying threat of abolition and anticolonialism underpinned the movement for white equality and how the enslaver ruling class was compelled to support it only to maintain the alliances of white counterrevolution.

While capital sponsored white equality to preserve the unity between white labor and capital to enact counterrevolution, this collided with capital's increasing appetite for wage labor and centralization. White equality would always remain an aspiration rather than a reality. This contradiction of white counterrevolution engendered an insurgent character in the movement of white equality. The vanguard elements of the movement for white equality openly defied and attacked the state where they did not see it supporting this aspiration. I see white equality's insurgent character surface in two moments in the antebellum period. The first was white filibustering of the 1850s and the second the New York City draft riots of July 1863.

FILIBUSTERING INSURGENCY

In November 1853 the notorious filibuster William Walker and his private army of mercenaries illegally invaded Mexico's Baja California and Sonora. Their aim was to seize these territories for US settlers. Walker recruited followers and launched this illegal invasion from his base area in San Francisco. Like so many settlers, as detailed in chapter 2, Walker had thrown in with the conquest of Indigenous and Mexican California to accumulate wealth through dispossession. Intoxicated with conquest, Walker had turned his attention to Mexico. Just months after Joaquín Murieta waged insurgent attacks against US settlers like Walker in California, Walker, for very different reasons, defied the US settler state to extend its imperializing mission on his terms. Walker trespassed into Mexico, in his words, to overturn it and establish his own nation: "Those engaged in the Lower California expedition gave proof of their desire not to destroy, but to reorganize society wherever they went."[50] The invasion was a debacle. It failed miserably. In fact, upon facing difficulties, some of Walker's recruits attempted to desert. "Several of the soldiers," writes Walker, "had formed a conspiracy to desert and to pillage the cattle-farms on their way to Upper California." Walker executed them for this.[51] Mexican forces eventually routed the filibusters from the territory. Despite violating the Neutrality Act of 1818, Walker did not face any punishment for his illegal incursion into Mexico.[52]

Only a few years later Walker organized a second filibustering invasion, targeting Central America. Walker won the trust of opposition leaders of Nicaragua seeking to overthrow the local ruling class of conservative landowners, known as the Legitimists. Their aspiration was to unfetter capitalist development in Nicaragua. The leaders of this opposition movement allegedly made a deal with Walker that in exchange for mercenary services, Walker's army would be provided land for settler plantations. Walker's army arrived and went to work waging insurgency against the local ruling class. Through manipulation and craftiness, Walker took advantage of the conflict between the two sides to emerge as the president of Nicaragua. Walker claimed that the local population embraced American justice, seeing American filibusters as those who effectively maintained law and order and protected the weak from crimes by the lawless.[53] However, Walker's ascendancy to power was short lived. He was dethroned, detained, and forced to return to the United States to face a grand jury indictment for his illegal filibustering actions.

According to Walker, he had invaded Mexico to "protect families on the border from the Indians," and he did not care if his invasion was "sanctioned or not by the Mexican government."[54] He believed the Apache nation held too much power over the region, in defiance of the Mexican state. Because of this, Walker argued, US settlers had the duty to seize control of Baja California and Sonora where the Mexican state had failed to do so properly.[55] Against accusations that his mission was only to loot and plunder, Walker claimed the objective was, as mentioned, not to destroy but to build a new society in Lower California.[56] In Nicaragua, Walker made very clear his intention of aiding the liberals in exchange for mercenary services. Filibustering was not reckless adventurism but the duty to use white force to conquer the "Hispano-Indian race" because European states were failing to do so in their use of indirect coercion through diplomacy, policy, and economic pressures. Walker contended that the colonized would not "meekly" yield to such indirect colonialism. Direct force was required, and he would bring it when the state refused to.[57]

On December 19, 1856, the *New York Herald* ran the article "Filibustering Sympathy for Gen. Walker—A Good Move," reporting on a meeting hosted in New York City to recruit men and funds for Walker's Nicaragua expedition. The irony in the title telegraphs the author's criticism of white filibustering. Walker's filibustering is described as a service to the public for luring the jobless surplus of New York City to faraway lands. Filibustering removed the unwanted classes of "loafers . . . vagabonds, ruffians, idlers." The author characterizes filibustering as the work of amateurs and opportunists. The article predicts that Walker's invasion would be a failure. However, it would be a success in vanquishing the unwanted jobless white surplus. In filibustering destinations like Central America, "white men die off there so fast." If this was the result of filibustering, the author proclaims, referring to the white surplus, "send them down" to Nicaragua to be used as fodder in filibustering wars.

Such a perspective on filibustering embodied capital's perspective on the rising industrial reserve army of wage labor. By not serving as productive labor, the surplus was redundant and thus a nuisance to remove. The role of the jobless as a lever to depress the wages of the waged in order to increase surplus value extraction reached a limit when the accumulation of the jobless surplus posed a problem to reproduction of capital accumulation. The *New York Herald*'s view of filibustering as buffoonish rather than professional white conquering—only useful to resolve the problem of the white surplus—was a symptom of the conditions from which filibustering emerged as a movement for white equality responding to increasing centralization of capital. The paper's mocking of the white surplus's attraction to filibustering indexed how it saw in Walker's campaigns the aspiration for white equality. The difference, however, between filibustering and homesteading was the former's insurgent character. Walker was dedicated to insurgent actions to win white equality where the state was perceived as failing to support such aspirations. This was Walker's appeal among the white surplus for which the *New York Herald* had such disdain. The author's condescension revealed a latent fear of New York City's white surplus and their attraction to reactionary insurgency rather than obedience to industrializing capital.

Like the mass meeting reported by the *New York Herald*, there were many events, balls, and rallies in major cities dedicated to fundraising and recruiting for filibustering in Central America. The principal recruiting strategy was to promise recruits land in exchange for mercenary work. In Walker's plan, after seizing control of Nicaragua, he would provide lands to new emigrant settlers, who were needed to fill the territory as armed occupiers, as we saw in the early homestead vision of Benton and others. Walker's Nicaragua expedition promised 250 acres of land per person, almost double the amount that was being proposed at the time in the emerging Homestead Bill.[58] According to historian Robert May, poor and jobless whites were the primary recruits.[59] It was the landless who were gripped by the vision of filibustering dreams for white equality. In fact, for Walker's first two campaigns to Mexico and then to Nicaragua his recruits were found among the strata of the gold rush's losers, the failed settler-miners and Indian killers rendered jobless by the expanding capital that followed settler conquest.[60] From violent Indian removal in California to pave the way for extraction and expropriation of lands and resources to doing the same work as filibusters, it was an easy move for landless settlers. They saw redemption through filibustering.

Historian Walter Johnson has examined the appeal of Walker's filibustering to poor whites. "Walker pitched his revolution," Johnson writes, "to those for whom the promise of a grant of 250 acres of unimproved land and a dream of bigger things was sufficient to get them to risk their lives." Walker's dream grasped discontented whites who saw capital was failing in its promises of sharing the spoils of empire and enslavement.[61] Walker agitated around this grievance among poor whites: "The question [is] whether you will permit yourselves to be hemmed in on the South as you already are on the North and on the West—whether you will remain quiet and idle while impassable barriers are being built on the only side left open for your superabundant energy and enterprise."[62] Like proslavery propagandists, Walker argued that the abolition of slavery would expose white workers to further depredations of capital, just as much as capital might be overtaken by wage labor. Slavery was the linchpin for maintaining a harmony between capital and white labor in which both would benefit. A society without slavery, wrote Walker, "would result in the subordination of one class of the white race to the other—capital to labor (anarchy) or labor to capital (despotism, also known as white slavery)."[63] Filibustering in Central America promised to resolve this problem, which seemed increasingly unsolvable in North America. Where the landless, the surplus, the underemployed European worker was denied the prospect of escape from proletarian life, which was increasingly the case in the 1850s, filibustering dreams emerged as a resolution.[64]

In his memoir, *The War in Nicaragua*, Walker tries to make the case that he never defied the US state. The state approved of his action, he argues, or led him to believe that it was sanctioned.[65] He claims that opposition leaders of Nicaragua offered him a contract for colonization or permission for his army to emigrate and settle in Nicaragua in their support for the campaign to overthrow the Legitimists. Walker contends that this contract adhered to the 1818 Neutrality Act.[66] Beyond the legal details, Walker argues that the state's mission of expansion and conquest was his same mission in Nicaragua. He shared with the US state the objective of spreading the dominance of Anglo-Saxons in the Americas. It was manifest destiny, not filibustering. For this, Walker asks, how could he be in violation of any law? If he has violated the letter of the law, it matters not, for he was fulfilling the spirit of the law. In a speech delivered January 25, 1858, in Mobile, Alabama, Walker claimed that President James Buchanan had met with him and supported his expedition to Nicaragua. "If I am the lawless person which the Message describes," Walker asked, "how should he, as the President of the United States, receive me, William Walker, a criminal, and offender against the laws of the county? . . . [W]as it proper that I should cross the threshold of his door, and that he should receive me as an equal? But this he did."[67] Walker questioned how he could be considered a criminal when the US president had received him warmly and promised that the Monroe Doctrine would provide cover for filibustering.

In the same breath, however, in which Walker appealed to the authority of the US state to justify filibustering, he undermined its legitimacy for criminalizing his mission and actions. Walker accused the US state not only of sabotaging his filibustering mission's potential victory but of dispossessing his property and invalidating his dignity:

> At the very moment when we were about to regain all we had lost through an officer of the United States the strong arm of the government again interferes, and takes us from the soil which we were entitled to call our own. But not satisfied with this act of violence against all constitutional and national law, it accompanies the acts of violence with a series of insults towards the men it was engaged in removing. The naval officers of the United States take occasion to trample us in the dust, and insult us with their epithets. . . . They not only style us pirates, but actually treat us as such, and take possession of the property we hold, as if it were the property of nobody.[68]

Walker also claimed that the US state had asked him to pursue filibustering in Mexico to form an alliance for the United States that would precipitate a war between Mexico and Spain to bolster US interests. As a proponent of the South's expansion, Walker saw this dangerously leading to Mexico seizing Cuba and making it a free state under Mexico's abolition policy. Walker suggested that for declining this request while nonetheless advancing US interests in Central America, he was betrayed by his country: "Here, at the very time that they are saluting us with all the epithets of our language, when we are denounced as men, lawless and without shame, violating the acts of Congress of the United States, at this very moment they propose an act I scorn even to think of. They propose that we shall do things to bring about a war between friendly nations."[69] Walker also pointed out that the new Nicaraguan president who succeeded him quickly signed a treaty with the United States to establish the Nicaraguan transit route, which for Walker was nothing but a scheme to enrich finance capitalism: "Who are the parties interested in this speculating mart? Go among the moneyed hucksters that throng the streets of your capital, and find, if you can, men more corrupt." His crime was not filibustering but fighting for less propertied white men of the South in the face of finance capital's power. "The great offence on our part? That we were born in the South, and were endeavoring to extend her interests. This is a great crime, and every wrong which they commit against us is a wrong against you." When the state served capital over white men rather making capital serve white men, white insurgency emerged as a viable strategy for Walker. He called for his followers to make the government pay for criminalizing his attempts to secure land and resources for landless Europeans. "Your Constitution has been trampled in the dust; your rights as Southern men and American citizens, have not only been ignored, but have been insulted. I venture to speak to you, and now call upon you, as you desire to see transmitted those rights, permit not these wrongs to go unpunished."[70] In this way, Walker's filibustering for dreams of white equality not only defied the US state and international law but became a potential insurgency against the state's attempt to criminalize white equality filibustering.

This insurgent character of Walker's filibustering, however, never betrayed counterrevolution. He ends his memoir by suggesting that when the state fails to wage counterrevolution effectively, white workers must do so because those conquered will not "meekly" yield. This was one of his justifications for filibustering in Central America. The US state was not properly guarding against anticolonial and abolition revolution. White workers were needed as filibusters to take over where the state was coming up short. As Gerald Horne has shown of this period, the South sought to expand its territories of slavery capitalism not only to accumulate but to curb abolition's power.[71] Counterrevolution drove expansion. Walker was also in this game. In fact, in one speech republished by William Lloyd Garrison's abolitionist newspaper the *Liberator*, Walker claims that it was an abolitionist plot that led to his detention and criminalization. He suggests that the British and Northern abolitionists have hijacked the US state to oppose the expansion of slavery in Central America. "The American Minister to England, and the Abolitionists at the North, determined that slavery should be excluded from a place over which Americans had no control." An abolition government has strong-armed Walker, he believes. In response to growing abolition power, filibustering carries the duty to expand slavery capitalism in Central America to amass greater counterrevolutionary power. The filibuster's calling is to impose white supremacy on such lands: "On whom rested the right of regenerating the amalgamated race? On no other than the people of the United States, and especially of the Southern States. I call upon you, therefore, to execute this mission. You cannot, in justice to yourselves, shrink from the endeavor."[72] Of course, when carrying out the duties of counterrevolution in alliance with capital, one also expects capital to uphold its end of the deal.

Where capital knew it was not upholding its end of the alliance, there arose fear of a breakdown in this alliance. That is, where white equality was foreclosed, disloyalty to upholding counterrevolution was on the table. Johnson explains how what emerged in the 1850s was a fear that white workers in the South would renounce their loyalty to policing for capital, as examined in chapter 1, because it was becoming clear that white equality was not possible. The South's trajectory of centralizing capital pushed out nonenslavers from escaping proletarian life. They were asked to police to preserve accumulation while facing limited prospects for white equality. "Thus it was the nonslaveholders," Johnson writes, "who came to be seen as 'a problem' in the era of the 'Negro Fever'. . . . Although few slaveholders had the bad judgment to come right out and say so, there were grave doubts circulating through the South about the loyalty of non-slaveholders to the existing order, especially after 1857."[73] It was in this way that Walker's filibustering insurgency was a movement to uphold slavery in response to abolition by securing land and resources to address this problem of a

Figure 6. *The Riots in New York: Destruction of the Coloured Orphan Asylum.* Woodcut illustration in the *Illustrated London News*, 1863. The Miriam and Ira D. Wallach Division of Art, Prints and Photographs: Picture Collection, The New York Public Library, New York City. b17149519.

foreclosure of white equality that if not addressed, risked derecruiting the policing forces necessary to repress Black revolt. There was once a time when the landless surplus were seen as useful armed occupiers for capital. That was the time of Benton and others who expounded white equality to secure counterrevolutionary forces on the "frontier." The 1850s was a time when capital expected counterrevolutionary service from white labor with no expectation to deliver white equality. The result produced an insurgent filibustering movement that capital could mock, detain, and criminalize, but could not solve the problem of why the movement emerged in the first place. A few years later in the North another form of white insurgency erupted in New York City, caused by similar contradictions stemming from white counterrevolution and the centralizing of capital.

NEW YORK CITY'S ANTI-ABOLITION INSURGENCY

In July 1863 for five days straight, white insurgent violence raged across New York City. White workers of diverse strata, occupations, and industries united to attack state institutions and free Black communities of New York City. The insurgency targeted police, military, and government leaders, while unleashing a pogrom against free Africans to drive them from the city. Some 105 people died from the violence. Eleven of the dead were Black men whom white mobs gruesomely lynched. The spark that ignited the five days of white insurgency was the Enrollment Act, better known as the Conscription Act, passed in March 1863. The Union government faced dwindling numbers of recruits for the army since Lincoln's signing of the Emancipation Proclamation in September 1862, which had gone into effect January 1, 1863. White soldiers were less enthusiastic to enlist in a war for abolition than for what they had perceived before as a war to stop the South's rebellion and reunify the nation. The Conscription Act made all men ages twenty to forty-five, both citizens and immigrants seeking citizenship, "liable to perform military duty in the service of the United States when called out by the President for that purpose."[74] A lottery system decided who would be called to duty. The act also provided commutation for those who could provide a substitute or pay $300. Mandating that they fight for abolition and that wealth could exempt citizens from this duty inflamed white workers. The $300 was a year's worth of wages for a common worker.[75] The onset of the war had also triggered inflation in goods but not wages, intensifying the class antagonism between labor and capital. Inflation had risen 43 percent since 1860, but wages had only increased 12 percent.[76] These were the conditions in which the prospect for white equality had been killed by the state that, it was perceived, had also adopted abolition as its mission.

On Saturday, July 11, 1863, officials at the Eighth District draft offices drew the first names to be conscripted for service. At 6:00 am on

Monday, July 13, white workers took to the streets instead of going to work. The insurgency's opening act was a white strike, a refusal to work, not in protest against capital but rather to riot for white equality.[77] Rioters assembled at the draft offices and shut down the lottery selection, routing officials and ransacking the building. They then directed their anger at the police and state officials. Crowds engaged in pitched battles with police, who tried in vain to suppress and break up the assembled. Their numbers had grown into the thousands. With the police weakened, rioters began burning buildings. By the afternoon, with smoke billowing into the sky overhead, the rioters had a taste for blood. They began to target free Africans. White workers attacked a Black fruit vendor and child who happened to be in their path of destruction. White rioters then set their sights on the Colored Orphan Asylum, which housed 237 Black children. Fortunately the children escaped out the back before the building was breached. The older children carried the young on their backs as they fled. They became refugees once again and sought sanctuary at the nearby police precinct for the next few days. After seizing anything of value, the rioters burned the Black orphanage to the ground. They came close to beating to death one of their own who had admonished the crowd to spare the Black children.[78]

All of this was a rehearsal for what was to come in the following days. Insurgent white workers made it their mission to rid New York City of free Africans. Rioters began to hunt down Black workers. The vanguard for this pogrom was made up of the white longshoremen and iron workers.[79] White insurgents set ablaze Black tenements, boarding homes for Black sailors, and houses of "amalgamation," or brothels where white women workers sold sex to Black workers. When Black workers defended themselves, it was considered a further affront to the white mob, for which the price was even greater violence. When a cluster of white workers confronted a Black worker named Costello, he drew his pistol and shot one of his attackers to defend himself. In response, Costello was strung up and hanged on a lamp post. The most barbaric killing was of Abraham Franklin, a disabled coachman. Franklin was extracted from his house and hanged. He was then cut down, and his body was dragged through the streets by his genitals while the white crowd jeered and cheered. After disembarking from his ship, Black sailor William Williams was violently attacked for asking for directions to nearby grocery stores. He was beaten and stabbed by multiple attackers, who made his killing a theatrical performance. As they had done to the revolutionary Nat Turner, white workers dismembered their victims to loot body parts as war trophies. They cut off the toes and fingers of lynching victims.[80] These rabid attacks against free Africans drove many to the woods in the surrounding areas. Most fled to police precincts for protection. Even the precincts, however, were not safe. On Tuesday night a white mob attacked the Fifth Precinct, where four hundred Black refugees had relocated. Police were desperate. They armed many of the Black refugees and braced for the attack. Luckily, reinforcements arrived in time to rout the white mob. This was a foretaste of what the Union government would be compelled to do, namely arm Black troops to win the war.[81]

White workers did not stop there. They went after the Republican propagandist Horace Greeley and his *New York Tribune*. Rioters amassed in front of Greeley's *Tribune* office, calling for him to meet them in the streets. Greeley wisely did not show up.[82] They broke through a small police line and raided the office, smashing furniture before setting the building ablaze. Insurgent whites saw the *Tribune* as the voice of abolition, for which it should pay the price of fire. They chanted "Jefferson Davis," while roaming the streets searching out the homes of propertied abolitionists to destroy. At one point, several rioters paused to shred a US flag, cursing "damn the flag." [83] Rioters stormed the Union Steam Works, where they appropriated more than three thousand carbines. Police mounted a counterattack and drove out the rioters. The rioters returned later and reduced the building to ashes. Armed with axes, shovels, clubs, and now carbines, the rioters engaged in a pitched battle in a race war for reactionary white equality.

In the aftermath, the city's Black population fell from 12,581 in 1860 to 9,943 in 1865.[84] Many Black refugees who returned to their homes and neighborhoods fell into extreme poverty resulting from the refusal by their landlords to continue to rent to Black tenants or employers denying employment to Black labor for fear of being attacked by white insurgents.[85] White workers had sought to make New York City a white man's city, much like the vision of a white man's country through homestead utopianism. The difference was that in the latter case, state policy supported white equality, but in the former white workers took matters into their own hands. It was estimated that three thousand white workers participated as rioters for this dream. Thousands more watched and lent support. Thousands more did nothing to stop white attacks against Black workers. Although it was an insurgent action, most participants were not prosecuted. Those who were charged were criminalized for destruction or theft of property, not for attacks against the state or Black workers.[86] Historian Adrian Cook details how before the draft riots, many of the rioters had "led quiet, respectable lives."[87] These were white workers who considered themselves free labor, entitled to land and ownership of the products of their labor. They became insurgent when facing conditions in which it was clear the state had renounced its commitment to white equality. Later that summer New York City passed an ordinance raising $2 million to pay the commutation fee of $300 per person for firemen, policemen, militia members, indigent workers, and any workers who could prove that being conscripted for military duty would cause economic hardship for their families. No public funds were raised or used to rehome Black refugees who survived the white riots.[88] White workers saw that it was their duty to correct what the state was not defending, namely the promise of white equality emerging from the alliances of counterrevolution. While the insurgency was not representative of all white workers, it did embody a vanguard position for white equality that had been the principal demand of the antebellum workers' movement for land reform and homestead utopianism.

Like filibustering, the draft riots were an insurgency of white counterrevolution. In response to the state's appearing to sponsor free Africans over white workers through the abolition agenda, white workers attacked free Africans to curb any possibility of Black power emerging in New York City. Historians often interpret white workers' attacks on Black workers in the draft riots in terms of labor competition. Historians have argued that the presence of cheaper Black labor suppressing the wages of white workers and increasing the competition for available jobs angered white workers enough to retaliate with violence.[89] Cook, however, shows that white workers during these years in New York City did not consider Black labor competition. In fact, imported Irish labor was becoming cheaper than Black labor. Yet Irish workers were not the targets of the rioters' ire.[90] Many of the Irish workers were rioters themselves. Competition in the labor market was not the cause. The rioters targeted Black workers to do the work of crushing abolition precisely where the state was perceived as not only abandoning the commitment to white counterrevolution but undermining it. It was the white worker who upheld white counterrevolution against Black workers where the state was seen as taking up the cause of an "antiwhite" abolition. In this way, white workers bloodied and murdered police, burned US flags, destroyed property, stole firearms, razed buildings, and lynched Black workers to protest the state's perceived failure not only to sponsor white equality but to curb the abolition struggle.

CONCLUSION

This chapter has argued that the alliances of white counterrevolution in which white labor demanded an impossible equality with capital clashed with the burgeoning centralization of capital in the 1850s. If capital required the loyalty of European workers to carry out counter-revolution to protect accumulation from abolition and anticolonialism, capital began to centralize through this very protection, resulting in the expanded exploitation of European workers' labor power. White labor's work in white counterrevolution upheld the very processes of capital accumulation that with the emergence of an incipient central-ization in the 1850s began to come home to roost to intensify the exploi-tation of white labor. The result of this contradiction was a movement for white equality that took on an insurgent character. While insur-gent in relation to the state, white equality remained a project loyal to white counterrevolution. It was an insurgency for white equality and counterrevolution, which European workers believed that the state had failed to deliver on both fronts.

This perspective expands how we understand the relationship be-tween white labor and capital. Whiteness studies has shown how Eu-ropean workers constructed white identities against the racialized subjugation of the enslaved and colonized. In these accounts, white-ness functioned as symbolic compensation for European wage workers, who faced increased centralization of capital. However, this chap-ter has illuminated how white counterrevolution was a structuring force in European workers' response to capitalism's emergent central-ization. It was the material necessity for capital to develop alliances with white labor in the counterrevolution against anticolonialism and abolition that served as the soil in which sprouted the reaction-ary aspirations for white equality as a utopian resolution to central-izing capital. Focusing on white counterrevolution sheds light on the role of Black and Indigenous class struggle in the history of European workers' confrontation with centralizing capital. Anticolonialism and abolition were the undercurrent motor forces shaping the conditions in which European workers organized movements for white equal-ity utopianism, which at moments erupted into insurgency against their own state. This was more than fashioning white identity against

Black suffering. White equality insurgency erupted from the irresolvable contradictions of white counterrevolution and capitalist development. While racial capitalism has passed through various stages, these contradictions remain. In the years that followed, abolition democracy of the Reconstruction era, in which a dictatorship of Black labor imposed its will on Southern capital, would awaken again the monster of white insurgency. It would terrorize in the name of counterrevolution to restore racial capitalism. In our contemporary conjuncture, the monster of white insurgency has again been set loose in the growing movements of neofascism. Yet we can better see its causes and predict its trajectories through a view of its origins during this period of white counterrevolution and the beginning of a centralizing capitalism.

4

ABOLITION SHOOTS BACK

John Brown, Osborne Anderson, Harriet Tubman,
and Black Revolution

JOHN BROWN was an ardent student of Black Study. He
researched the Haitian revolution, the revolts and maroon
societies of Jamaica, Denmark Vesey's plot, Joseph Cinqué
and the Amistad rebellion, Nat Turner's insurrection, Black
marronage of the Seminole insurgencies, and other events
of Black militancy to discover their insights on the enemy of
slavery and revolutionary strategy. Historian Kellie Carter
Jackson highlights how Brown solicited political education
and mentorship from Black radical abolitionists of his day.[1]
He sought counsel from Frederick Douglass, James McCune
Smith, Jermain W. Loguen, Martin Delany, Lewis Hayden,
Henry Highland Garnet, and Harriet Tubman, among
others. What Brown learned from Black Study was not only
a commitment to justice but also the art of people's war.

When he last spoke with his longtime friend Frederick
Douglass, Brown petitioned Douglass to join him as a military leader in the plan to raid the South at Harper's Ferry,

Virginia. As Brown envisioned it, the raid would initiate a guerrilla warfare campaign in the Appalachian Mountains to destroy slavery. In August 1859 Douglass and Brown met at an "old stone quarry near" Chambersburg, Pennsylvania, to discuss the tactics of Brown's "Virginia" plan. Also present was Shields Green, a fugitive slave and Underground Railroad organizer working closely with Douglass. Many referred to Green as the "Emperor." John Kagi, the secretary of war in Brown's militia, attended as well, accompanying Brown. Though he was a strategist, planner, and advocate for Brown's abolition war strategy, Douglass doubted the proposed tactics of the raid at Harper's Ferry. "It would be an attack upon the Federal Government," warned Douglass, "and would array the whole country against us." He believed Brown "was going into a perfect steel-trap" at Harper's Ferry. Brown countered that intensifying the class war of slavery was precisely his objective, and that the attack would inspire those held captive already fighting slavery to join his program to abolish it. "The capture of Harper's Ferry," Brown promised, "would serve as notice to the slaves that their friends had come, and as a trumpet, to rally them to his standard." Concerning the problem of escaping the steel trap, Brown was prepared to take hostage the "best citizens of the neighborhood as his prisoners" as leverage to "dictate terms of egress from the town." Douglass warned that "Virginia would blow him and his hostages sky-high, rather than that he should hold Harper's Ferry an hour." After a day and half of rigorous debate, Douglass made his final decision not to join the raid. Brown was planning a different set of tactics than what Douglass claimed had been Brown's previous proposal of "gradually . . . drawing off the slaves to the mountains."

As Douglass prepared to depart, he asked Shields Green "what he had decided to do, and was surprised by his coolly saying in his broken way, 'I b'leve I'll go wid de ole man.'" If the change of tactics inspired Douglass to withdraw to a rear-base role, for Green, it invited him to move to the front lines of abolition war. Green enlisted on the spot to serve as a soldier in the campaign, knowing its risks but also the potential rewards of slavery's destruction. Brown had met Green during one of Brown's visits to Douglass's home in Rochester.[2] Douglass knew Green as someone not "to shrink from hardships or dangers," and that during Brown's visit in Rochester Brown "saw at once what 'stuff' Green 'was made of,' and confided to him his plans and purposes." At Harper's Ferry, Green would live up to these characterizations. He would prove to be one of the fiercest fighters in the raid. He helped mobilize local enslaved people to join the raid, guarded captured proslavery hostages, and in a decision that tragically, led to his arrest and execution, chose to remain and defend the raiders retreating to safety when they came under siege by federal troops.[3] While those who joined Brown's militia are often characterized as his followers, won over by his commanding persona, in truth it was Brown's theory of abolition war and program for carrying it out that attracted recruits like Shields Green. He signed up to fight not for John Brown, but for the strategy of abolition war that Brown was centralizing into an armed military campaign with the capacity to overthrow slavery.[4]

Black radical thinkers who have studied Brown emphasize that he should be studied for the ways that his armed campaign from Kansas to Harper's Ferry was a major advancement of abolition war, building on the long history of slave revolts, maroon societies, and fugitivity.[5] Brown is often remembered for his prophetic warning that it would require apocalyptic violence to abolish slavery. Moments before his execution following his capture at Harper's Ferry, Brown scribbled his famous last words on a note passed to a nearby prison guard: "I, John Brown, am now quite *certain* that the crimes of this *guilty land* will never be purged away but with *blood*. I had, as I now think vainly, flattered myself that without very much bloodshed it might be done."[6] Regarding the question of what strategy was correct for ending slavery, Du Bois proclaimed that "John Brown was right."[7] Abolition war thinkers, like Brown, could see that slavery—as a violent war of accumulation targeting Africans—called into being its negation: war for the liberation of Africans. Following the example of Nat Turner, Brown understood that it would take waging armed abolition war to end the war that was slavery.

Historians and theorists of abolition have studied the role and impact of abolition war in the broader antislavery movement of the nineteenth century.[8] Abolition war is seen as one strategy among many adopted by abolitionists in the struggle for the extension of civil rights to those of African descent. However, when abolition war is folded into the framework of civil rights, its objectives are concealed. Through its aim to destroy enslavement as a primary engine of capital accumulation and win self-determination for people of African descent, abolition war's trajectory, I contend, was to abolish racialized class society itself. In this way, abolition war was constituted by a revolutionary horizon. It was the armed movement of Black workers to overturn the power of their exploiters standing at the helm of US class society. If Marx and Engels had written in 1848 that the movement for the revolutionary overthrow of capitalism had emerged among Europe's industrial working classes to haunt Europe's ruling classes, Black revolution housed in abolition war was the specter terrorizing North American racial capitalism.[9] The African revolutionary Amilcar Cabral argued that "we would recall that every practice produces a theory, and that if it is true that a revolution can fail even though it be based on perfectly conceived theories, nobody has yet made a successful revolution without a revolutionary theory."[10] This chapter asks: If abolition war was a revolutionary movement, what was its revolutionary theory? How did the partisans of armed abolition war represent and theorize not only the racialized class society of slavery they sought to abolish, but also the class struggle or dialectics of abolition's confrontation with white counterrevolution? In the following, I examine how abolition war produced a theory of Black revolution that has been understudied and underappreciated both in studies on abolition and Marxism. Within the history of abolition war, I focus on the campaigns of John Brown and Harriet Tubman, approaching these as collectives of abolition war thinkers who thought, theorized, and fought together as units rather than individuals.

This chapter argues that abolition war thinkers of Brown's and Tubman's campaigns theorized the enslaved as a vanguard force for cutting a path and pulling together a movement to overthrow not merely formal enslavement but racialized class society. In the same years when Karl Marx and Fredrich Engels conceptualized the European industrial proletariat in such terms as the advanced sector of the dispossessed leading the international working class in a revolution to overthrow capitalism, abolition war thinkers saw the enslaved as the gravediggers of North American racial capitalism. It was this theory of the enslaved as the political and military vanguard for waging insurgency against slavery that guided abolition war strategy and tactics. Abolition war thinkers did not consider the enslaved a vanguard force through a moral framework of suffering. Rather, they saw the enslaved through a historical materialist lens. The enslaved were positioned in racial capitalism not only as its fulcrum for capital accumulation, but also as its strongest foe, as the class whose only available course of action to become free was the strategy of overthrow. Accordingly, like what Delany's *Blake* (see chapter 1) envisioned, the campaigns of Brown and Tubman sought to organize a political program in the image of the slave's insurgent orientation to guide abolition war.

This reading of abolition war sees the campaigns of Brown and Tubman in a new light. They were not social reform struggles seeking to redeem US democracy. Rather, they were efforts to centralize Black revolution in North America, where the enslaved as a vanguard force pulled, like a tugboat, other classes toward the overturning of the class society of slavery. In this way, the chapter also illuminates how abolition war thinkers analyzed the dialectics of class struggle in similar yet distinct ways from European communism at the time. Where Marx theorized the abolition of slavery in North America as the struggle to end formal enslavement of African workers in ways that would unite them with European free laborers under the shared position of wage labor, abolition war theorists saw the inverse. It was the enslaved Africans' abolition war for Black revolution that would wrench free labor into a movement to abolish capitalism. Abolition war was thus a history in which theories of anti-capitalist struggle were developed, stretched, and practiced in antebellum North America, both paralleling but also expanding the historical materialist thought of European communism. Through their militant confrontation with slavery, abolition war thinkers also perceived the vulnerabilities, points of weakness, and fragility of white counterrevolution guarding slavery.

"THE JOHN BROWN WAY"

In chapter 1 we learned how Nat Turner kick-started radical abolition in the 1830s. His insurrection gave confidence to others to demand not only immediate abolition but abolition by any means necessary. Counterrevolutionary repression followed in the form of consolidating white alliance policing and the anti-abolition riots. It was this inability or weakness of the abolition movement to challenge white counterrevolution that pushed John Brown into the fray of abolition war. Historians often note that the vigilante murder of antislavery publisher Elijah Lovejoy precipitated John Brown's commitment to abolition war. Famously, after receiving news that Lovejoy had been killed in Illinois by proslavery Missourians, Brown swore an oath to dedicate his life to waging a war to destroy slavery. As explored in chapter 1, the attack on Lovejoy should be seen in the context of anti-abolition counterinsurgent riots of the 1830s following Nat Turner's insurrection and in response the antislavery movement's construction of a much more sophisticated propaganda infrastructure that was reaching and influencing a sizable portion of the public. Du Bois points out that Brown had personal experience confronting this wave of anti-abolition violence. Brown was a participant in the defense against an anti-abolition mob that attacked the Marlborough Chapel in Boston. Brown was "present fighting back the people" and had seen some of the "'principal Abolition mobs.'"[11] As Brown would demonstrate during his years in Kansas—such as when he learned that Lawrence had been razed by proslavery forces without a fight—he was agitated by abolition's lack of militancy to defend against the violence of counterrevolution. Instead of reading these counterrevolutionary attacks as signs of defeat, Brown considered them actions within the dialectic of resistance and repression. White counterrevolutionary repression demanded more advanced forms of abolition resistance.

After the passing of the Fugitive Slave Act, many abolitionists feared its repercussions. As discussed in chapter 1, it was a counterrevolutionary law designed to curb the advances made in the organizing of the Underground Railroad and free Black communities of the North. It angered, and for some radicalized, many white moderates, who saw that "Slave power" had formally extended into their neck of the woods. Abolitionists leaders condemned the law for what it was and braced for its impact. John Brown interpreted the law much differently. In the fall of 1850, while in Springfield, Massachusetts, Brown wrote to his wife, "It now seems that the Fugitive Slave Act was to be the means of making more Abolitionists than all the lectures we have had for years. It really looks as if God had His hand on this wickedness also. I of course keep encouraging my colored friends to 'trust in God and keep their powder dry.' I did so to-day at Thanksgiving meeting publicly."[12] Brown perceived how white counterrevolution produced the very conditions in which a more militant form of abolition could emerge. He saw how repression transformed the terrain of struggle and, if read correctly, it could be seized as an opportunity for growing resistance. Through the language of liberation theology, Brown's response to the Fugitive Slave Act indicates that he believed it had only moved the dialectic between resistance and repression forward and thus closer to a favorable terrain on which abolition war could emerge to confront slavery capitalism.

In the wake of the Fugitive Slave Act, abolitionists rallied around the position of intentional defiance, militant resistance, and, for many, armed defense. The organizing to defend against the Fugitive Slave Act was a rehearsal for later forms of more open abolition war. As Sinha argues, "Confronting slaveholders and their agents in their own backyard prepared abolitionists for a revolutionary, remorseless war against slavery."[13] In his public speeches following the passing of what Douglass called the "Bloodhound Law," he repeated the refrain that "the only way to make the Fugitive Slave Law a dead letter, is to make a few dead slave-catchers." In what he termed the "John Brown Way," Douglass called for abolition in a way that would make enslavers fear for their lives, to raise the cost of perpetuating slavery. "We need not only to appeal to the moral sense of these slaveholders; we have need, and a right, to appeal to their fears."[14] As mentioned in chapter 2, Martin Delany promised to shoot in self-defense federal agents if they attempted to enter his home to enforce the Fugitive Slave Act. In a speech at Allegheny City, Pennsylvania, only days after the passing of the law, Delany warned, "If any man approaches that house in search of a slave,—I care not who he may be, whether constable or sheriff, magistrate or even judge of the Supreme Court—nay, let it be he who sanctioned this act to become a law, . . . if he crosses the threshold of my door, and I do not lay him a lifeless corpse at my feet, I hope the grave may refuse my body a resting-place."[15] In August 1850, at the Cazenovia Fugitive Slave Law Convention, where two thousand abolitionists attended, Garret Smith coauthored a speech with formerly enslaved organizers that called for armed defense and for mass insurrection in the South, a vision that echoed David Walker and Henry Highland Garnett and that Delany, as we saw, novelized in *Blake*.[16] Black abolitionist James McCune Smith argued that "our white brethren cannot understand us unless we speak to them in their own language; they recognize only the philosophy of force. They will never recognize our manhood until we knock them down a time or two; they will then hug us as men and brethren."[17] In this context Brown, who had already been an active participant in the Underground Railroad for years, organized a project of Black community defense called the League of Gileadites.[18]

While this project is most remembered for its requirement that Black members were to always be armed, what is overlooked is how the League of Gileadites was premised on understanding the Black worker as the most advanced fighter in this struggle to repel invading waves of slave catchers and to perform slave rescues. In Brown's "Words of Advice" to League members, he suggests that Black militancy sparks greater solidarity and support than representations of Black suffering. "The trial for life of one bold and to some extent successful man, for defending his rights in good earnest, would arouse the sympathy throughout the nation than the accumulated wrongs and sufferings of more than three million of our submissive colored population."[19] Similar to Harriet Tubman's critique of the politics of Harriet Beecher Stowe's *Uncle Tom's Cabin*, that it overrepresented Black suffering while erasing Black militancy, here Brown contends that daring resistance was the best propaganda for inspiring meaningful solidarity from others. Appealing to suffering to garner support would elicit words condemning slavery but not solidarity actions dedicated to its destruction. Resistance prompted the recognition of the Black worker's humanity without solely focusing on Black suffering, which reinscribed white supremacist logics underpinning modern definitions of bourgeois humanity, as Sylvia Wynter and Saidiya Hartman have theorized.[20] As Robert and Mabel Williams and Frantz Fanon would later theorize comprehensively, Brown understood that it was through violent resistance that the white world would be compelled to see the enslaved as human.[21]

Brown also analyzed how Black militancy was the catalyst for piercing the armor of white alliance policing. He suggested that Black members of the League of Gileadites seek refuge from assailants among their white friends with status and resources, with or without their permission. For Brown, this would compel whites to align with the objectives of Black defense and slave rescue: "After effecting a rescue, if you are assailed, go into the houses of your most prominent and influential white friends with your wives, and that will effectually fasten upon them the suspicion of being connected with you, and will compel them to make common cause with you, whether they would otherwise live up to their profession or not."[22] Black militancy would pull in and provide leadership to whites who otherwise would not, on their own, align with armed abolition's attack on slave catcher counterinsurgency. While these instructions to find refuge in the homes of friendly whites without permission appear to be have been more about political theater and sleight of hand criticism of moderate abolitionists not willing to take action that risked their well-being, they nonetheless reveal how Brown conceptualized Black militancy's role in sharpening the contradictions of class struggle in ways that drew the lines in the sand between Black revolution and white counterrevolution. The command to seek refuge among the well-resourced forced their hand to commit to abolition war or be revealed as untrustworthy.

Brown counsels that the League of Gileadites should include all members of the Black community regardless of age, ability, or gender: "We invite every colored person whose heart is engaged for the performance of our business, whether male or female, old or young. . . . [Their role] shall be to give instant notice to all members in case of an attack upon any of our people."[23] The League members were not a specialized and separate militia from the community. Rather, the free Black community was to serve as a fighting force itself, with everyone playing a role. This strategy of recruiting all members of the free Black community for defense against slave catchers indicates how Brown conceptualized Black worker vanguardism in the abolition movement. Free Black communities were already organically organizing to provide mutual aid, relief, refuge, and defense for those escaping from slavery. Brown's League of Gileadites model approached this organic frontline defense work and formalized it into a military machine.

A few years later, the Black novelist and abolitionist William Wells Brown visited Springfield and reported that the League of Gileadites was very successful in defending against slave catchers. He explained that in response to the threat of armed Black defense, the local "authorities, foreseeing a serious outbreak, advised [the slave catchers] to leave, and feeling alarmed for their personal safety, these disturbers of the peace had left." It was the formerly enslaved women, William Wells Brown noted, who were the most eager to attack menacing slave catchers. He described the scene of a "hot room," where formerly enslaved African women were organized to attack any slave catcher using instruments of the kitchen, including throwing boiling water. "Each of these Amazons was armed with a tin dipper," observed Wells Brown, "a woman of exceedingly large proportions—tall, long-armed, with a deep scar down the side of her face, and with a half grin, half smile— was the commander-in-chief of the 'hot room.' This woman stood by the stove, dipper in hand, and occasionally taking the top from the large wash-boiler, which we learned was filled with boiling water, soap, and ashes. In case of an attack, this boiler was to be the 'King of Pain.'" Wells Brown also reported that not a single person had been kidnapped by slave catchers and that the area was known for its militant defense, which had a deterrent effect on would-be pursuers of fugitive slaves.[24]

Brown developed his theory of Black worker vanguardism through the study of Black revolution. John Hinton, the abolitionist reporter and later one of the first biographers of Brown, recalled that while in Kansas Brown would tell "stories of 'Isaac,' 'Denmark Vessey,' 'Nat Turner,' and the 'Cumberland Region' insurrectionary affairs in South Carolina, Virginia, and Tennessee. He showed himself perfectly familiar with the sometime resistance to slave-catchers in Pennsylvania, and he knew the story of Hayti and Jamaica, too, by heart."[25] Du Bois's biography of Brown is, in many ways, the study of how Black revolutionary strategy and theory shaped Brown's political development. Recently, Kellie Carter Jackson emphasizes how Brown made himself a student of slave revolts, marronage, and Black militancy. He studied this history to learn its revolutionary lessons.[26] From his study of the Haitian revolution, Brown theorized that militant leadership defying white terror inspired mass mobilization as the key weapon of the enslaved for overtaking their enslavers. One of Brown's soldiers, Richard Realf, shared that Brown was "thoroughly acquainted with the wars in Hayti and the islands round about; and from all these things he had drawn the conclusion . . . that upon the first intimation of a plan formed for the liberation of the slaves, they would immediately rise all over the Southern States."[27] Brown observed this same lesson from Nat Turner, who himself had been inspired by the strategy of the Haitian revolution. Turner initiated his revolt with only a handful of leaders. Yet their militancy quickly inspired the support of around seventy fighters. Turner, like Haitian revolutionaries, exposed the mutability of slavery in ways that inspired further rebellion. This militancy, as we have seen, also compelled enslavers to weigh the risks and rewards of enslavement as a mode of capital accumulation. Brown is reported to have remarked that "Nat Turner, with fifty men, held Virginia five weeks. The same number, well organized and armed, can shake the system out of the State."[28] It was not simply Turner's courage or sacrifice that interested Brown. It was Turner's ability to organize a campaign powerful enough that it came close to compelling enslavers to abolish slavery in Virginia using only a handful of leaders and very few resources that resonated with Brown. Turner's strategy taught Brown that militancy and organization were the principles around which to devise a campaign to scale up abolition war in North America. Synthesizing these lessons into a theory and strategy while in conversation with Black militant leadership of the abolition movement, Brown crafted a plan for going on the offensive against slavery in the South.

The point of entry for his plan was Harper's Ferry, Virginia (today West Virginia), where Brown's militia aimed to seize the town's federal arsenal. The surprise attack was meant to paralyze the local white community with fear, destabilizing their ability to guard the area and police their enslaved. With this breakdown in white alliance policing, the enslaved of nearby plantations could mobilize en masse to join Brown's abolition army. Famously, custom-made pikes, Sharp's rifles, revolvers, and the expropriated arms from the arsenal would be distributed to the newly liberated. From there, the campaign's goal was to retreat to what were called at the time the "Alleghenies," what today are the Appalachian Mountains. This was the "Great Black Way," a stretch of mountainous and heavily wooded terrain that provided strategic cover and concealment for those liberating themselves and escaping to the North.[29] Underground Railroad organizers, including Brown, referred to this region as the Subterranean Pass Way. At one point early in his abolition career, Brown had posed for a daguerreotype holding a flag with the insignia "SPW."[30] Many have analyzed Brown's plan in terms of its potential for military success. Historians seem to agree that while the Harper's Ferry raid was a failed military operation, it succeeded politically. It galvanized support for abolition and set in motion the chain of events that would lead to the Civil War, which ended in slavery's defeat. However, I consider Brown's plan both a representation of Black futurity and a theoretical reflection on Black revolution in the context of North America. Brown's plan was a synthesis of his study and application of Black thought, reading the enslaved as a revolutionary class.

Brown's plan demonstrates that he understood the strategy of abolition war was already underway in organic form in North America. The Great Black Way was already the terrain of raids and battles waged by the fugitive fighters of the Underground Railroad. Brown's plan recognized these fighters as the frontline revolutionary actors in the abolition war strategy. In his plan, the seizure of Harper's Ferry was secondary to the more principal tactic of retreating into the Alleghenies as a terrain already in use among the enslaved. Brown had examined how fugitive fighters used the Great Black Way in their strategy of flight. From this, his plan considered the Great Black Way a rear base from which to launch guerrilla attacks on slavery. Brown explained to Douglass the role of the Alleghenies: "God has given the strength of the hills to freedom, they were placed here for the emancipation of the negro race; they are full of natural forts, where one man for defence will be equal to a hundred for attack; they are full also of good hiding places, where large numbers of brave men could be concealed, and baffle and elude pursuit for a long time."[31] From the rear base of the Alleghenies, the campaign would expropriate food, resources, and property from enemy plantations. Most importantly, it would liberate further recruits, growing the abolition army and weakening the South's economy.

Brown envisioned an internal colony or maroon community forming, not as a commune as an end unto itself, like the antebellum utopian projects of the Northeast, but rather as a Black revolutionary nation in the way that Fanon would later theorize revolutionary nationalism: a vehicle for steering forward revolutionary struggle. As Du Bois argued, "Brown knew guerrilla warfare. . . . The raid was not a foray *from* the mountains, which failed because its retreat was cut off; but it was a foray *to* the mountains with the village and arsenal on the way."[32] In this way, Brown's plan envisioned the extending of the Underground Railroad into a more open form of warfare. "When I asked him how he would support these men," Douglass writes, "he said emphatically, he would subsist them upon the enemy. Slavery was a state of war, and the slave had a right to anything necessary to his freedom."[33] Brown's plan sought to bring the war from below ground to the surface, where the antagonists would meet more on an equal footing for once, anticipating Fanon's dialectics of decolonization.[34] Encountering the enslaved on such a terrain would undermine the very function of white alliance policing, which hinged, in part, on terror and assumed invincibility.

Brown's plan also anticipated that if the Underground Railroad could be brought to the surface in open abolition war, it would radically destabilize the reproduction of accumulation in the South's economy. Brown told Douglass, "The true object to be sought is first of all to destroy the money value of slave property; and that can only be done by rendering such property insecure."[35] Here Brown understood the relationship between production relations and their reproduction. If Marx argued that the social relations of slavery are what made Africans "slaves"—or as he put it, "a Negro is a Negro. Only under certain conditions does he become a slave"—Brown saw how the reproduction of these social relations would easily break down once a certain portion of the enslaved broke out.[36] If conditions of such instability indicated that future valorization was not feasible because of the potential for unrest and revolt, enslavers would lose confidence in the enslaved as value-producing commodities. When Brown says "insecure," he means not only uncontrollable property but also unreliable or risky investments. His plan envisioned how abolition insurgency could devalorize the commodity of the enslaved worker in order to undermine confidence in the future valorization of slavery capital. Without this confidence or assumption of future valorization of capital, the reproduction of production relations was at risk of unraveling.

Douglass understood this dynamic and suggested that enslavers of the Upper South, where Brown intended to strike first, would answer by selling their capital farther in the South, where such future valorization was not under jeopardy. Douglass related that Brown had anticipated this from enemy enslavers: "'That,' said he, 'will be first what I want to do; then I would follow them up. If we could drive slavery out of *one county*, it would be a great gain; it would weaken the system throughout the state.'"[37] Here Brown hoped to exploit the contradiction between individual enslaver capitalists and capital as a system. Seeking self-interest and immediate profits, individual enslaver capitalists would be interested in selling their enslaved workers to avoid their devalorization. However, their tunnel vision or inability to see or think structurally prevented them from apprehending how their individual self-interest undermined their class interest as enslavers. As a class, they lost not only territory but also counterrevolutionary power. As we saw in chapter 3, expansion was key to amassing counterrevolutionary capacity. Less territory meant risking losing the obedience of European workers in policing for slavery. Brown saw how forcing enslavers to perform self-abolition, much as Turner had come close to bringing about in Southampton, weakened slavery in the long term.

Above all, Brown's vision of a future Black army anchored in the Alleghenies indicates—like what he envisioned for the League of Gileadites but on a larger and more advanced scale—that abolition war thinkers considered the enslaved a vanguard force whose organic struggle should be formalized into a political and military project guiding the larger abolition movement. Brown explained how his militia sought to recruit those among the enslaved who were more eager and ready to join an abolition army: "My plan then is to take at first about twenty-five picked men . . . supply them with arms and ammunition, post them in squads of fives on a line of twenty-five miles, the most persuasive and judicious of whom shall go down to the fields from time to time, as opportunity offers, and induce the slaves to join them, seeking and selecting the most restless and daring."[38] Brown's plan sought to unite with the most rebellious sectors of Black labor to harness the power of their experience, knowledge, and existing networks. This was not a top-down affair, as many have often read the structure of Brown's militia. Instead, Brown's envisioned abolition army rested on developing leadership from the most advanced fugitive, maroon, and rebel fighters among the enslaved and formerly enslaved.

John Kagi captures this when sharing the details of the plan with Richard Hinton while in Kansas following the Chatham Convention: "Kagi spoke of having marked out a chain of counties extending continuously through South Carolina, Georgia, Alabama, and Mississippi.

He had travelled over a large portion of the region indicated, and from his own personal knowledge, and with the assistance of Canadian negroes who had escaped from those States, they had arranged a general plan of attack. The counties he named were those which contained the largest proportion of slaves, and would, therefore, be the best in which to strike."[39] Here Kagi reveals how fugitive slaves as veterans of abolition war coplanned Brown's plan. Many had committed to mobilizing as reinforcements once the plan was set in motion. Martin Delany and, as we will see later in more detail, Harriet Tubman were recruiting such reinforcements. "They anticipated, after the first blow had been struck, that, by the aid of the free and Canadian negroes who would join them, they could inspire confidence in the slaves, and induce them to rally."[40] Brown saw how a military force capable of overthrowing slavery would have to draw into its ranks those who were already leaders confronting enslavement at its points of production and reproduction. Brown could see how racial capitalism produced its own gravediggers in a Black proletariat. His campaign was made in the image of these gravediggers, the success of which rested on their participation and leadership.

Proslavery forces also knew that the strength and thus danger of Brown's plan was its theory of Black worker vanguardism. We see this precisely in how the South mocked Brown for the alleged lack of support from the enslaved for the raid. Proslavery responses to the raid characterized it as an utter failure to mobilize the enslaved. They argued that the enslaved had little interest in a fanatic's lone crusade. Proslavery propaganda suggested that the enslaved did not want to rebel and did not support abolition. This perpetuated the myth of the content slave, happier in bondage than "free" to be exploited as a wage earner in the North. Proslavery forces had to conceal that there was or could have been mass support from the enslaved for Brown's raid. However, others sounded the alarm that abolitionists, like Brown, were on the cusp of invading and carrying off large portions of the enslaved, for

Osborn Perry Anderson,
who escaped to write *A
Voice from Harper's Ferry*
and fight in the Civil War.

Figure 7. Portrait of Osborn Perry Anderson. Photograph. Schomburg Center for Research in Black Culture, Photographs and Prints Division, The New York Public Library. New York City. b16104370.

Figure 8. Portrait of John Brown. Daguerreotype reproduction from Martin M. Lawrence, New York City, May 1859. Library of Congress Prints and Photographs Division, Washington, DC. LC-DIG-ppmsca-23764.

which the South should secede to stave off this attack.[41] Such was the contradiction of their propaganda. Abolitionists were threats for their potential to incite mass insurrection, even as they were lone fanatics with no following and rejected by the very people they espoused to liberate. The contradiction embodied their fear of Black worker vanguardism. It was either disavowed or overrepresented through demonization. Historians have shown that there is substantial evidence demonstrating that enslaved Africans in the surrounding area of Harper's Ferry participated in the raid and were ready to take further action depending on how events unfolded. In the weeks that followed a series of arson fires struck several plantations, targeting the jurors who had convicted Brown of treason.[42] In these same weeks, proslavery forces were on edge in fear of slave insurrection. Despite their own propaganda, they believed the raid had laid the groundwork for a larger uprising. What they feared the most was precisely what Brown had intended to achieve—namely, striking a blow that would provide the opening for enslaved fighters to join and advance the program of abolition war.

OSBORNE ANDERSON AND THE DICTATORSHIP OF ABOLITION

One of the members of this Black worker vanguard in Brown's collective was Osborne Anderson. The other Black fighters who joined the raid were Shields Green, John Copeland, Dangerfield Newby, and Lewis Leary.[43] After joining Brown's campaign, Anderson was an attendee at the Chatham Convention, where Brown proposed his plan to invade the South and establish his provisional abolition government. At Harper's Ferry, Anderson was the only Black member to evade capture and successfully retreat to the North. He returned to Chatham, Canada, and reunited with the editor and writer Mary Ann Shadd, for whom Anderson had previously worked as a subscription salesman and printer for Shadd's newspaper the *Provincial Freeman*.[44] Shadd helped Anderson compose and publish his account of the raid, *A Voice from Harper's Ferry*. Anderson's narrative is considered one the best first-hand accounts of the raid. One objective of the narrative was to debunk the misconceptions, distortions, and mystifications of Brown's militia and campaign. Anderson disproves the proslavery allegation that the enslaved did not support Brown's call to action. He documents the many instances of the enslaved participating in the raid. He also suggests that many more were ready to join if Brown had followed the plan to strike and quickly retreat to the Alleghenies.

Anderson's narrative also offers an elaboration on Brown's theory of Black worker vanguardism. Anderson conceptualized Black worker vanguardism as the vehicle for establishing what I read as the strategy of winning a dictatorship of abolition over slavery. That is, Anderson's narrative expresses a dialectics of class struggle in which he sees that the task of the Black proletariat during the revolutionary process of abolition war was to seize political power and use it to subordinate slavery in a dialectical reversal necessary to turn abolition war into overthrow. His narrative registers a theory of a dialectics in dialogue with Marx and the European communist movement's concept, at the time, of the dictatorship of the proletariat. Following the revolutions of 1848, Marx argued that for the proletariat to carry out revolution, it would need to conquer power or win a worker's state to use this power to stave off a counterrevolutionary restoration of power by capital.[45] I am not suggesting that Marx or European communism were in direct conversation with abolition war thinkers like Anderson. While Marx wrote for Horace Greeley's *New York Tribune* as its European correspondent, a newspaper that was read by many abolitionist thinkers, European communists before the Civil War, as mentioned in chapter 3, were more interested in land reform movements of white labor than abolition.[46] It was through struggle and the study of conditions—practicing a form of historical materialist thinking—that Anderson shared an understanding of class struggle similar to Marx's, but for the context of North American racial capitalism. Anderson's narrative highlights moments in which Brown's collective not only seized and held power over the enslaver class at a local scale, but also performed political theater that rehearsed a dictatorship of abolition over slavery. Anderson and others in Brown's collective believed, like Marx, in the necessity of the proletariat subordinating the class rule of capitalists in the process of winning liberation or the end of a racialized class society.

As Anderson details, on the morning of October 16, 1859, Brown's militia held one last council meeting at the Kennedy Farmhouse, their base of operations a few miles from Harper's Ferry, before setting in motion their plan for seizing control of the town and its arsenal. In the meeting, tasks were divided and assigned. One task was for a small team, after seizing Harper's Ferry, to visit nearby plantations to capture enslavers as hostages. "Captain Stevens, Tidd, Cook, Shields Green, Leary," writes Anderson, "and myself went to the country," where the "first prisoner taken by us was Colonel Lewis Washington."[47] Anderson notes that en route to Washington's plantation, their team encountered enslaved rebels, who joined their party upon learning of its objective. "They said they had been long waiting for an opportunity of the kind."[48] Brown's collective had selected Lewis Washington for a few specific reasons. He was one of the wealthiest enslavers of the county and a descendant of George Washington, whose valued life could be leveraged in strategic negotiations at a later point with the enemy. More importantly, he best symbolized the US slavery state. The capture of Lewis Washington was an act of political theater rehearsing a dialectical reversal of power that the raid was designed to achieve in its objective of kick-starting Black revolution.

In the memoir, Anderson represents Washington as a crushed and broken enemy in the face of abolition power over him. Anderson observes that after Washington's house was invaded and he was told he was now a prisoner of abolition, "he stood as if speechless or petrified."[49]

Anderson notes that as the enslaved on his plantation were liberated and the team prepared to return to the town with the enslaved now free and the enslaver Washington imprisoned as a hostage, "Washington was walking the floor, apparently much excited." A key ritual in the political theater of the action was to command Washington to transfer ownership of two family heirlooms gifted to him by George Washington to Osborne Anderson. They were a pistol from Lafayette and a sword from Frederick the Great. "The Colonel cried heartily," writes Anderson, "when he found he must submit, and appeared taken aback when, on delivering up the famous sword formerly presented by Frederic to his illustrious kinsman, George Washington, Capt. Stevens told me to step forward and take it."[50] There is cheer and pleasure in Anderson's representation of Washington's cowardice, panic, and emotional breakdown when confronting his imprisonment by abolition. And the political theater was meant to be pedagogical. "Anderson being a colored man, and colored men being only things in the South, it is proper that the South be taught a lesson upon this point."[51] The command for Washington to surrender his family heirlooms as symbols of white power to Anderson, a Black man, forced Washington, as a stand-in for the enslaver class, to confront the humanity of the enslaved, which could not be denied in the face of the enslaved now holding power over their former enslavers. If slavery turned people into objects, this performance of abolition dictatorship in Lewis Washington's home made enslavers recognize the humanity of the enslaved for the first time, precisely through the enslaved's power over them.

The political theater made an example out of Washington, showing that abolition war was about a Black proletariat seizing political power over enslavers. Lewis Washington was made a captive of those whom he had held captive in slavery. Washington's weapons for waging war against Africans were seized and turned into weapons of abolition war for liberation. In fact, Brown would later take possession of the sword and use it in the last hours of the raid when he was under siege by federal troops in the engine room. Anderson reads this as symbolic of abolition dictatorship, or the attempt of abolition to conquer the slave state: "Capt. Brown, in anticipation of further trouble, had girded to his side the famous sword taken from Col. Lewis Washington the night before, and with that memorable weapon, he commanded his men against General Washington's own State."[52]

"TURNING THE TABLE ON THE OVERSEER"

Brown, Anderson, and others involved in the Harper's Ferry raid were not anomalies in this thinking. Others enmeshed in abolition war strategy articulated a similar theory of a dictatorship of abolition. The influential Black editor Thomas Hamilton, who as we saw in chapter 1 published Martin Delany's novel *Blake*, circulated essays and propaganda celebrating the prospect of a dictatorship of abolition. Following the Harper's Ferry raid, Hamilton penned an essay for his *Anglo-African Magazine* comparing John Brown and Nat Turner to memorialize the two revolutionaries. The essay served as a preface to the republication of Turner's *Confessions*. Hamilton argued that at Harper's Ferry John Brown was mild in his use of revolutionary violence, speculating that if Nat Turner had been in command of the raid, the entire South would be drenched in blood.[53] Hamilton also edited the *Weekly Anglo African*, which he cultivated to be a platform of debate among its Black readership. As discussed in chapter 1 regarding the publication context of Delany's *Blake*, while Hamilton was reluctant to impose editorial positions, he used the *Weekly Anglo-African* to incubate analysis, reporting, and theory on abolition war strategy—especially with the onset of the Civil War following the Harper's Ferry raid.[54] During these years, Lincoln initially refused to adopt the aim of abolishing slavery as part of the Union's strategy for defeating the Confederates. Facing defeat, dwindling recruits, and mounting abolitionist pressure, Lincoln shifted the Union's strategy closer to the aims of abolition war.

TURNING THE TABLES ON THE OVERSEER.

Figure 9. *Turning the Tables on the Overseer.* Woodcut stand-alone print from Richard and Thomas Hamilton, New York City, 1863. Library Company of Philadelphia. 5780.F.

Marking this shift was Lincoln's release of the Emancipation Proclamation in September 1862, which went into effect January 1, 1863. It authorized the raising of Black troops and granted freedom to the enslaved in states that were in open rebellion against the Union. In November 1863 the *New York Illustrated News* published a woodcut titled "Turning the Table on the Overseer." Shortly after its publication, Thomas Hamilton and his brother Richard repurposed and published the woodcut as a stand-alone or "loose" print for individual purchase at the offices of the *Weekly Anglo-African.* Later they announced that it could also be purchased from anywhere in the United States by mail-in payment.[55]

The print depicts a white overseer bound to a tree with his back exposed, encircled by several recently liberated Black workers. One Black worker holds a whip and is pulling up his sleeve, preparing to strike the overseer, who already bears the marks from a few lashes.

The whipping of the overseer is also a family affair, in which formerly enslaved women and children are the audience, appearing to enjoy watching the overseer receive his punishment. One of the freedmen is wearing a Union Army uniform. Benjamin Fagan interprets Hamilton's choice to distribute the print as a response to the "limited expectations and strategic exemptions of Lincoln's Proclamation." If the Emancipation Proclamation did not free all enslaved people and put Black militancy under the command of the US state, the print in Hamilton's hand calls for "unauthorized black violence" to fight for Black liberation rather than reconciliation in ways that "whites would be held to account for their actions."[56]

While "Turning the Table on the Overseer" certainly supported Hamilton's call for the enslaved to fight for liberation under their own terms and criticized Lincoln's war strategy, it also articulates precisely what Brown and Anderson at Harper's Ferry understood about the dialectics of abolition war. The print portrays a moment *after* the enslaved have won their liberation. In the scene, they hold power over white power, embodied by the overseer. For the freedmen to be in a position of power to whip their former overseer is not simply punitive revenge or practicing the same violence of the enslaver that abolition war partisans were fighting to abolish. It rehearses the enslaved seizing power from enslavers and using this power to subordinate them as a class to defend the recently won liberation. The image of the formerly enslaved unifying as a community to impose their power over enslaver power allegorizes what Du Bois later theorized was the relationship between a dictatorship of Black labor and abolition democracy. To construct and defend abolition democracy, Black labor would need to impose its power over slavery capital following emancipation. Hamilton's repurposed print also relishes in its articulation of the dialectics of abolition war. Like the pedagogical acts of dominating enslavers of Brown's armed campaign, Hamilton's "Turning the Table on the Overseer" was meant to demoralize enslavers while inspiring further Black militancy.

Learning from Black abolition war thinkers like Anderson and Hamilton, Brown had expressed this vision of a dictatorship of abolition in his "Provisional Constitution and Ordinances for the People of the United States." The year before the Harper's Ferry raid, Brown had convened a conference inviting leading abolition war thinkers and organizers to propose, discuss, and vote on Brown's vision for forming an alternative government under the command of abolition. Anderson opens his memoir at the Chatham Convention, providing the minutes of the two-day event. It was through this convention that Anderson joined in the leadership of Brown's militia. In January 1858, during the months leading up to Chatham, Brown lodged at Douglass's home in Rochester for a few weeks during which Brown drafted the "Provisional Constitution" as a solution to the problem of how to coordinate across the abolition war movement. The "Provisional Constitution" called for the creation of a new abolition government that could steer and direct abolition war in the next steps of escalating the campaign to go on the offensive against slavery by raiding the South: "the better to protect our Persons, Property, Lives and Liberties, and to govern our actions."[57] Historians have often interpreted Brown's provisional government in the vein of utopian projects of the time. It is read as a vision of the future America that Brown wanted to create. David Reynolds sees the provisional government as evidence of Brown's aim to win an integrationist future in which the ideals of US democracy would be achieved through full racial equality among Europeans and Africans.[58]

However, if we consider Brown and Anderson's understanding of abolition war dialectics, their support for a provisional government was less a utopian endeavor of forming an ideal society at a distance from the United States than a necessary instrument of class war for shepherding the strategy of abolition war. It would do the work of centralizing abolition war strategy in the next stage of struggle following the strike against Harper's Ferry. Kagi described the importance of this centralized organization in the campaign to raid the South. It provided not only the power of coordination, but the appearance of such sophisticated organization descending upon the South would work to demoralize the enemy: "It was not anticipated that the first movement would have any other appearance to the masters than a slave stampede, or local insurrection, at most. The planters would pursue their chattels and be defeated. The militia would then be called out, and would also be defeated. It was not intended that the movement should appear to be of large dimensions, but that, gradually increasing in magnitude, it should, as it opened, strike terror into the heart of the Slave States by the amount of organization it would exhibit, and the strength it gathered."[59] Similar to how Marx and Engels theorized the role of a communist organization centralizing and guiding worker rebellion into a strategy of socialist revolution to overturn the capitalist class, Brown's "Provisional Constitution" sought to guide the abolition movement toward revolutionary insurrection against capitalist enslaver power.

In this way, Brown's provisional government might be thought of as an embryonic form of the revolutionary party that Lenin would later theorize and help construct as a vehicle for the people of Russia to establish a worker's state in 1917. Brown's provisional government was envisioned as functioning as a form of dual power, as Lenin theorized it, in relation to the United States.[60] It would be a competing form of governance in North America composed of the enslaved and oppressed, which to overthrow slavery would by necessity need to take power away from the enslaver class and impose its governance over it to defend ongoing Black revolution from white counterrevolution. Brown's provisional government anticipated Lenin's contention that the "proletariat needs state power, a centralized organization of force, an organization of violence," not as an end in itself but rather as a means "both to crush the resistance of the exploiters and to *lead* the enormous mass of the population . . . in the work of organizing a socialist economy."[61] A provisional abolition government initially entrenched in the

Appalachian Mountains would provide the enslaved with the military and political capacity to defend the unfolding Black revolution against what would be the inevitable efforts of the enslaver state to restore the class rule of slavery capital.

Anderson is keen to highlight the impact of abolition dictatorship on the local white community at Harper's Ferry. He spotlights numerous examples of extreme panic and fright among whites that induced them to scatter and flee:

> Monday, the 17th of October, was a time of stirring and exciting events. In consequence of the movements of the night before, we were prepared for commotion and tumult, but certainly not for more than we beheld around us. Gray dawn and yet brighter daylight revealed great confusion, and as the sun arose, the panic spread like wild-fire. Men, women and children could be seen leaving their homes in every direction; some seeking refuge among residents, and in quarters further away, others climbing up the hillsides, and hurrying off in various directions, evidently impelled by a sudden fear, which was plainly visible in their countenances or in their movements.[62]

Anderson reminds readers how, in the aftermath of Brown's militia driving away Virginia troops and Shields Green shooting and killing a person in defensive retaliation for shooting a fellow Black soldier, Dangerfield Newby, this show of force among the abolitionists terrorized the whites of Harper's Ferry: "There was comparative quiet for a time, except that the citizens seemed to be wild with terror. Men, women and children forsook the place in great haste, climbing up hill-sides and scaling the mountains. The latter seemed to be alive with white fugitives, fleeing from their doomed city."[63] Armed Black fugitives turned enslavers into white fugitives, fleeing from a dictatorship of abolition at Harper's Ferry. Anderson's choice to focus on scenes in which abolition terrorized whites in the raid spoke to the broader role or function of terror in the dialectics of abolition dictatorship. Abolition war thinkers

Figure 10. *Harper's Ferry Insurrection—The Battle Ground—Captain Alberts' Party Attacking the Insurgents—View of the Railroad Bridge, the Engine-House, and the Village/from a sketch by our special artist.* Woodcut illustration in *Frank Leslie's Illustrated Newspaper,* November 5, 1859, 358. Library of Congress, Washington, DC. LC-USZ62-115350.

grasped how the dialectical reversal of terror worked to radically undermine and destabilize the work of counterrevolutionary whiteness. If abolition dictatorship was the strategy, abolition terror was its principal tactic. It worked to liquidate the power of white terror to repress Black rebellion. This is what Anderson surfaces in his narrative to demonstrate the points of weakness or fragility in whiteness, which otherwise narrates itself as invincible.

Before Harper's Ferry, Brown's militia most notoriously used tactics of terror and intimidation within this strategy of abolition dictatorship in Kansas. Brown had waged a campaign from the spring to summer of 1856 to drive proslavery settlers out of the territory to stop their attempts to make it a slave state. Unlike most free soil settlers who, as examined in chapter 3, opposed slavery not to support Black

THE STORMING OF THE ENGINE-HOUSE BY THE UNITED STATES MARINES.—[Sketched by Porte Crayon.]

Figure 11. David H. Stother, *The Storming of the Engine-House by the United States Marines* [Sketched by Porte Crayon]. Woodcut illustration in *Harper's Weekly*, November 5, 1859. New York City: Harper's Weekly Co. The Miriam and Ira D. Wallach Division of Art, Prints and Photographs: Picture Collection, The New York Public Library. New York City. b17613361.

freedom but to win white equality, Brown brought abolition war to Kansas. Brown's campaign gained national fame when it defeated proslavery forces at the Battle of Black Jack.[64] He and his fighters further proved themselves a formidable military force for abolition at the Battle of Osawatomie (as mentioned in the introduction), where despite being greatly outmatched by proslavery forces, Brown's forces inflicted heavy losses on the enemy with minimal cost to them. What became retroactively more well-known than these victories was Brown's attack on proslavery settlers at Pottawattamie creek. Following the proslavery forces' razing of the free state capital of Lawrence and making threats to decimate Brown's camp, known as Brown's Station, near Osawatomie, Brown had selected certain proslavery settlers to attack as a form of what could be considered anticipatory defense.

On the night of May 24, 1856, Brown's group, under the cover of night, captured and killed five proslavery settlers, some of whom not only were enslavers but also were sex trafficking Indigenous women.[65] Brown directed his sons to slash to death each enslaver with military broadswords. The choice of broadswords over firearms was symbolic. Swords were weapons of enslaved rebels. The attacks were not only about anticipatory defense; they were also political theater: a performance of slave revolt.[66] In this way, Brown was making his Kansas campaign in the image of the slave insurgency. In the aftermath, both proslavery and antislavery forces were shocked by the violence. Many white Northern abolitionists also decried the methods even if they agreed with the goal of ejecting slave power from Kansas territory. However, the military-political consequence of the attack on the five proslavery settlers was a precursor to what Anderson describes at Harper's Ferry: making enslavers into white fugitives fleeing from abolition power.[67] Later John Brown Jr. would write to his family describing how his father was referred to as the "Terror of Missouri" and "Old Terrifier." John Brown Jr. claimed that "the mere report that John Brown is coming broke up many proslavery meetings."[68]

While Brown never apologized for this abolition terror, he did not revel in it. In fact Brown, in all his public writing and commentary, worked hard to minimize his abolition terror. "God is my judge. It was absolutely necessary as a measure of self defence, and for the defence of others."[69] A few years later, when Brown returned to Kansas following the Chatham Convention, his group helped liberate a family of enslaved people from a plantation in Missouri. An enslaved person, Jim Daniels, had traveled into Kansas to request help. His family was set to be sold south. Brown's militia took on his request and not only easily liberated the man's family and other enslaved people held captive, but also expropriated property from the plantations where the rescue took place. They also killed an enslaver, who as Brown said, "fought against liberation."[70] Brown would later write a summation of the rescue for the *New York Tribune* in which he instructed the public on the difference between righteous and reactionary violence. He compared the reception of his rescue to that of a recent proslavery massacre of free state men, known as the Marais des Cygnes massacre. He argued that those who condemned his violence had nothing to say about the violence of enslavers. Brown's narrative of the rescue justified his use of violence in the defense of the enslaved.[71]

Those who did revel in such tactics and their work of destabilizing white terror were members of the Black worker vanguard of Brown's campaigns. One of the liberated from Missouri, Samuel Harper, offered a much different representation of Brown's violence than Brown himself. Instead of straining to justify it, Harper extolled the power it had to terrorize proslavery forces and thus subordinate them to abolition. Harper recounts how, when after the escape from Missouri a posse of slave catchers approached the home where the enslaved were hiding out across the border in Kansas, Aaron Stevens, a captain in Brown's militia, intercepted them and appeared to agree to allow the posse to search the premises. Harper relates that the fugitives were fearful they would be discovered. As Stevens led one of the posse's leaders to the cabin where the fugitives were hiding, Stevens opened the front door and grabbed his double-barreled shotgun. "'You want to see your slaves, does you? Well, just look up them barrels and see if you can find them.'" Harper notes the response of the posse's leader, "That man just went all to pieces. He dropped his gun, his legs went trembling, and the tears most started from his eyes. Stevens took and locked him up in the house. When the rest of his crowd seen him captured, they ran away as fast as they could go."[72] Harper emphasizes the fear of the enslaver and how it disarmed him, reducing him to a state of feebleness. He notes that when Brown returned and later confronted the slave catcher, the man again fell apart: "'I'll show you what it is to look after slaves, my man.' That frightened the prisoner awful. . . . [H]e began to cry and beg to be let go."[73] Harper highlights how abolition terror supported Brown's guerrilla warfare strategy.

Later, US marshals led a posse into Kansas to attempt to recapture the enslaved and arrest Brown's militia, but Brown, as Harper spotlights, leveraged abolition terror to paralyze and thus defeat a much more formidable force. "There was only fourteen of us altogether, but the captain was a terror to them, and when he stepped out of the house and went for them the whole seventy-five of them started running." Brown pursued members of the posse and captured a few of them as hostages. He forced the hostages to give up their horses to the fugitive slaves, like Harper: "Then he told five of us slaves to mount the beasts and we rode them while the white men had to walk. It was early in the spring, and the mud on the roads was away over their ankles. I just tell you it was mighty tough walking, and you can believe those fellows had enough of slave-hunting. The next day the captain let them all go."[74] Harper's choice, like Osborne's, to focus on these moments of abolition terror disarming white terror, and the pedagogical role of reversals performing abolition dictatorship, express an abolition war dialectics that illuminates points of weakness, fragility, and frailty of white counterrevolution. Black radical thinkers of Brown's campaigns theorized how abolition violence against and power over enslavers pierced the veneer of invincibility and inevitability of slavery. They saw the potential for the destruction of slavery in the feebleness and cowardice of the weeping and crushed proslavery forces of Kansas and Harper's Ferry when they encountered abolition forces that shot back, expropriated property, seized towns, captured hostages, and killed in battle those who fought against liberation.

If we return to a scene from Kansas territory that opened the introduction, the Battle of Osawatomie, we see that what Osborne and Harper spotlight in their narratives relating to abolition dictatorship and its tactic of using a political theater of intimidation did not merely expose the weakness of white counterrevolution. Abolition dictatorship and its intimidating effects pushed white counterrevolution into a position of vulnerability. That is, abolition war moved forward the dialectic of class struggle into a stage of open civil war that slavery's supporters wanted to avoid until they could not. Following the Battle of Osawatomie, despite proslavery forces winning that battle and razing the town, the Kansas governor, John Geary, who supported slavery, called off proslavery forces as they were preparing for further attacks, particularly against Lawrence. The governor did this because he dreaded the presence of Brown's militia and knew that it would surely bring, as it was already doing, costly counterattacks and harassment, leading to a dynamic that would spiral into civil war in which the advantages of white counterrevolution would be lost. The Kansas governor chose to cool down the movement of the class war that was playing out, but this meant providing concessions and momentarily admitting defeat to abolition forces. Brown and his militia were forgiven of any "crimes" in exchange for the expectation that abolition forces would not reignite their campaigns in Kansas.[75]

Historians often read John Brown's abolitionism through the framework of anti-racism and civil rights. They consider his objective to have been ending formal slavery and winning a racially inclusive US democracy. The cultural historian Reynolds argues that "viewed as a whole, Brown's career anticipated a panoply of civil rights goals, some of which America is still struggling to achieve. The right to vote; the right to participate in government; the right to be paid equally for equal work; and the right to live in an integrated society free of prejudice—John Brown had envisaged all these rights for blacks and other minority groups."[76] Through this lens of civil rights, Brown's campaign is thus understood as a movement for the reform of US society. Brown did at times state that his mission was not to overturn but to redeem the United States from slavery.[77] At the Chatham Convention, attendees debated this very question of reform or revolution when deliberating over Article 46 of Brown's "Provisional Constitution." It stated that the provisional government "shall not be construed so as in any way to encourage the overthrow of any State Government or of the General

Government of the United States . . . but simply to amend and repeal."[78] One attendee, George J. Reynolds, opposed the article, arguing that destroying slavery and winning Black liberation required the overthrow of the United States. Martin Delany initially seconded Reynolds's motion to remove Article 46, but after some debate, Delany sided with Brown to carry the article. Brown argued that the overthrow of slavery was disentangled from the US state, and that his abolition war sought to create a new United States founded on racial equality and holding property in common.[79] This was a widely held position among the abolition movement to expand the promises of US democracy to those classes it enslaved and excluded.

Yet the abolition war dialectics that Brown's collective practiced betrayed his words calling for a reformed United States. That Brown advanced a strategy of abolition war organized around a Black worker vanguardism demonstrates that his campaign's trajectory was not reform but overthrow. If Brown's abolition war was about transforming Black revolt into a formal political and military project of Black revolution, reform was never its object. This is precisely what George J. Reynolds had pointed out at the Chatham Convention. He questioned how the provisional government and abolition war strategy could be interpreted to mean reform. Perhaps the article was retained to provide cover against allegations of treason, for which state execution was the penalty, in the buildup to the raid at Harper's Ferry. Or perhaps Brown did believe in a reformed US society. Either way, abolition war and the racialized class society of the United States were incompatible. Brown's strategy did not merely seek to formally include the enslaved in US civil society; it sought to build a military strategy in the image of enslaved Africans' revolt against US society. Brown put Black revolutionary politics in command of a strategy in which, as Kellie Carter Jackson argues, Brown made himself a soldier, as he expected others to do as well.[80] This was not an anti-racist integrationism, but rather dialectical materialism applied to the context of North American racial capitalism. Abolition

Figure 12. *The Execution of John Brown, in a Stubble Field, Near Charleston, [W.] Va. [men on horseback in foregrd.]*. Woodcut illustration in *Frank Leslie's Illustrated Newspaper* 9, no. 210 (December 10, 1859), 24–25. Library of Congress Prints and Photographs Division, Washington, DC. LC-USZ62-11424.

war thinkers, like Brown, Anderson, and others, read the class relations of slavery and saw how the enslaved were positioned as its gravediggers, for whom the task was to organize a political and military strategy that would carry out this class's historical mission.

HARRIET TUBMAN: "THE GENERAL OF ALL OF US"

When John Brown first met Harriet Tubman at her home in St. Catherines, Canada West, he greeted her by addressing her as "General Tubman" three times.[81] Later, when describing Tubman to a friend, Brown said that she was "the General of all of us."[82] Brown recognized that Tubman's work waging guerrilla raids through the Underground Railroad into the South to extract those held captive by slavery had made her one of the most effective leaders among abolition war's Black worker vanguard. Brown and Tubman found in each other a shared objective of destroying slavery. Brown met Tubman when he traveled to Canada to build relationships with one of the largest bases of Black worker vanguardism, the free Black community of Canada West, home to veteran fugitive fighters of the Underground Railroad like Tubman. He chose Canada West to hold his national abolition convention as the place to propose, discuss, and approve his provisional government because it was home to the fiercest fighters and leaders in the abolition war movement. Brown sought their consultation, feedback, and leadership. After their meeting, at which Brown shared his plan to invade the South, Tubman was an enthusiastic supporter.[83] She offered her insights and committed to joining. This was the case for many Black organizers in Canada West. They had made the commitment to mobilize for Brown's raid when the plan was ready. Tubman would meet and plot with Brown a year later in Boston in May 1859, in preparation for the attack on Harper's Ferry. Their mutual friend and abolitionist Frank Sanborn remembered that "she had several interviews with Captain Brown, then in Boston. He is supposed to have communicated his plans to her, and to have been aided by her in obtaining recruits and money among her people. At any rate, he always spoke of her with the greatest respect, and declared that General Tubman, as he styled her, was a better officer than most whom he had seen, and could command an army as successfully as she had led her small parties of fugitives."[84] In the end, there is no record that Tubman was able to join or participate in Brown's raid. Many believe she fell ill or was forced to go underground around the time of the raid, preventing her from participating.[85] Perhaps she played a clandestine role in the raid. Nonetheless, even if Tubman may not have directly participated, her imprint on the raid's tactics was apparent.

As Sanborn highlighted, Brown recognized that Tubman's raids into Maryland to liberate captives were guerrilla warfare attacks against the enemy, slavery. Her planning, preparation, and execution of these missions proved she was a skilled military leader of abolition war. Theorist Butch Lee's study of Tubman argues that she should be understood not as a humanitarian or civil rights leader but rather as a military leader in a people's war. "Harriet and the rest of the Underground Railroad," writes Lee, "had military goals, had military strategy and tactics. It wasn't any accident that Harriet and many of the other guides were armed. They were armed as front-line guerrillas who moved through a genocidal terrain. They were soldiers on a military mission."[86] As a leader of abolition war, Tubman was a theorist of Black revolution and whiteness. Tubman's thoughts on Black revolution and whiteness, I contend, can be found in a reading of her strategy and tactics in attacking slavery via the Underground Railroad, her relation to Brown's plan, and her later insertion in the Union Army's campaign to defeat Confederates.

Tubman understood racial capitalism as a Manichean formation, anticipating Fanon.[87] When asked how she would characterize slavery, Tubman once responded, "I think slavery is the next thing to hell."[88] Freedom was the world beyond this hell. To move from slavery to freedom was to move across zones or worlds. She compared her experience breaking out of slavery to that of an imprisoned person who after twenty-five years of being held captive exits prison and returns to the free world but finds it both unfamiliar and uncanny. As Tubman described, "He leaves the prison gates—he makes his way to his old home, but his old home is not there. The house has been pulled down, and a new one has been put up in its place; his family and friends are gone nobody knows where; there is no one to take him by the hand, no one to welcome him. . . . I was free; but there was no one to welcome me to the land of freedom. I was a stranger in a strange land."[89] Here Tubman articulates how slavery was the constitutive other to the free world. When those in enslavement break out and enter the free world, they enter a zone that is the product of the unfreedom they have escaped. The free world could not be a true home to them when the perpetuation of enslavement engendered by negation the meaning and infrastructure of the "free world."

This analysis of the Manichean relationship between slavery and the free world guided and shaped Tubman's commitment to the strategy of guerrilla raids into the South to liberate her family and others. "But I was free, and [Tubman's family] should be free. I would make a home in the North and bring them there, God helping me."[90] When her first biographer, Sarah Bradford, asked Tubman how she had the courage to return to slavery in these raids to liberate people, knowing the risks of recapture and violent retaliation she would most assuredly face, Tubman answered through the apocalyptic language of liberation theology: "Now look yer! John saw the city, didn't he? Yes, John saw the city. Well, what did he see? He saw twelve gates—three of dose gates was on de north—three of 'em was on de east—and three of 'em on de *South* too; an' I reckon if dey kill me down dere, I'll git into one of dem gates, don't you?"[91] Like Brown, who made it clear after bounties were issued for his capture that he would sacrifice his life before submitting to his enemies, Tubman's intention was to remain free from her former captors by any means necessary. She would not be taken alive. Tubman's choice of apocalypse as a metaphor for the confrontation with slavery also suggests that she understood abolition to be a world-ending endeavor. It was a struggle to turn upside down the world that slavery had created as foundational violence of US society.

It was Tubman's theory of slavery as the unfree zone or position against which the free world was defined and constructed that called forth, for her, the strategy of abolition war. Tubman explains that in the months before her flight from slavery, she prayed daily for her enslaver to have a change of heart and not separate her family at the auction block. When she learns that he plans to go forward with the sale, her prayer changes. She begs God to kill her enslaver: "Den we heard dat some of us was gwine to be sole to go wid de chain-gang down to d e cotton an' rice fields, and dey said I was gwine, an' my brudders,

HARRIET TUBMAN.

Figure 13. Drawing of Harriet Tubman. Woodcut frontispiece in Sarah Bradford, *Scenes in the Life of Harriet Tubman* (Auburn: W. J. Moses, 1869). General Research Division, The New York Public Library. New York City. b11616598.

Figure 14. Portrait of Harriet Tubman. Photograph by Benjamin Powelson, Auburn, New York, 1868 or 1869. Collection of the Library of Congress and the National Museum of African American History & Culture, Washington, DC. LC-DIG-ppmsca-54230.

an' sisters. Den I changed my prayer. Fust of March I began to pray, 'Oh Lord, if you ant nebber gwine to change dat man's heart, kill him, Lord, an' take him out ob de way.'"[92] A rehearsal for her commitment to the abolition war to come, Tubman's demand for a higher power to kill her enslaver paralleled other abolition war thinkers like Brown, who argued that slaveholders had forfeited their right to live in their war against Africans.[93] In fact, Tubman also claimed to have the power to predict future war. Bradford represented this discernment as super-stitious, even absurd:

> She says she always knows when there is danger near her,—she does not know how, exactly, but "'pears like my heart go flutter, flutter, and den dey may say 'Peace, Peace,' as much as dey likes, *I know its gwine to be war!*" She is very firm on this point, and ascribes to this her great impunity, in spite of the lethargy before mentioned, which would seem likely to throw her into the hands of her enemies. She says she inherited this power, that her father could always predict the weather, and that he foretold the Mexican War.[94]

What Bradford implies is a silly superstition is Tubman's historical materialism. She could predict war because she correctly read the class relations of slavery. Tubman's concepts of hell and freedom were zones of nonbeing and being, as Fanon would later describe in the colonial context. It took war to make and maintain this racialized class struc-ture. From this, Tubman could predict that it would require a war of liberation to end slavery's war on Africans.

RAID AS STRIKE

By her count, Tubman commanded nineteen raids against the South to liberate captives.[95] These were well planned and executed opera-tions, carried out with precision, skill, and speed. They rested on the sophisticated networks of trust and mutual aid that composed the Underground Railroad. I read these raids as a form of strike against slavery. I mean *strike* both as a blow or hit and a refusal or withdrawal of labor. As discussed in chapter 1, Du Bois described the fugitivity of the Underground Railroad as a "Safety Valve of Slavery." Without it, he argued, more slave revolts would have taken place in the South.[96] However, Tubman understood her raids to be instrumental in increasing the pressure, that is, sharpening the contradiction between Black revolution and white counterrevolutionary repression. Tubman's practice of fugitivity in her guerrilla raids was a precursor to what became an organic general strike that Du Bois identified took place at the onset of the Civil War, when the enslaved used the instability as an opportunity to refuse their labor and retreat from the plantations.[97] Tubman's raids not only liberated enslaved people, whose absence was a withdrawal of labor from plantation production, but also catalyzed further fugitive flights to become what enslavers called "stampedes," in which a mass exodus would take place in counties and regions where they would greatly impact slavery capital.[98] Later this ability to trigger a mass exodus would be the key tactic in the Combahee River raid. It was also the reason Tubman was so valued by the Union Army. She not only provided intelligence on the enemy but sparked "stampedes" of the enslaved, who escaped into Union camps, where many became Union soldiers.

In this way, Tubman's strikes undermined white alliance policing. The underground network of safe houses, mutual aid, and intelligence sharing combined to out-organize the alliances of whiteness conscripting the white community to police fugitivity. While this horizontalism and decentralization of the Underground Railroad was one of its sharpest weapons, Tubman also practiced a strict centralism of action to ensure a solidarity strong enough to combat white terror. Tubman was extremely disciplined when carrying out her raids. For example, once the raid was set in motion, she would not wait for anyone or risk jeopardizing the entire mission. Tubman also required that those who joined her party make the commitment not to turn back or break from the mission. Tubman enforced this centralism with her revolver, promising to shoot anyone who broke away. "'Go on or die'; and so she compelled them to drag their weary limbs on their northward journey."[99] Such disciplined unity of action was what gave her raids the power to outmaneuver and outpower white alliance policing. The power of white alliance policing called for this practice of centralism in Tubman's raids. It was an indication of how she read or conceptualized whiteness as a project that organized and mobilized the entire white community to be the police, to surveil, to be prison guards and slave catchers. This situation could only be overcome with strict unity in action. Tubman represented her raid strategy as an inversion and thus an undermining of white policing's power to surveil the enslaved and maintain a carceral landscape. "Sometimes, when she and her party were concealed in the woods, they saw their pursuers pass, on their horses, down the high road, tacking up the advertisements for them on the fences and trees. 'And den how we laughed,' said she. 'We was de fools, and dey was de wise men; but we wasn't fool enough to go down de high road in de broad daylight.'"[100] Here Tubman pointed out the gaps or blind spots of white policing in its arrogance or assumed mastery over space and bodies. White policing didn't know its enemy as well as Tubman knew hers. White policing assumed a lack of sophistication in the fugitive's retreat, and it was this arrogance that Tubman took advantage of.

In undermining counterrevolutionary whiteness, Tubman's raids targeted the reproduction of slavery capital. She was already putting into practice the tactics Brown had discussed with Douglass on how his raid would devalorize slavery capital, leading to its crippling breakdown. The flight of unfree labor to rear bases in the North not only incurred heavy losses of capital to enslavers, both immediate and in the future valorization of the enslaved as commodities and their labor power, but also threatened to break down the hierarchy between free and unfree labor. Black labor liberated from the plantation, from hell as the zone of nonbeing, was not simply absorbed into a free labor position. As Du Bois says, the freedman was a contradiction in slavery capital.[101] Liberated Black labor destabilized the category of free labor as nonenslaveable. Free labor, as we saw in previous chapters, confronted this destabilization by aligning with and following the lead of either abolition or the opposite, reactionary white insurgency. These factors, losing capital and future valorization, uncontainable Black fugitivity, and ungovernable free laboring classes combined to threaten the reproduction of capitalism. In this way, Tubman's strategy of the raid as strike was a force that fomented a crisis of reproduction for slavery capital, and this crisis of reproduction became the entry point for insurgent abolition war. In other words, the raids were not only about liberating individuals. Often Tubman's raids are understood as having been motivated solely by her desire to free her family members. While this was her focus, the raids were actions within a larger strategy of abolition war in which, by triggering a crisis in the reproduction of capitalism, they aspired to cut a path to a gravedigger situation for capitalism, led by Black revolution. When she met Brown and they coplotted how to carry out a plan to raid the South, Tubman saw this as an opportunity to scale up her raids as strike strategy. In doing so, she theorized the crisis points of slavery capital and how to use this critical understanding to trigger them into openings for revolutionary ruptures.

As such Tubman, like other abolition war thinkers, should be read alongside Marx, who was also thinking about crisis and revolution. Or perhaps, Marx should be read alongside thinkers like Tubman. Marx theorized crisis as the opening for revolution led by wage labor. Marx saw how the strike or a refusal of labor that demanded and won improved conditions like a shorter workday to recapture a greater share of the value of workers' labor product drove forward capitalism's industrialization or transition from formal to real subsumption of labor by capital. The battle over the workday length was one lever compelling capital to find ways to increase productivity to augment the extraction of surplus value in response to granting the concession of reducing the length of the workday. Investment in machinery, management strategies, and the organization of the production process—the elements of industrialization—were the tactics used by capital to increase productivity without lengthening the workday. This dynamic would lead to the trend of capital shedding labor from the production process, with machines replacing workers. Greater production output could be achieved, but with less labor. In this way, the strike for a shorter workday dialectically turned into its opposite, expanded exploitation, in which capital extracted greater surplus value while spending less on the cost of labor. For Marx, this contradiction spirals into an accumulation crisis for capital. Yet this crisis also presents the opportunity for the industrial proletariat to wage revolutionary overthrow.[102] Capital's pursuit of surplus value through industrialization results in the discarding of its very source of surplus value, namely labor power. The result is growing surplus populations at one pole and at the other capital stagnating in its ability to produce increasing rates of surplus value extraction. Capital creates a class of laborer dependent on the wage and then makes this class wageless. In so doing, however, capital creates the industrial proletariat as its gravediggers. Through this contradiction, the industrial proletariat is in a position where it increasingly has nothing to lose but its chains, and the revolutionary seizure of the world that labor has created is the resolution to the contradiction.[103]

Abolition war thinkers like Tubman had a similar but stretched theory of crisis of slavery capital. She saw how capital positioned the enslaved as an unfree class for which rights, inclusion, and life were never on the table. The reproduction of slavery capital rested on white counterrevolution to administer the direct force of policing and repressing Black rebellion. The crisis of slavery capital emerged through this contradiction between counterrevolution and the external rebellion of the unfree. This was the contradiction that had always haunted slavery capital. Tubman, Brown, and other abolition war thinkers read this as well. Tubman's strategy of the guerrilla raid as strike, attacking and undermining counterrevolutionary forces—scaled up in Brown's attack on Harper's Ferry—placed pressure on this contradiction, turning it into crisis. In the face of this strike, slavery capital lost faith in white counterrevolution's ability to control the situation. From this, its leaders took counterrevolution to the next level, formalizing it into a white dictatorship in their decision to secede from the Union and form the Confederate States of America. But in this state, slavery capital became weaker or vulnerable. It was blundering, thinking about immediate preservation rather than long-term strategy. In a dictatorship of white counterrevolution enforcing slavery capital, the lines between white supremacy and liberation were more clearly drawn. This was where insurgent abolition war had an advantage. Here was where it could pull together various sectors and strata of classes under its revolutionary trajectory, which was harder to do before.

These dialectical steps are precisely what happened following Brown and Tubman's planned raid at Harper's Ferry. Staring down a rising abolition war entering a phase of anticipatory defense, the administrators of slavery capital attempted to form a counterrevolutionary dictatorship to stop Black revolution. In turn, if slavery attempted to form a counterrevolutionary dictatorship in the form of the Confederate States of America, abolition war became the guiding force of a united front to defeat it. That is, following the raid on Harper's Ferry, where Brown with Tubman's planning help scale up abolition war, counterrevolution made its move toward dictatorship, but in doing so, what was a conflict between competing factions of capital turned into a crisis, that is, a protracted class war between the enslaved with other classes in tow or under the direction of their militant political orientation, and racial capitalism.

Tubman would be called on to lead and participate as a frontline leader in the Union forces when their strategy became subordinated to abolition war. As mentioned earlier, initially Lincoln and other moderates endeavored to disavow abolition war. After confronting the potential outcome of defeat, the very strategy they had considered madness when Brown deployed it at Harper's Ferry was taken up by Union forces to defeat the Confederates. Douglass and other Black radicals had worked tirelessly to persuade Lincoln to make the war about abolition rather than reconciliation.[104] While Tubman may not have directly participated in Brown's raid at Harper's Ferry, she planned and led a very similar raid attacking proslavery forces only a few years later on the Combahee River near Beaufort, South Carolina. The Combahee River raid best embodied this larger dynamic of abolition war rooted in a Black worker vanguardism emerging as the unofficial political leadership in what became a united front to destroy slavery.

In spring 1862 Massachusetts governor John Andrew solicited the help of Tubman. She was asked to join the Union forces as a spy and guerrilla leader on the front lines in the South.[105] She was sent to Port Royal, South Carolina, with the official mission, along with social reformers, educators, and physicians, of helping the "contraband," or the formerly enslaved who had escaped to Union camps, adjust to a new life of freedom. In truth, Tubman's role was to do what she had already been engaged in, which was guerrilla raids as strikes against the enemy. After she arrived and used her time to build networks of mutual aid and intelligence gathering among the freedmen at Port Royal and the enslaved in nearby plantations, General Hunter asked Tubman to lead a raid up the Combahee River with the goal of locating and disarming Confederate "torpedoes" or floating mines, destroying enemy infrastructure, and cutting off supply lines. Tubman agreed to take on the mission if she was allowed to select her cogeneral in the raid. Tubman requested that General Montgomery, "who was one of John Brown's men, and was known to Harriet" cocommand the raid.[106] General Montgomery had worked closely with John Brown in Kansas and was known as an abolition war strategist who used tactics of terror and destruction like those of Brown and Tubman to deliver blows against proslavery forces. For this, Montgomery was almost not allowed to take up a post in the South because many of the Republican Union leaders found his methods and strategy too extreme. However, this is precisely the reason Tubman sought out and selected Montgomery as a coleader of the raid. It was a return to working with Brown's collective through one of its trainees, Montgomery.

Receiving intelligence from networks among the enslaved across enemy lines about the location of Confederate torpedoes, Tubman was able to chart a course that led the Union gunboats carefully around any potential deadly obstacles. As the gunboats arrived at the section of the river lined with lucrative rice plantations, the enslaved workers recognized their arrival as the signal to make their escape. In the days before, Tubman had used her networks to pass on information that Union gunboats would be coming to extract and liberate the enslaved. Despite overseers' best efforts to prevent the mass escape, whipping and shooting at people, the enslaved broke through and made their way to the shore, where oar boats were used to ferry them from the shore to nearby anchored gunboats. Tubman provided directions through song and chants to those waiting to be ferried to maintain a disciplined escape without panic and thus prevent mistakes. She also directly assisted the escapees with their belongings and livestock, remarking that she tore her dress while trying run while carrying a couple of pigs to the boats.[107] She would later ask her friend Sanborn for a new dress better fashioned for military operations.[108] The raid also inflicted severe damage on Confederate targets. Black soldiers destroyed a key bridge upriver, razed dozens of plantations, and burned property. Tubman described how "the masters fled; houses and barns and railroad bridges were burned, tracks torn up, torpedoes destroyed, and the expedition was in all respects successful."[109] The raid is often recognized for Tubman's role as the first woman to lead a US military operation. However, the significance of the raid lies in its success being rooted in Black worker vanguardism. It repeated and extended similar operations that Tubman had already completed for years in the South, and which Brown's collective had carried out in Kansas, in Missouri, and at Harper's Ferry.

Later Tubman would write to her friend Sanborn about the raid and how he and others represented it in the press:

> Don't you think we colored people are entitled to some credit for that exploit, under the lead of the brave Colonel Montgomery? We weakened the rebels somewhat on the Combahee River, by taking and bring away *seven hundred and fifty-six* head of their most valuable live stock, known up in your region as "contrabands" and this, too, without the loss of a single life on our part, though we had good reason to believe that a number of rebels bit the dust. Of these seven hundred and fifty-six contrabands, nearly or quite all the able-bodied men have joined the colored regiments here.[110]

Here Tubman was not asking for the enslaved to receive recognition in terms of fame or notoriety. Rather, she was reminding Sanborn that it was the slave insurgency as the vanguard force that had made the raid successful. The raid demonstrated how slave insurgency in command had pulled together a spectrum of different sectors and strata of society into alignment with its objective. It was a microcosm of a larger trend in which the Union was compelled to take up the abolition war strategy of Tubman and Brown or face defeat at the hands of the Confederates.

In this way, the Combahee River raid embodies how Black revolution through abolition war was the force leading and unifying all other classes in a movement toward overthrow. Marx had theorized that this was the historical mission of the European proletariat. He saw abolition as the movement in which the enslaved would win formal abolition and join with European workers as fellow wage laborers. The Combahee River raid, like the Harper's Ferry raid, suggested that in North American racial capitalism it was the inverse where the enslaved with their insurgent orientation in command would be the force to pull in others, including white workers. For example, white workers were

Figure 15. *Raid of Second South Carolina Volunteers (Col. Montgomery) among the Rice Plantations on the Combahee, S.C.* Woodcut in *Harper's Weekly* 7, no. 340 (July 4, 1863), 429. *2nd South Carolina Infantry Regiment Raid on Rice Plantation, Combahee, South Carolina, and Escaped Slave Named Gordon*, Library of Congress Prints and Photographs Division, Washington, DC. LC-DIG-ds-05099.

not confronting capital in their worker movements until they were conscripted and compelled to align with abolition war in the Union armies, commanded to defeat slavery capital, which the Confederates were attempting to enshrine through a white counterrevolution dictatorship. It was this very compelled alignment with abolition war that provoked the white insurgency against the state among some white workers that is discussed in chapter 3. While the Union would take credit for the military victory against the Confederates, it was abolition war thinkers and leaders like Tubman and Brown who had read the contradictions of slavery capital from which they developed a strategy to trigger crisis as an opening for slavery's overthrow. Du Bois tells the story of how this opening for overthrow developed into abolition democracy, which was met by a renewed white counterrevolution that regrettably contained it. But it is important to see when and how this opening was created.

CONCLUSION

In his essay "Marxism and Third World Ideology," Walter Rodney argues that Marxism is not a European phenomenon. It is a science for understanding class society and revolutionary struggle. It takes root wherever there are poor, dispossessed, exploited, and excluded people who seek out tools to help them get free.[111] This chapter also has shown how abolition war thinkers, organizers, and fighters practiced and developed theories of race, class, counterrevolution, and revolutionary struggle that advanced a dialectics paralleling but also stretching Marxist dialectics emerging from European communism. In a later version of his biography of John Brown, Du Bois adds further analysis in the conclusion, where he argues that while Brown probably never read the *Communist Manifesto*, he had put into practice its principles.[112] However, David Reynolds has argued that Brown was no revolutionary anti-capitalist. Rather, Brown was cut from the cloth of utopian socialism. For Reynolds, Brown was an antebellum social reformer embedded in the same contexts that produced other social reform movements at the time. Brown was anomalous, for Reynolds, in his radical commitment to racial equality.[113] In a similar way, Tubman has been understood as a radical reformist of US nationalism. She is read as an ant-racist reformer who fought for a better US democracy. This view has led to the Central Intelligence Agency rewriting history to memorialize Tubman as one of the agency's first spies, celebrating her work advancing US interests in her role in the South when she was inserted into the Union forces.[114]

However, Brown and Tubman's centralizing abolition war was not a movement of anti-racist reform. It was a revolutionary anti-capitalist project with a corresponding theory of Black revolution as the standard leading the way. Abolition war thinkers like Brown, Tubman, Anderson, and others studied here read this revolutionary trajectory and took action to hasten it along. Lenin later argued that in hindsight class society works to transform revolutionaries into "harmless icons, to canonize them . . . and to hallow their names to a certain extent for the 'consolation' of the oppressed classes and with the object of duping the latter, while at the same time robbing the revolutionary theory of its substance, blunting its revolutionary edge and vulgarizing it."[115] This chapter has rediscovered the revolutionary theory of abolition war thinkers to mark their contributions to the traditions of anti-capitalist and anti-imperialist critique, which US class society has worked hard to erase, not only to disavow that such thinking and strategy occurred in these lands but also out of fear of their reemergence.

Conclusion

WHITE COUNTERREVOLUTION TODAY

Crisis, Repression, and Insurgent Fascism

<hr/>

DURING THE SUMMER OF 2020, the fires of abolition war were rekindled at a Wendy's restaurant in Atlanta, Georgia, and in the Third Precinct police building in Minneapolis, Minnesota—and in countless other locations of militant protest against state violence in these months of uprisings. Millions of people flooded the streets to exact a cost for the police murders of George Floyd, Breonna Taylor, Rayshard Brooks, and so many others extrajudicially executed by the state. Real estate capital around the nation was reduced to ashes. The George Floyd uprisings proved once again what John Brown had said about the injustice of slavery: that there will be no more peace in this land until police stop murdering Black, Indigenous, colonized, and other poor people. They displayed the power of mass mobilization to challenge the hegemony of US class society. This power to destabilize, disrupt, and do damage to racial capitalism that so frequently kills with impunity those it exploits and dispossesses signaled the uprisings' latent revolutionary potential.

While the police murder of Floyd triggered the uprisings, they were a collective rebellion responding to capitalism's sharpening contradiction of valuing accumulation over life that in the past decades has entered a stage of terminal crisis. The outbreak of the COVID-19 pandemic in the spring of 2020 further exposed and intensified this crisis. Marx theorized capitalism's accumulation crisis as the tendency of capital to shed labor from the production process through automation and management strategies that increase productivity while decreasing costs of production to maximize profit.[1] Competition among individual capitalists accelerates this tendency. Expelling labor power from production to reduce costs results in what Marx calls "surplus populations" or sectors of the working class excluded from earning necessary wages to live in capitalism. What capitalists exploit to accumulate surplus value—labor power—is also what is increasingly removed from the production process. That is, capitalism's source of value, labor power, is also considered a cost that capitalists seek to reduce, leading to systemwide diminished rates of surplus value extraction. The less surplus value is accumulated, the less capital is put into motion to accumulate more capital. This internal contradiction of capitalist accumulation leads to systemic crisis. Built into capitalism's process of accumulation is the undoing of accumulation. And with the breakdown of accumulation, the very reproduction of capitalism as a social system enters crisis.[2]

With large portions of the population without access to wages to reproduce their lives, capitalism fails to provide for the social reproduction of its workforce. The swelling ranks of the under- and unwaged are treated as redundant and made disposable. From the point of view of capital, the labor power of the unwaged is no longer useful. There is no place for them in capitalism or its assumed future. The state abandons any concerns it might have had during previous stages of industrial capitalism about the reproduction of workers' lives to maintain a stable workforce. Sylvia Wynter argues that this class of the unwaged in late capitalism has become the newest category of "Human Otherness" upholding Western bourgeois definitions of who counts as human or not, or free or not.[3] The racialized and colonized remain overrepresented among the unwaged as capitalism's accumulation crisis unfolds, overlaid on settler colonialism and slavery.

While the state renounces any concern to reproduce the life of the unwaged, it remains very worried about how their superfluous existence impedes capital accumulation and holds the potential for costly rebellion. People without access to wages such that they cannot provide for their basic needs to reproduce their lives do not accept these unlivable conditions without resistance. They rebel to live, whether in the form of survival strategies or through collective action, as they are increasingly doing across the globe in our era of uprisings. The state's response to the collective rebellion against these conditions of crisis during the George Floyd uprisings was naked repression and criminalization of righteous protest. Protesters were killed, maimed, and caged by police, who operated as "counterterrorism" forces. The state also deployed several counterinsurgency strategies. For instance, the demand for police and prison abolition that was voiced and enacted so strongly in the uprisings has been met not with less but with *more* funding for police and prisons.[4] The most infamous example of this is the City of Atlanta choosing to fund the construction of a colossal police training center to be erected in the Weelaunee Forest (South Forest River) of DeKalb County. Known by those who oppose it as "Cop City," the project is predicted to cost $67 million and serve as a "tactical training compound featuring a mock city."[5] To construct Cop City, builders plan to clear-cut three hundred acres of old growth forest.[6] A powerful campaign to block the construction of Cop City has mobilized and has had much success, for which its leaders have faced intense state repression. In January 2023 a police raid targeting Stop Cop City protesters murdered activist Manuel "Tortuguita" Terán who was camping in the Weelaunee Forest. The police shot Tortuguita fifty-seven times, appearing to execute them by firing squad.[7] In addition, Georgia's attorney general has levied felony indictments against more than sixty Stop Cop City activists for allegedly violating the state's Racketeer Influenced and Corrupt Organizations (RICO) law. The grand jury indictment suggests that merely sharing the goal of protesting the building of Cop City constitutes a "criminal conspiracy."[8] At the time of writing, there are plans to construct more than sixty similar police training centers across the nation.[9] The state is preparing, training, and amassing resources to manage, contain, and repress future uprisings, which state administrators know will inevitably re-erupt in the context of an accelerating crisis of capitalist reproduction.

Intersecting with abolition uprisings, Indigenous land defenses have forcefully confronted extractive industries that invade, plunder, and threaten to destroy Indigenous land bases. Water protectors at Standing Rock, South Dakota, have waged the #NODAPL campaign, risking life, limb, and imprisonment to stop the illegal trespass involved in Energy Transfer's construction of the Dakota Access Pipeline on Oceti Sakowin treaty lands.[10] In British Columbia, the Wet'suwet'en First Nation has resisted the construction of the Coastal GasLink Pipeline (CGL).[11] Anishinaabe communities have mobilized land defenders to block the expansion of the Enbridge corporation's Line 3 tar sands oil pipeline, which spans from Alberta, Canada, to Minnesota and Wisconsin.[12] Native Hawaiians have fought to stop the construction of the industrial Thirty Meter Telescope to protect the dormant volcano Mauna Kea from desecration.[13] Beyond North America, Indigenous and colonized peoples have engaged in similar struggles to defend against extraction, enclosure, and removal. They face a rising tide of right-wing authoritarian regimes that seek to intensify fossil fuel industries' assault on Indigenous lands. From Bolivia to Brazil to most recently Peru, Indigenous people combat both capital and Western-backed states that unleash violent repression against those who dare to resist the destruction of their lands, water, and lives.

These struggles highlight how capitalism targets Indigenous territories for dispossession as a resolution to its accumulation crisis. While the accumulation crisis has sparked the pursuit of surplus value through speculation and financialization found in fictitious capital, resulting in market crises like the one in 2008, it has also renewed the "extraeconomic" direct dispossession campaigns that Marx characterized as modes of primitive accumulation.[14] Indigenous lands are some of the richest in resources that Western corporations and their states seek to plunder.[15] Accumulators see Indigenous territories as capital waiting to be valorized to transform it into surplus, as a fix to their problem of stagnating growth. Iyko Day argues that Indigenous lands are also treated as exterior wastelands in relation to internal productive sites of industrial and financial accumulation. "Wastelanding," writes Day, "targets Indigenous lands that represent an 'outside' of capital that, through the racialized regimes of ownership, remains an outside. These racialized sacrifice zones are necessary for capitalist social reproduction in reaction to Indigenous modes of relation."[16] Whether it is to accumulate lands, resources, and labor as wealth or to treat as wasteland sacrifice zones, imperial expansion continues to play the role of resolving the internal contradictions of capitalism.

If abolition uprisings and anticolonial land defenses have taken place in the domestic context of US imperialism, at the time of writing we are seeing, at its periphery, the Palestinian people fighting to defend themselves from genocidal war waged by the Israeli settler state, acting as a proxy for Western capitalism. The siege of Gaza and the constant violent incursions in the West Bank and occupied territories are meant to serve, as we saw in the history of anti-Indian counterrevolution discussed in chapter 2, as collective punishment of a colonized people who dare to defend their homeland in the face of annihilation.

As scholars and organizers point out, Israeli and US state violence are constant collaborators; they share and train together in the strategies and tactics they develop in waging counterinsurgency against the respective populations whom they police and occupy.[17]

Related to the state's repressive response to recent uprisings, we are also amid what is popularly referred to as a period of white backlash but is better understood as the acceleration and consolidation of a coalition of white counterrevolutionary forces from spontaneous white reactionary mobilizations to organized neofascist insurgency. The more obvious faces of these forces have been the rise of Trumpism and the campaigns of white militias, neo-Confederates, and neofascists that struck at the "Unite the Right" Rally in Charlottesville, Virginia, in 2017 and stormed the Capitol on January 6, 2021. This white reaction has also reenergized a new counterinsurgent McCarthyism targeting institutions of education, the aim of which is to rid such spaces of educators and students dedicated to anti-capitalist and anti-imperialist thought stemming from traditions of Black, Indigenous, and working-class struggles that had only made their way into higher education through militant protest in the first place.[18] At the time of writing, a violent campus counterinsurgency has been unleashed across the nation against students protesting Western imperialism's unfolding genocide in Palestine. University administrators have closely collaborated with federal, state, and local police to brutalize student protesters who are demanding that universities divest from war industries that directly contribute to genocidal policies.

I review these recent events to show that we are in a time when the dialectic of resistance and repression is heating up. The question of how US class society manages its accumulation crisis and the rebellion for life among the exploited, dispossessed, and surplus is paramount. The history of the struggle between abolition and anticolonial wars and white counterrevolution of the antebellum nineteenth century that has been studied and theorized here serves as an important source of insights for understanding our current conditions of crisis, repression, and resistance. The modes of repression unleashed today to protect capital accumulation in crisis owe their origins to white counterrevolution in the nineteenth century. The eruption of violent white reaction and neofascism stem from the same contradictions that spawned antebellum white insurgency. Yet these very forces of renewed white counterrevolution today also reveal the rekindling of abolition and anticolonial wars whose rehearsals have been our era's uprisings and rebellions. What *No More Peace* has shown is that where we see the presence of white counterrevolution, so too the assembling of revolutionary activity manifests, but it often goes unacknowledged, hidden, or even disavowed. Our tools of analysis, modes of critique, and methods of reading must be sharpened for the task of these accelerating class struggles unfolding. If not, we risk offering misreadings of our material conditions in ways that are not accountable or useful to those risking it all in movements for liberation. Abolition and anticolonial war thinkers discussed in this study remain a model for us today of how to read the world in order to transform it.

WHITE COUNTERREVOLUTION AND STATE REPRESSION

White alliance policing and settler mass militarism serve as the foundations of the state's strategies for managing resistance and the crisis of capitalist reproduction in the terrain of surplus life today. If white alliance policing was devised to repress revolt and fugitivity of the enslaved, it aids the state's strategy to do the same for the populations of the jobless, underwaged, and excluded, who occupy a similar unfree, disposable position in capitalism, most of whom are disproportionately Black, Indigenous, and colonized people. In other words, the state depends on white alliance policing for controlling the unfree surplus classes of its accumulation crisis. White alliance policing organizes people to participate in and support the direct policing and incarceration of the growing ranks of the unwaged, as well as the methods of soft control enacted through education, state services, and the nonprofit-industrial complex. Geo Maher's study of policing and abolition describes this as the "pig majority," which "includes the police, but it exceeds them as well. It comprises all those volunteer deputies eagerly doing their violent work alongside them. It is the judges, the courts, the juries, and the grand juries. It is the mayors and the district attorneys who demand 'law and order' and denounce those who protest police brutality as 'mindless rioters and looters.' It is the racist media apparatus that bends over backward to turn victims into aggressors."[19] In the stage of wageless life, white alliance policing recruits and organizes the necessary prison guard and slave catcher labor in all their various forms, whether in uniform or not, to control the unwaged and ensure that their exclusion from the formal economy and thus potential for rebellion do not create obstacles to the reproduction of capitalism in terminal crisis.

For instance, the rise of the carceral state has rested on a cross-class alliance among white workers, petty bourgeois whites, and capital in opposition not only to the Black and colonized working classes, but also to those made wageless, including poor whites. Following the uprisings in Ferguson, Missouri, Baltimore, Maryland, and across the nation in the summer of 2020, there has been a consolidation of reactionary support for policing and prisons under the slogans "Back the Blue" and "Blue Lives Matter." The state builds prisons near labor pools where white alliances are the strongest. Police continue to murder and brutalize the poor and unwaged with the mass support of the securely waged and petty bourgeois classes. While these classes remain disproportionately white, the forces of white alliance policing have also become increasingly multiethnic, taking on a neocolonial form in which whiteness organizes people of color of the petty bourgeois classes to administer and enforce state repression. In this way, white alliance policing continues to cultivate unity across difference for the aim of protecting capitalism from formidable resistance.

Intertwined with white alliance policing, settler mass militarism provides the base on which rest today's imperial wars of counterinsurgency protecting extractive capitalism and repressing progressive anticolonial movements. The largest single employer in the world is the US Department of Defense, employing over 3.2 million people.[20] US arms manufacturers that receive contracts to supply weapons, munitions, and technology, not only for the US military but also for proxy foreign militaries extending the work of Western imperialism, are some of the leading corporations and employers of the US economy. Most major universities serve as research hubs for war industry contractors, both designing new technology for counterinsurgency wars and training the future leaders of these wars. As universities face austerity policies, they increasingly rely on federal funding earmarked for research, development, and training in support of war industries. Universities also seek direct private funding from weapon manufacturers, so that entire colleges, departments, and programs serve at the pleasure of companies like Raytheon, Boeing, and Lockheed Martin. These industries and institutions are embedded in US life to such a degree that they appear as one among many employers providing jobs and service for US communities. Settler mass militarism normalizes the manufacturing of weapons for imperial war. It is experienced the same as manufacturing cars, electronics, or textiles.

Settler mass militarism also explains how, while in the US settler metropole there may exist conflict, disagreement, and discord over domestic policies related to wealth distribution, there is, for the most part, alignment for an imperial agenda in foreign policy that ensures superprofits are extracted from the Global South and that colonized populations in the periphery are subjugated and subdued through sanctions or military occupation and policing (either directly or through proxy states). In other words, while US politics might debate the ills of the unequal distribution of wealth of the metropole, it remains difficult for these debates to engage questions of imperialism in which Global

South nations continue to be underdeveloped to serve as resource and labor colonies for the Global North. Furthermore, by organizing large portions of the working class to support US imperialism, settler mass militarism provides the footing and legitimacy for the US military to serve as a force of global counterinsurgency, repressing decolonization movements and destabilizing competing nations who attempt to undermine Western capitalism.

WHITE INSURGENT FASCISM

Today's accumulation crisis and resurgence of abolition and anticolonial resistance have also conjured the monster of white insurgency that we encountered in chapter 3. It has reemerged in the form of accelerating movements of neofascism. Dominant liberal discourses characterize Far Right violence as exceptional to US society. A longue durée approach to white counterrevolution helps us understand that neofascism is not a form of extremism or exception in the United States. Rather, it is a force that emerges from the very conditions of US class society itself.

Black revolutionary theorist and political prisoner George Jackson argued that US fascism was a stage of capitalism's development in relation to revolutionary movements for liberation. Fascism was a counterrevolutionary force that around the globe followed movements for liberation to crush them with repressive violence. It was consolidated in the centralized state following the failure of international socialism to seize power. In this way, fascism cannot be understood separately from the insurgent movements for liberation that it seeks to end. For Jackson, liberation movements call into existence fascism.[21] The roots of this relationship lie in the history of abolition and anticolonial wars and white counterrevolution. Modern fascism is the mode of mass white counterrevolution in the terrain of contemporary capitalism. While fascism operates through the centralized state, as Jackson argues (as we see in how the state responded to the George Floyd upris-ings and the efforts to build Cop Cities across the nation), it also is car-ried out by mass-based, reactionary, and insurgent fascist movements. These forces extend and supplement the fascist state repression of liber-ation movements, while also working autonomously from state power. This is the same tension that emerged in the antebellum period be-tween white counterrevolution's mass character and the state's efforts to centralize it.

It is beyond the scope of this conclusion to comprehensively analyze contemporary US neofascism. Yet reading the convergence of its forces in the January 6, 2021, US Capitol attack reveals the tensions between centralized state fascism that Jackson theorizes and the mass-based fas-cism of white counterrevolution's long history. While January 6 was much more of an organic white riot than a prepared and organized at-tempt to bring about a coup d'état to install a neofascist dictatorship, the event was nonetheless a show of force and escalation by neofas-cism. A striking image emerged from the Capitol attack. White riot-ers brandished Blue Lives Matter flags as weapons in their battles with Capitol police.[22] White insurgents used the very symbols supporting white counterrevolutionary policing to attack and kill those very po-licing forces. One of the organizations that led the Capitol attack was the Oath Keepers. In its ranks are cops and military personnel, who by joining this group pledge to defend the Constitution over obeying any potential commands from their superiors that might violate the Con-stitution, according to their interpretation. This is understood to mean that cops and military members who join the Oath Keepers will not enforce potential gun bans that would disarm neofascism's white reac-tionary base. While the Oath Keepers is not an advanced underground paramilitary group, it is nonetheless an organization that recruits the policing and military forces of the state to be insurgent against their own state.[23] How do we make sense of this contradiction, which mani-fested in deadly ways on January 6, in which those normally committed to "backing the blue" orient themselves as insurgent to the state and its policing forces, who share the same aims of repressing liberation and anti-capitalist movements?

January 6 was a symptom of how the decentralized, mass character of white counterrevolution lends itself to insurgency against its own state in the context of capitalism's worsening accumulation crisis and era of progressive uprisings. Insurgent white nationalism and neo-fascism are movements oppositional to the state in their aim to wage white counterrevolution on their own terms and win control of US racial capitalism to impose the long-held dream, discussed in chapter 3, of white equality capitalism. In other words, there are two aims of this new white insurgency. The first is to continue to do the work of repressing liberation movements to protect settler racialized class society, but doing so beyond the oversight or control of the centralized state. They seek to dissolve the concessions that Black, Indigenous, and Third World revolts won in the mid-twentieth century, which resulted in the dismantling of Jim Crow and limited inclusion in US democracy. In this way, while insurgent fascism aligns with the neoliberal state's goal of undoing these concessions, it reads the state as inept or compromised in achieving this. In response, insurgent fascism seeks to install itself as the administrator of white counterrevolution rather than following the lead or being under the command of what white insurgency perceives is a compromised state.[24] These forces "back the blue" to support state fascism's counterrevolutionary repression of liberation movements but will kill police who do not appear loyal or who stand in the way of this objective, like what took place on January 6. The second aim is to wrest control of the state away from neoliberal administrators to retool capitalism in the image of the aspiration for white equality.[25]

Historians note that there was a shift in the contemporary white power movement to adopt an insurgent objective of waging war against its own state beginning in the decades following Third-World national liberation struggles of the 1960s–1970s, the inception of capitalism's deindustrializing accumulation crisis, and the subsequent rise of neo-liberal policies. Kathleen Belew writes that beginning in the early 1980s, the white power movement "declared war on the state. This marked a tectonic shift for the movement, which until then had featured populist and reactionary Klan mobilizations and vigilante violence. Rather than fighting on behalf of the state, white power activists now fought for a white homeland, attempted to destabilize the federal government, and waged revolutionary race war."[26] Revolutionary decolonization movements had forced imperial states to make concessions like the dismantling of legal apartheid in the United States. In the same moment capital launched its neoliberal strategy that unraveled the New Deal welfare state, resulting in increasing proletarianization of petty bourgeois whites and securely waged white workers. Insurgent fascism has sought to capture and articulate a program around the grievances of reactionary workers and petty bourgeois subjects who are unnerved at the sight of the state granting concessions to racialized and colonized peoples and by the dying prospects of white equality capitalism.[27] The fear of descending into permanent proletarian life, marked by chronic joblessness and underwaged work, drives petty bourgeois whites and the securely waged to see fascism as a weapon for combating these trends in contemporary capitalism. For instance, a grassroots militia movement grew and spread in the 1990s, producing Timothy McVeigh's insurgent terrorist attack against the federal government. With a copy of the white power movement's sacred text, *The Turner Diaries*, in hand, McVeigh bombed the Federal Building in Oklahoma City, an act he believed would kick-start a race war or a white insurgency, whose fantasy is to eliminate and/or enslave the colonized and racialized and seize control of the US state.[28]

More recently, the case of white vigilante shooter Kyle Rittenhouse offers an illustration of this dual character of white insurgency today. On August 25, 2020, Rittenhouse shot three Black Lives Matter protesters at a demonstration in Kenosha, Wisconsin. He killed two and seriously wounded the third. Protesters had flooded the streets of Kenosha to demand justice for the police shooting of Jacob Blake and in solidarity with the national George Floyd uprisings. Rittenhouse was later charged with murder and stood trial, at which his defense attorney argued that he had acted in self-defense when shooting the protesters. The jury delivered a not guilty verdict. In the days leading up to the shootings, Rittenhouse had traveled from his nearby home in Antioch, Illinois, to Kenosha to aid the state in repressing the protests. He has described witnessing the George Floyd uprisings sweep across the nation that summer. Alarmed that they were erupting in his own backyard of Kenosha, Rittenhouse joined with friends to carry out white alliance policing of Black revolt. "The thought that this community was in danger of suffering the same problems that had happened in other cities over the last few months made me very sad. Kenosha did not deserve what was happening to it."[29] Rittenhouse was a former participant in a Public Safety Cadet Program run by local police departments to recruit youth into careers in "law enforcement." Rittenhouse went on "ride-alongs" with police and shadowed them in their day-to-day tasks, learning the ins and outs of police work. He recalls, "Here, I began to find a purpose and direction in life. I met adults interested in mentoring me and showing that I could be something more than I was."[30] At the time of the shootings, he was working as a lifeguard at a YMCA to gain skills to become a paramedic or firefighter to work as a "first responder" alongside police. Since the shootings, Rittenhouse has characterized his actions as the work of a selfless street medic and neutral peace-keeper who was victimized by unhinged Black Lives Matter protesters.

After arriving in Kenosha and witnessing a night of protests that left extensive property destruction in their wake, Rittenhouse walked the town with friends to survey the damage. He helped clean graffiti slogans protesting state violence off a local school. He describes this experience uniting with strangers around the goal of removing the traces of militant protest for Black lives as akin to a religious experience, in which he found for the first time a community he could call home. It was the volunteerism for white alliance policing that inspired him. "They would not sit at home and just 'say a quick prayer.' They would not just wait and give $5 for some community drive. They were not waiting for someone else. . . . I watched the community come together to fix what a group of outside agitators wanted to destroy."[31] In his memoir, Rittenhouse also styles himself as a poor white whose parents' irresponsible decision-making, he emphasizes, not their poverty, led to a broken home, alienation, and lack of community. The community coming together for white counterrevolution at Kenosha redeemed him from this past.

It was during this community building for counterrevolution that Rittenhouse made plans with fellow white reactionaries and militia members to guard the property of a car dealership later that night. He remarks that the area "looked like the pictures of war zones in a third-world country," and that observing "all the vehicles that had been destroyed, I felt a little angry and a lot sad."[32] The police would refer to Rittenhouse and others as "friendlies" for their role in the armed policing of the protests, at one point saying, "We really appreciate you guys, we really do."[33] While operating outside of a formal organization, Rittenhouse's actions nonetheless align with many of the neo-Confederates, neofascists, and patriot militias organizing independent movements to do what they believe the state is failing to do effectively, namely the repression of the rebellion of Black, Indigenous, colonized, and unwaged classes. In most cases, the state depends on this supplementary help and welcomes white insurgency with its mass character when it extends state power, as we saw in previous chapters. During moments of uprisings, as in Rittenhouse's case, armed white militias and neofascists commonly conduct patrols with permission or in coordination with police. Under the guise of "peacekeeping" or counterprotesting, these forces have attacked and murdered those protesting state violence while police watch. In fact, in many cases police provide security for Far Right antagonists at protests to ensure they are not driven away by the mobilizations of anti-racist protesters.

Rittenhouse's case also articulates an insurgency for reactionary white equality. As discussed in chapter 3, the cross-class alliances of white counterrevolution engendered the dream among white workers of white equality as the resolution to industrializing capitalism that augments the class antagonism between free labor and capital. White equality remained aspirational, always clashing with the logics of capital to expand the exploitation of free labor. White insurgency surfaced to challenge the state that enforced this expanding exploitation of free labor rather than deliver white equality. In today's context of accumulation crisis, the expansion of surplus life and the waning of capital growth is felt by sectors of white workers and petty bourgeois classes as the death of the dream of white equality capitalism. In his memoir, Rittenhouse emphasizes that he was not a wealthy white teenager from the suburbs, which he claims the media characterized him as following the shootings. As mentioned, he details how he grew up in poverty. He lived in a homeless shelter for an extended period. He recounts that his family was evicted from their housing on several occasions. He focuses on his father's drug addiction and arrest, which led to his parents' divorce. Rittenhouse also bizarrely describes the Black Lives Matter protesters he sought to police as "rich white kids" protesting for the sake of adventurism and not for a legitimate moral cause.[34] While he sought to repress Black revolt, he also displaces his anger and frustration related to the class antagonism among whites onto white protesters participating in rebellions for Black lives: "The troublemakers around the BLM movement were rich white kids. Maybe they were rebelling against driving a new BMW rather than a new Porsche. I never understood their anger."[35] This transformation of his anger about class antagonism into the policing of whites who betray their whiteness by joining protests challenging white supremacy captures how from the perspective of white alliance policing, not only should whites be policing not supporting Black rebellion, but also white alliances should translate into white equality.

Rittenhouse showed up in Kenosha to stop Black revolt and teach fellow whites the meaning of white alliance policing: that it should engender a white equality like what he found in the spontaneous community coalescing around restoring "law and order" and censoring street art protesting racist state violence. For this, his case drew widespread support from white reactionary forces, especially due to the state criminalizing his efforts to fulfill his duties of white alliance policing to protect US class society. For his services, Rittenhouse was not only found not guilty by the same state his violence was extending on the night he killed two protesters and wounded a third, but he has become a Far Right celebrity and speaker, doing propaganda work for white counterrevolution for hefty royalties and endorsements. It does not appear his career goal now is to become a paramedic.

As the accumulation crisis continues to eject white labor from waged life and threatens to proletarianize portions of the white petty bourgeoisie, like small business owners, labor aristocrats, and small and midsize white farmers, white insurgency will continue to surge. While the aspiration for white equality emerges from the alliances of white counterrevolution, white equality also recursively becomes its own autonomous objective. Like homestead utopianism of the antebellum period, white equality in the context of its death caused by today's accumulation crisis becomes the movement for an alternative future from the current status quo of neoliberal capitalism. For many white workers and petty bourgeois classes, capitalism is experienced as reaching a stage where white equality exists only in the past, for which reactionary overthrow of the bourgeoisie and the state to install a fascist dictatorship is required.[36] In this way, we see how the very conditions of capitalism that have developed guarded by white counterrevolution, produce movements today of white insurgents who seek to wrest control of capitalism from the bourgeois ruling class by capturing full control of the state, to use its power to restructure capitalism to deliver white equality.

Rittenhouse's case also demonstrates how the state today continues to depend on the mass character of white counterrevolution. His vigilante armed policing extended state power to repress and terrorize. Yet this same mass character on which the state depends also becomes unmanageable. This was the contradiction examined in chapter 2, illustrated by the colonization of California and captured in John Rollin Ridge's novel *Joaquín Murieta*. The mass character and decentralized orientation of white alliance policing and settler mass militarism, which allowed for a more effective execution of repression of abolition and anticolonial wars, were also what led to an anarchy of white counterrevolution. This works in excess of centralized state authority, a force that is unleashed but cannot be controlled.

This contradiction has manifested in deadly ways through the massacres that go by the name of mass shootings. These massacres play a counterrevolutionary role in attacking anti-imperialist and abolition struggle.[37] They are forms of white terror that serve a punitive and pedagogical function. The shooters' manifestos indicate as much. From Dylan Roof in Charleston, South Carolina, to Patrick Wood Crusius in El Paso, Texas, to Payton S. Gendron in Buffalo, New York, to so many others, the shooters have been explicit in their manifestos that they sought to murder the colonized and racialized as punishment for perceived challenges to whites. Like armed occupiers of the nineteenth century, these white male settler mass shooters consider themselves soldiers, waging a genocidal counterrevolutionary war on colonized and racialized peoples to "defend" against what is fantastically believed to be their role in a conspiracy to eliminate whites. These fears of "white genocide" and the "great replacement theory" are the newest versions of the same colonial story that said settlers must decimate the colonized and racialized to "defend" their settlements and plantations from liquidation. Estes, Yazzie, Denetdale, and Correia write that from the perspective of the settler position, "The bordertown is always under attack. . . . This is the recipe for an always present settler fear and anxiety stoked by the terror of a coming 'great replacement' fantasy, a 'white genocide' in which Native and Black people are in constant rebellion, always threatening to do to the settler what the settler did first. To the settler, the only reasonable response to this is violence. Destroy the Native before the Native destroys you."[38] In their counterrevolutionary function, then, mass shootings align with the state's aim of repression and counterinsurgency against unfree and colonized populations. This is why the state is reluctant to disarm its white settler mass base through gun bans. It still needs the support of white alliance policing and settler mass militarism to supplement its efforts to repress liberation movements and the rebellions of the unfree and colonized. Mass shootings are also an accelerated version of the violence that the state is already perpetuating against the colonized and racialized working classes, both in the domestic context and abroad, using its prisons, police, and militarism. On the other hand, however, school shootings are costly to the legitimacy of US settler racialized society, which promises security and safety for its citizen-civilians in a democracy defined as "civilized" against nations that are usually the targets of imperial wars. As examined in chapters 1 and 2, this uncontrollable excess of white settler violence emerges from the contradiction between the need for counterrevolution to have a mass character in response to revolutionary abolition and anticolonialism and the state's efforts to centralize counterrevolutionary violence to place it under its monopoly command. This contradiction remains irresolvable in a context today in which the state continues to depend on white alliance policing and settler mass militarism, which exceed the state's control as mass-based, decentralized formations.

Scholars of contemporary fascism argue that if we understand the insurgent and autonomous character of fascism today, what follows is seeing that our context is defined by a "three-way fight" among progressive forces, the neoliberal conservative status quo, and insurgent neofascism. Their contention is that fascism is much more than a tool for protecting bourgeois power.[39] It also has, as I have detailed, its own independent agenda of seizing state power and operating independently from any oversight of the state. Joining these conversations, I have argued that this autonomous character of insurgent fascism has always been an element of the longue durée of white counter-revolution precisely because of racial capitalism's need to repress the revolutionary challenge from Black abolition and Indigenous anticolonialism. The viable threat of revolutionary alternatives and challenges from these traditions of struggle gave rise to enlisting, hailing, and organizing the masses of white settlers to be racial capitalism's police and military forces who, as such, could never be fully under the command or oversight of a centralized state. Tragically, the deadly consequences of this contradiction will continue until revolutionary transformations take place in the conditions causing them.

ABOLITION WAR THEORETICIANS

Antebellum abolition and anticolonial wars produced revolutionary theory, strategy, and imagination that this book has attempted to unearth. Rediscovering a tradition of revolutionary anti-capitalist and anti-imperialist thought from these movements illuminates their radical rather than reformist trajectory. There was always the potential for armed abolition and anticolonialism to win freedom from US class society despite facing extreme forms of violence, destruction, and terror. This is a reminder that these movements arose from the very conditions of slavery and settler colonialism that are the foundations of US class society. The insights of these movements anticipated revolutionary anti-capitalist theory of the twentieth-century national liberation movements. Yet abolition and anticolonial wars were also movements practicing historical materialism in the specific context of North

America that both preceded and paralleled the development of forms of revolutionary theory and strategy taking root in other contemporaneous contexts such as European communism. These movements were the anti-capitalist negation of slavery and settler colonialism as the primary modes of accumulation composing North American racial capitalism. As such, they evince a much longer history of revolutionary anti-capitalism in these lands than is often recognized.

From their vantage point of revolutionary insurgency, abolition and anticolonial wars could perceive the points of potential undoing of racial capitalism. Through their militant orientation, the partisans of abolition and anticolonial wars exposed the weaknesses of capitalism as the openings for revolutionary futures. They spotlighted racial capitalism's fragility and liability precisely in how it was compelled to devise mass-based, cross-class counterrevolutionary strategies of protection. Abolition and anticolonial war thinkers analyzed the workings of slavery, settler colonialism, and white counterrevolution not merely to interpret them for the sake of doing so but to understand how to defeat these projects—to paraphrase Marx's famous slogan. Such militancy, it should be noted, guided their thought and strategy, enabling them to arrive at the crucial insights and knowledge studied here, which were not available through other routes. Their methods of reading the worlds they worked to transform are models for how to read for the weak points of class society that irrepressible resistance exposes and that counterrevolution disavows. Today, when study and critique are all too often marked by defeatism, cynicism, or nostalgia for times before crisis, the history of abolition and anticolonial war invites us to read for the ways that not only is class society not inevitable or invincible, but also its very conditions of contradiction produce its own gravediggers.[40] *No More Peace* has attempted to do this kind of reading, illuminating histories in which people rebelled, advanced revolutionary change, and won against their exploiters and oppressors, even in the most terrible of conditions.

Abolition and anticolonial wars also invite us to recognize rather than disavow or, worse, demonize those who carry on these unfinished movements today. An example from the end of John Brown's life illustrates this point. Following the US Marines' siege and storming of the engine room at Harper's Ferry that led to the capture of John Brown and members of his militia, Virginia authorities—including Colonel Robert E. Lee, Virginia governor Henry Wise, and Senator James M. Mason—interrogated Brown and Aaron Stevens at the paymaster's office as they lay wounded and bloodied awaiting their imprisonment at the nearby Charles Town jail. Brown had suffered saber cuts on his head and stab wounds from marine bayonets. Stevens received similar injuries.[41] Governor Wise's public account of the interview suggested that Brown was a fanatic, even as Wise conceded that Brown was a worthy foe in his sincerity of purpose to liberate the enslaved. What Wise did not include in his public account was the mention of a portion of the conversation in which Brown shared insights on the aims of the raid. Later, a jailer questioned Brown about his conversation with Governor Wise, asking what Brown meant when he told Wise that Brown had expected reinforcements to arrive from several Northern states following the inception of the raid.

JAILER: What did you tell him that could have made that impression on his mind?

BROWN: Wise said something about fanaticism, and intimated that no one in full possession of his senses could have expected to overcome a State with such a handful of men as I had, backed only by the struggling negroes; and I replied that I had promises of ample assistance, and would have received it too if I could only have put the ball in motion.[42]

Attempting to entrap Brown to divulge names of accomplices, while also contradictorily minimizing the organized power behind the raid, the jailer doubted that Brown had the support to call on from the North or that enslaved Africans were inspired to join him. Brown's response to these doubts crystallized the dialectics of abolition war: "No; I knew, of course, that the negroes would rally to my standard. If I had only got the thing fairly started, you Virginians would have seen sights that would have opened your eyes; and I tell you if I was free this moment, and had five hundred negroes around me, I would put these irons on Wise himself before Saturday night."[43] Brown's vision of abolition placing slavery's leaders in irons in a reversal of positions if his raid had been able to scale up as planned before the forces of counterrevolution could stop it articulated the understanding of what was required for revolutionary change. It was not solely violence (for which Brown is most remembered), but the organized power to overturn the class rule of those at the helm of slavery. Brown, like all the thinkers and organizers of abolition and anticolonial wars studied here, knew that wars of liberation were necessary to end capitalism's wars of accumulation.

In class society, such militancy is always characterized as monstrous. From the Stono rebels to Nat Turner to the Seminoles, Black Seminoles, and Black maroon insurgents of Florida, to Harriet Tubman, John Brown, Osborne Anderson, and other abolition and anticolonial war thinkers and organizers of this study, they were all vilified, demonized, and deemed murderable in their time. In fact, in the interview just mentioned, John Brown was accused of seeking to kill all white people in the South in the name of Black liberation. At the end of the interrogation, an officer asked Brown what he would have done if he had recruited all the enslaved in his abolition army. Brown answered emphatically, "Set them free, sir!" A bystander interjected, "To set them free would sacrifice the life of every man in this [white] community." Brown disagreed. The bystander then called Brown an unhinged extremist: "I know it. I think you fanatical."[44] The specter of Black revolution that abolition war conjured at Harper's Ferry was experienced by white supremacist enslavers as a program of white extermination. Yet this fear of abolition indiscriminately targeting all whites was projection. Enslavers feared that the same genocidal violence they unleashed on Black and Indigenous people would be turned on them if they lost their power to abolition or anticolonialism. From the perspective of white counterrevolution, the world looks only like wars of retributive death and destruction. This is all capitalism and imperialism know as they proceed through their wars of genocide. From the perspective of abolition and anticolonial wars, however, the destruction of slavery and settler colonialism was a life-giving act. It was the destruction of oppression to win life. As class struggles sharpen today, abolition war theorists remind us that while such militancy is always demonized in its time, it is only from militant struggle that people arrive at forms of thoughts and methods of reading that are up to the crucial task of understanding class society in ways that can assist movements to bring about its abolition.

Acknowledgments

I COMPOSED THIS PROJECT in the aftermath of surviving state repression. In response to my involvement in community organizing against state violence and white supremacy, the state seized an opportunity to bring charges against me that threatened years of imprisonment. Yet as the very history that I have examined in this project teaches us, repression tends to inspire, not stunt, further mobilization, action, and commitment. With the unwavering support of the same communities whom the state sought to weaken through repression, I was eventually, after several months, exonerated of all charges and recovered from their impact. Compared to the violence that the state regularly unleashes on those it seeks to repress, my case was minor, even as it was serious. I express my deepest appreciation and thanks to all those who took action to defend me from this repression. From signing petitions to marching in the streets to all the other ways that people advocated for me that resulted in my exoneration, I am honored to have received this support. Many of those who took action are the same to whom I give thanks below for shaping this project. For those whom I can't name in these acknowledgments, know that I recognize your solidarity. It was inspiring to see how from the repression I experienced bloomed further irrepressible struggle.

Before these events, the ideas for this project emerged from my dissertation and graduate coursework at the University of New Mexico. I owe so much and offer my deepest appreciation to my dissertation adviser and mentor, Professor Jesse Alemán. His seminars on nineteenth-century American literature and history were instrumental in shaping my research interests, methods, and commitment to the study of history and literature. Professor Alemán embodies what it means to serve the people in his work at the university. His dedication to helping students learn and succeed is unmatched. His courses, conversations, feedback on seminar papers and dissertation drafts, and frameworks were formative for developing my understanding of race, class, colonialism, and capitalism. Professor Alemán also understood the laboring conditions of academia and the university. This perspective guided how he provided support and mentorship. It made all the difference. I cannot think of a better example of how to be a mentor to students, especially those from working-class communities trying to navigate the arcane and unwritten codes of conduct, expectations, and rules of university culture. Simply put, Professor Alemán's teaching, mentorship, and knowledge changed my life.

Along with Professor Aleman's support, I am deeply indebted to the members of my dissertation committee, Daniel Worden, Alyosha Goldstein, and its unofficial member Bernadine Hernández. Their feedback prompted me to take the work of my dissertation in directions that led to this project. Although she joined the UNM faculty after I had assembled my committee, Bernadine nonetheless offered crucial support for my work, providing pivotal feedback, suggestions, and perspectives related to questions intersecting with her work on racial capitalism. Many of our conversations served as the foundation for questions explored in this project. Like Professor Alemán, Bernadine is a revolutionary scholar and educator dedicated to serving social movements and communities in struggle. I was blessed to have the opportunity to work with her at UNM, and I value our friendship and ongoing collaboration.

In the English department at UNM, I was also very fortunate to take courses and learn from professors Melina Vizcaíno-Alemán and Kathleen Washburn, who provided invaluable support and mentorship. I also found guidance and support from the American Studies Department at UNM. I am deeply indebted to Dr. Jennifer Denetdale. Her seminar on Indigenous critiques of colonialism has been a bedrock to my thinking informing this project. Dr. Denetdale also modeled for her students how university study should serve liberation struggles. I was also fortunate to be a fellow graduate student of Nick Estes, who is now a faculty member at the University of Minnesota. In American studies seminars and reading groups, Nick's sharp insights on colonialism and class struggles expanded how I thought about capitalism. Nick exemplified how to do work in history and theory that advanced revolutionary understandings and perspectives. I also thank Tania Balderas, Emma Mincks, David Puthoff, Joshua Heckman, Chrysta Wilson, and Amy Gore. I am grateful for our conversations and for the many lessons we learned together in our efforts to initiate a graduate worker unionization campaign at UNM.

At Penn State, I am deeply indebted to my colleague mentors, some of whom are now at different institutions: Cynthia Young, Ebony Coletu, Tina Chen, Sean Goudie, Mark Morrisson, Janet Lyon, Michael Bérubé, Hester Blum, Jonathon Eburne, Christian Haines, John Marshall, Julia Kasdorf, Alex Lubin, Michael West, Gary King, Jennifer Black, Timeka Tounsel, Abraham Khan, Becky Tarlau, Manuel Rosaldo, Zachary Morgan, and Michelle Rodino-Colocino. I thank them for their indispensable guidance, advice, and support over the last few years. Cynthia Young provided essential mentorship in my first years in State College. She not only encouraged my work and teaching but was a lifeline in times of need, for which I cannot thank her enough. Michael West, Gary King, and Jennifer Black have been tremendous mentors and friends both on campus and in the activist community. It has been an honor to learn from and work alongside them in campaigns for racial justice. Hester Blum and Jonathon Eburne have offered vital guidance on teaching and research. They are gifted community builders on and off campus in ways that inspire me in my work. I also thank all my colleagues in the English and African American Studies Departments at Penn State, especially Janelle Edwards, Dara Walker, Gabrielle Foreman, Jim Casey, Sam Tenorio, Matt Tierney, Debra Hawhee, Elizabeth Kadetsky, Samuel Kólawolé, Kevin Bell, Aldon Nielsen, Benjamin Schreier, Scott Smith, and Paul Kellerman.

My deepest thanks to Shama Rangwala at York University for our years of friendship, collaboration, and many conversations related to the topics of this project. Shama's insights and wisdom have shaped so much of my work. She has also been a lifeline in times of need, for which I am forever in debt to her solidarity. I also express my deepest gratitude to Alex Lubin, who has helped me in countless ways in the last years, from sponsoring my work and offering critical feedback, to mentoring support, to community building on and off campus. Without his mentorship, friendship, and selfless assistance, I simply would not have been able to complete this project. Our conversations and discussions on topics related to this project, university study, and community organizing are always energizing and inspiring.

I received generous feedback on this project from a manuscript workshop sponsored by the English Department's Mentoring Program. I thank Alex Lubin, Hester Blum, Sean Goudie, Christian Haines, Dylan Rodríguez, and Bernadine Hernández for taking the time to read, comment, and offer incredibly useful suggestions for improvement. For offering additional help at various stages of the project, I appreciate the ongoing feedback from Alex Lubin and Michael West. I also deeply appreciate detailed feedback from Geo Maher, Manu Karuka, and anonymous reviewers of University of California Press. Maher and Karuka offered crucial advice and perspective for improving the framing of the project. They also helped me better grasp its contributions to discussions on class struggles, whiteness, and abolition.

It has been a delight and honor to work with the University of California Press. I thank my editor Niels Hooper for his wise direction, guidance, perspective, and seeing the potential in this project in our first conversations. I also thank Nora Becker for help and support in navigating the process of preparing the manuscript for production. I am deeply appreciative of Sharon Langworthy's superb work as a copy editor of the manuscript.

This project also developed out of my experience of community organizing. I am deeply indebted to the many grassroots organizations and their members with whom I have worked over the years. These are the organizations whose leaders trained, mentored, and inspired me to get involved in community defense work and anti-imperialist organizing. In Albuquerque, I thank the members of the Industrial Workers of the World (IWW), Albuquerque General Membership Branch and the John Brown Breakfast Club for helping me learn how to do workplace organizing and revolutionary community defense. I was incredibly fortunate to work in a coalition with and learn from The All-African

People's Revolutionary Party, the Red Nation, and Millions for Prisoners. These organizations not only provided training, political education, and revolutionary leadership that transformed me, but they also came to my aid from afar when I was facing state repression. In central Pennsylvania, I have been inspired by and honored to support the work of revolutionary students of the United Socialists at Penn State, the Student Committee for Defense and Solidarity, and Students for Justice in Palestine. Student leaders in these organizations advanced efforts to defend me against state repression. I would not be in a position to compose this project without their help. I owe them everything and continue to be inspired by their revolutionary work. They also are committed organizers on campus, waging campaigns in support of racial justice and anti-imperialism. I also thank those in People's Defense Front–Northern Appalachia for their anti-capitalist organizing in the wider Centre County area. PDF members are in the trenches every day, organizing workers and tenants in the region to win a better world. It has been an honor to work with them over the years.

I thank my family for everything they do. They always ground me in what matters. I am from rural, working-class Missouri and grew up in a large family. I am one of six children. My parents and siblings have always modeled how to be selfless and serve the people in ways that inspired me to do the same in my work, teaching, and organizing. It was from seeing how my family and people I grew up with try their best with what they had but still struggle to make ends meet, while working at jobs they put their lives into, only to be fired or laid off on a whim, that motivated me to study class oppression. I wrote this project with these things in mind to offer something useful for people trying to win a better world.

Above all, I thank my partner Laura for all her support, feedback, and suggestions on this project. Laura is a fighter and survivor. Her militancy in confronting injustice is unparalleled and has pushed me to be better in this regard. We first got to know each other while working the same job of cleaning the houses of the wealthy for low wages in Missouri. From those days to now, I continue to be amazed by her resilience and dedication to others, for which I am forever grateful we found each other.

Notes

INTRODUCTION. ABOLITION WAR
AND WHITE COUNTERREVOLUTION

1. W. E. B. Du Bois, *John Brown* (1909; New York: International Publishers, 1996), 133–138; and David Reynolds, *John Brown, Abolitionist: The Man Who Killed Slavery, Sparked the Civil War, and Seeded Civil Rights* (New York: Random House, 2005), 195–202.

2. Oswald Garrison Villard, *John Brown, 1800–1859: A Biography Fifty Years After* (Boston: Houghton Mifflin, 1910), 247–248; and Reynolds, *John Brown*, 202.

3. John Brown, "Provisional Constitution and Ordinances for the People of the United States," in *The Tribunal: Responses to John Brown and the Harpers Ferry Raid*, ed. John Stauffer and Zoe Trodd (Cambridge, MA: Harvard University Press, 2012), 26.

4. Gerald Horne, *The Counter-Revolution of 1776: Slave Resistance and the Origins of the United States of America* (New York: New York University Press, 2016).

5. Horne, *Counter-Revolution of 1776*; and Walter Johnson, *River of Dark Dreams: Slavery and Empire in the Cotton Kingdom* (Cambridge, MA: Harvard University Press, 2013).

6. See Kellie Carter Jackson, "Black Leadership: The Silenced Partners of Harpers Ferry," in *Force and Freedom: Black Abolitionists and the Politics of Violence* (Philadelphia: University of Pennsylvania Press, 2019), 85–106.

7. Reflecting on the role of peasants and the industrial proletariat in the 1848 upheavals against European monarchies, Marx observes that such classes learned precisely through engaging in class struggle that capital was their common enemy and that it would require an "anti-capitalist" or "proletarian government" to "break [their] economic misery," leading Marx to contend that "revolutions are the locomotives of history." *The Class Struggles in France, 1848 to 1850*, 1850, 1895, pt. 3, Marxist Internet Archive, www.marxists.org/archive /marx/works/1850/class-struggles-france/.

8. Neal Shirley and Saralee Stafford, *Dixie Be Damned: 300 Years of Insurrection in the American South* (Chico, CA: AK Press, 2015), 17–50.

9. Brown had a history of assisting and defending Indigenous sovereignty before his Kansas campaign. While living in Meadville, Pennsylvania, during the 1820s, John Brown combatted efforts of local white settlers to displace Indigenous nations. When a group of local white settlers approached Brown and others to recruit help for violently repelling Indigenous people hunting on their own land bases in the area, Brown threatened to use violence against the white settlers, promising, "I will have nothing to do with so mean an act. I would sooner take my gun and help drive you out of the country." See Reynolds, *John Brown*, 157–158, 168–170, 173–174. Brown was also not devoid of contradictions related to Indigenous peoples. Kathryn Walkiewicz points out that in Kansas Brown embraced the nickname "Osawatomie Brown," in ways approaching performing Redface. See Kathryn Walkiewicz, "Kansas Bleeds in Cuba," in *Reading Territory: Indigenous and Black Freedom, Removal, and the Nineteenth-Century State* (Chapel Hill: University of North Carolina Press, 2023), 112–150.

10. Quoted in John Stauffer, *The Black Hearts of Men: Radical Abolitionists and the Transformation of Race* (Cambridge, MA: Harvard University Press, 2002), 206.

11. Lewis Brownstein, "The Concept of Counterrevolution in Marxian Theory," *Studies in Soviet Thought* 22, no. 3 (August 1981): 175–192. See also V. I. Lenin, *The State and Revolution* (1918; Chicago: Haymarket Books, 2014).

12. For example, the reception of Patrick Wolfe's work on settler colonialism exhibits an overemphasis on its character as a structure of violence, with less attention to Indigenous resistance as a motor force in settler colonialism's development. "Settler Colonialism and the Elimination of the Native," *Journal of Genocide Research* 8, no. 4 (2006): 387–409. See also Lorenzo Veracini, *Settler Colonialism: A Theoretical Overview* (London: Palgrave Macmillan, 2010). Harry Harootunian argues that Western Marxism has attempted to totalize capitalism in its models of how it works, resulting in critiques of capitalism that see it as completed rather than uneven, unfinished, and contested. Harry Harootunian, *Marx after Marx: History and Time in the Expansion of Capitalism* (New York: Columbia University Press, 2015).

13. Karl Marx and Frederick Engels, "Manifesto of the Communist Party," 1848, Marxist Internet Archive, 14, www.marxists.org/archive/marx/works/download/pdf/Manifesto.pdf.

14. Nick Estes and Roxanne Dunbar-Ortiz, "Examining the Wreckage," *Monthly Review* 72, no. 3 (July–August, 2020), https://monthlyreview.org/2020/07/01/examining-the-wreckage/#en7backlink.

15. Marx writes, "The discovery of gold and silver in America, the extirpation, enslavement, and entombment in mines of the indigenous population of that continent, the beginnings of the conquest and plunder of India, and the conversion of Africa into a preserve for the commercial hunting of blackskins, are all things which characterize the dawn of the era of capitalist production." *Capital: A Critique of Political Economy* (1867, New York: Vintage Books, 1977), 1:915.

16. Class struggle," writes Losurdo, "is the genus which, in determinate circumstances, takes the specific form of 'national struggle.'" Losurdo also points out that Marx and Engels refer to class struggle in the *Communist Manifesto* and elsewhere in their work in the plural, arguing that "the meaning of the expression 'class struggles' . . . is not employed to denote repetition of the identical, the continual recurrence of the same class struggle in the same form. It refers to the multiplicity of shapes and forms that class struggle can assume." *Class Struggle: A Political and Philosophical History* (New York: Palgrave Macmillan, 2016), 14, 15.

17. See C. L. R. James, *The Black Jacobins: Toussaint L'Ouverture and the San Domingo Revolution* (New York: Random House, 1963); Frantz Fanon, *The Wretched of the Earth* (New York: Grove Press, 1965); Walter Rodney, *How Europe*

Underdeveloped Africa (1972; London: Verso, 2018); Sylvia Wynter, "Unsettling the Coloniality of Being/Power/Truth/Freedom: Towards the Human, after Man, Its Overrepresentation—an Argument," *CR: The New Centennial* Review 3, no. 3 (2003): 257–337; and Cedric J. Robinson, *Black Marxism: The Making of the Black Radical Tradition* (1983; Chapel Hill: University of North Carolina Press, 2020).

18. Roxanne Dunbar-Ortiz, *An Indigenous Peoples' History of the United States* (Boston: Beacon Press, 2014); Gerald Horne, *The Apocalypse of Settler Colonialism: The Roots of Slavery, White Supremacy, and Capitalism in 17th Century North America and the Caribbean* (New York: Monthly Review Press, 2018); Horne, *Counter-Revolution of 1776*; Manu Karuka, *Empire's Tracks: Indigenous Nations, Chinese Workers, and the Transcontinental Railroad* (Oakland: University of California Press, 2019); Nick Estes, *Our History Is the Future: Standing Rock Versus the Dakota Access Pipeline, and the Long Tradition of Indigenous Resistance* (London: Verso, 2019); Christina Heatherton, *Arise! Global Radicalism in the Era of the Mexican Revolution* (Oakland: University of California Press, 2022); Bernadine Marie Hernández, *Border Bodies: Racialized Sexuality, Sexual Capital, and Violence in the Nineteenth-Century Borderlands* (Chapel Hill: University of North Carolina Press, 2022); Charisse Burden-Stelly, *Black Scare/Red Scare: Theorizing Capitalist Racism in the United States* (Chicago: University of Chicago Press, 2023); Nikhil Pal Singh, *Race and America's Long War* (Oakland: University of California Press, 2017); Geo Maher, *Anticolonial Eruptions: Racial Hubris and the Cunning of Resistance* (Oakland: University of California Press, 2022); and Iyko Day, *Alien Capital: Asian Racialization and the Logic of Settler Colonial Capitalism* (Durham, NC: Duke University Press, 2016).

19. Jean McMahon Humez, *Harriet Tubman: The Life and the Life Stories* (Madison: University of Wisconsin Press, 2003), 94–110.

20. Sarah Bradford, *Scenes in the Life of Harriet Tubman* (Auburn, NY: W. J. Moses, 1869), 22.

21. See the correspondence between Frederick Douglass and Martin Delany on Stowe's novel in Martin Delany, *Martin R. Delany: A Documentary Reader*, ed. Robert S. Levine (Chapel Hill: University of North Carolina Press, 2003), 224–237.

22. Saidiya V. Hartman, *Scenes of Subjection: Terror, Slavery, and Self-Making in Nineteenth-Century America.* (Oxford: Oxford University Press, 1997).

23. Bradford, *Scenes in the Life*, 40–41.

24. See Stephen B. Oates, *The Fires of Jubilee: Nat Turner's Fierce Rebellion* (New York: Harper Perennial, 1975); David F. Allmendinger Jr., *Nat Turner and the Rising in Southampton County* (Baltimore, MD: Johns Hopkins University Press, 2014); Patrick H. Breen, *The Land Shall Be Deluged in Blood: A New History of the Nat Turner Revolt* (Oxford: Oxford University Press, 2015); Kenneth S. Greenberg, *Nat Turner: A Slave Rebellion in History and Memory* (Oxford: Oxford University Press, 2003); and Vanessa M. Holden, *Surviving Southampton: African American Women and Resistance in Nat Turner's Community* (Champaign: University of Illinois Press, 2021).

25. Nat Turner, *The Confessions of Nat Turner: The Leader of the Late Insurrection in Southampton, VA*, ed. Thomas Grey (Baltimore, MD: Lucas & Deaver, 1831), 10.

26. Turner, *Confessions*, 11.

27. See Vanessa M. Holden, "Intimate Rebellion," in *Surviving Southampton*, 3–10. Fanon writes, "The zone where the natives live is not complementary to the zone inhabited by the settlers. The two zones are opposed, but not in service of a higher unity. . . . [T]hey both follow the principle of reciprocal exclusivity. No conciliation is possible, for the two terms, one is superfluous." *Wretched of the Earth*, 38.

28. Fred Hampton, "You Can Murder a Liberator, but You Can't Murder Liberation," April 27, 1969, Marxist Internet Archive, www.marxists.org /archive/hampton/1969/04/27.htm.

29. See Henry Highland Garnet, "An Address to the Slaves of the United States of America," in *Electronic Texts in American Studies Libraries at University Nebraska-Lincoln*, 1843, https://digitalcommons.unl.edu/etas/8/.

30. Manisha Sinha writes that "Turner's rebellion put emancipation on the agenda of Virginia's legislature in 1831–32. William Henry Roane, the grandson of Patrick Henry, presented, among other measures, a Quaker petition for gradual abolition, and Thomas Jefferson Randolph, Jefferson's grandson, introduced a plan for gradual emancipation and the deportation of free blacks." *The Slave's Cause: A History of Abolition* (New Haven, CT: Yale University Press, 2016), 212. Oates writes that "out in the western part of the state, where antislavery and anti-Negro sentiment had long been smoldering, whites held public rallies in which they openly endorsed emancipation—yes, the liberation of all of Virginia's 470,000 slaves—as the only safeguard in these dangerous times."

Oates, *Fires of Jubilee*, 135. There were also several petitions from local citizens demanding gradual abolition and/or the removal of the enslaved population through African colonization. See "Petition from the Citizens of Hanover County," December 11 and 14, 1831, Nat Turner Project, www.natturnerproject .org/petition-hanover-county; and "Petition from Women of Augusta County to the Hon. the General Assembly of the State of Virginia," January 19, 1832, Nat Turner Project, www.natturnerproject.org/petition-augusta-county.

31. For more on white vigilante retaliatory violence, see Oates, who writes that "in all directions in upper North Carolina and southeastern Virginia, whites took Negroes from their shacks and tortured, shot, and burned them to death and then mutilated their corpses in ways that witnesses refused to describe. No one knows how many innocent Negroes perished in this reign of terror—at least 120, probably more. Several whites publicly regretted these atrocities but warned that they were the inevitable results of slave insurrection. Another revolt, they said, would end with the extermination of every black in the region." *Fires of Jubilee*, 99–100. See also Thomas Wentworth Higginson, "Nat Turner's Insurrection," *Atlantic*, August 1861, www.theatlantic .com/magazine/archive/1861/08/nat-turners-insurrection/308736/.

32. Maher, *Anticolonial Eruptions*, 18.

33. Dunbar-Ortiz, *Indigenous Peoples' History*, 99

34. Martha L. Finch, *Dissenting Bodies: Corporealities in Early New England* (New York: Columbia University Press, 2010), 30–35.

35. C. S. Monaco, *The Second Seminole War and the Limits of American Aggression* (Baltimore, MD: Johns Hopkins University Press, 2018), 176.

36. Karuka, *Empire's Tracks*, 176.

37. Karuka, *Empire's Tracks*, 174, 185.

38. Estes also explains how the #NoDAPL resistance camps at Standing Rock were both a challenge to capitalism and a model of how to enact an alternative to it. "In the absence of empire," Estes writes, "people came together to help each other, to care for one another. The #NoDAPL camps were designed according to need, not profit. . . . [I]t was here abundantly evident that Indigenous social systems offered a radically different way of relating to other people and the world." *Our History Is the Future*, 248, 252.

39. Joanne Barker, *Red Scare: The State's Indigenous Terrorist* (Oakland: University of California Press, 2021), 23.

40. Barker, *Red Scare*, 23–24.

41. Nick Estes et al., *Red Nation Rising: From Bordertown Violence to Native Liberation* (New York: PM Press, 2021), 75–76.

42. Barker, *Red Scare*, 24.

43. Karuka, *Empire's Tracks*, 185,

44. Karuka, *Empire's Tracks*, 181.

45. W. E. B. Du Bois, *Black Reconstruction in America* (1935; New York: The Free Press, 1998).

46. Horne argues that when the British empire signaled its intentions to abolish slavery in response to costly slave revolts and placed restrictions on further western land enclosures to prevent provoking war with Indigenous nations, the settler colonies revolted to form their own nation, dedicated to slavery and settler colonialism's expansion. Most recently, Horne's *The Counter-Revolution of 1836: Texas Slavery and Jim Crow and the Roots of American Fascism* demonstrates how Anglo settlers and enslavers who colonized the lands of what became Texas conducted a similar counterrevolutionary revolt against Mexico to preserve and extend slavery and settler colonialism. This pattern of settler revolt against abolition and Indigenous sovereignty, Horne suggests, has served as the origin for later reactionary white nationalist movements that reshaped the terrain of late twentieth-century US politics. Horne, *Apocalypse of Settler Colonialism*; Gerald Horne, *The Dawning of the Apocalypse: The Roots of Slavery, White Supremacy, Settler Colonialism, and Capitalism in the Long Sixteenth Century* (New York: Monthly Review Press, 2020); and Gerald Horne, *The Counter-Revolution of 1836: Texas Slavery and Jim Crow and the Roots of U.S. Fascism* (New York: International Publishers, 2022).

47. Here I also draw on the concept of "recursive dispossession" from the work of theorist Robert Nichols, who analyzes the historical processes of dispossession in settler colonialism. Nichols reveals how the settler theft of Indigenous lands works recursively to create conditions in which Indigenous grievances against dispossession are forced to play into the hands of settler meanings of private property possession, which end in reproducing those very categories and thus reinforcing Indigenous dispossession. I also consider that white counterrevolution works according to a similar recursive logic. While it is a reactionary formation emerging in response to abolition and anticolonial war, white counterrevolution also recursively becomes its own motor force

from the necessity to always be anticipatory in relation to future resistance from the enslaved or colonized. See Nichols, *Theft Is Property! Dispossession and Critical Theory* (Durham, NC: Duke University Press, 2019).

48. Marx, *Capital*, 1:899.

49. In his early work, Marx argued that African slavery was a stage of "original" or "primitive" accumulation whose character was not purely capitalist and thus was supplanted by wage labor exploitation as the principal mode of accumulation in capitalism. He considered the ongoing presence of slavery in capitalism an exception or "anomaly" that would give way to expanding wage labor exploitation. See Karl Marx, *Grundisse: Foundations of the Critique of Political Economy* (1939; New York: Penguin, 1973), 459–471, 497–501. However, in his later work Marx recognized and highlighted the motor force role Black worker struggles played in the transformations of capitalism. In a letter to Engels on the eve of the US Civil War, Marx writes, "In my view, the most momentous thing happening in the world today is the slave movement—on the one hand, in America, started by the death of [John] Brown, and in Russia, on the other. . . . I have just seen in the *Tribune* that there's been another slave revolt in Missouri, which was put down, needless to say. But the signal has now been given. Should the affair grow serious by and by, what will become of Manchester?" Marx, "Marx to Engels, January 11, 1860," in *The Civil War in the United States*, ed. Angela Zimmerman (1937; New York: International Publishers, 2016), 17.

50. Lisa Lowe demonstrates how this costly Black resistance compelled British enslavers of the Caribbean to import Chinese and Indian indentured workers, who were characterized as "free" laborers as a way of answering calls for the abolition of enslaved labor, while still serving as a coerced and thus highly exploitable workforce for capitalism. *The Intimacies of Four Continents* (Durham, NC: Duke University Press, 2015), 21–41, 44–45.

51. Marx, *Capital*, 876.

52. Rodríguez describes white reconstruction as the "historically pervasive logic of reform/rearticulation/adaption/revitalization that periodically surges into the aspirational hemispheric-to-global projects of White Being." Rodríguez examines the period of the post–civil rights era, in which white reconstruction has worked through reform to reassert global white power in the wake of global decolonization movements and the dismantling of apartheid

Jim Crow in the United States. *White Reconstruction: Domestic Warfare and the Logics of Genocide* (New York: Fordham University Press, 2021), 17.

53. For more on the role of settler colonialism in the history of Bacon's rebellion, Kevin Bruyneel offers a detailed examination of how anti-Indian violence and settler occupation are often disavowed in anti-racist studies of Bacon's rebellion. See Bruyneel, "The Settler Memory of Bacon's Rebellion," in *Settler Memory: The Disavowal of Indigeneity and the Politics of Race in the United States* (Chapel Hill: University of North Carolina Press, 2021), 21–44.

54. See Theodore Allen, *The Invention of the White Race*, vol. 2 (London: Verso, 1994).

55. David Roediger, *The Wages of Whiteness: Race and the Making of the American Working Class* (London: Verso, 1991). For an updated assessment of the field of critical white studies, see David Roediger's recent "Accounting for the Wages of Whiteness: US Marxism and the Critical History of Race," in *Class, Race, and Marxism* (London: Verso, 2019), 47–72.

56. See Alexander Saxton, *The Rise and Fall of the White Republic: Class Politics and Mass Culture in Nineteenth-Century America* (London: Verso, 1990); Noel Ignatiev, *How the Irish Became White* (New York: Routledge, 1995); Cheryl Harris, "Whiteness as Property," *Harvard Law Review* 106, no. 8 (June 1993): 1707–1791; and Roediger, *Wages of Whiteness*.

57. See the late Noel Ignatiev's *Treason to Whiteness Is Loyalty to Humanity* (London: Verso, 2022).

58. Heatherton, *Arise!*

59. Estes, *Our History Is the Future.*

60. Hernández, *Border Bodies.*

61. Holly Jackson, *American Radicals: How Nineteenth-Century Protest Shaped the Nation* (New York: Crown, 2019).

1. SLAVE REVOLT, FUGITIVITY, AND WHITE ALLIANCE POLICING

1. James, *Black Jacobins*, 85–90.

2. Maher, *Anticolonial Eruptions*, 30.

3. An Act Providing for the Relief of Such of the Inhabitants of Saint Domingo, Resident within the United States, as May Be Found in Want of Support,

6 Stat. Ch. 2 (February 12, 1794); William Patterson, "To George Washington from William Patterson et al.," January 30, 1794, Founders Online, National Historical Publications & Records Commission, https://founders.archives.gov /documents/Washington/05-15-02-0120.

4. Du Bois, *Black Reconstruction in America*, 12.

5. Du Bois, 12. Du Bois also traced how it was this collaboration between poor whites and enslavers of the antebellum period that later, along with the unification of Northern and Southern capital through monopoly after emancipation, undermined the abolition democracy of Reconstruction. White workers pledged their allegiance to capital rather than supporting, organizing, and unifying with Black workers to topple capital.

6. Horne, *Apocalypse*, 24.

7. Horne contends that it was only in response to the enslaved Africans' efforts to destabilize slavery that poor Europeans were recruited into alliances with the capitalist class by way of whiteness. "Pressure from Africans," Horne writes, "led to a profoundly material alteration of [European] indentured status to a kind of overseer that was accompanied by referring to these poorer Europeans in racial terms." *Apocalypse*, 132.

8. Horne, *Apocalypse*, 175. See also Sally Hadden's study on slave patrols, which tracks the construction of slave patrols in the early colonial period. *Slave Patrols: Law and Violence in Virginia and the Carolinas* (Cambridge, MA: Harvard University Press, 2001). Nikhil Pal Singh argues that the long history of policing of blackness was what generated and maintained the value of whiteness as a political status promising a set of freedoms and privileges in the first place. "The Whiteness of Police," *American Quarterly* 66, no. 4 (2014): 1097. Geo Maher's study on policing and abolition succinctly argues that "if whiteness were a job, it would be the police." *A World without Police: How Strong Communities Make Cops Obsolete* (London: Verso, 2021), 26.

9. For works examining repression and racial capitalism, see Jackie Wang, *Carceral Capitalism* (Cambridge, MA: MIT Press, 2018); Ruth Wilson Gilmore, *Golden Gulag: Prisons, Surplus, Crisis, and Opposition in Globalizing California* (Berkeley: University of California Press, 2007); and Susan Koshy et al., *Colonial Racial Capitalism* (Durham: Duke University Press, 2022).

10. Rodney, *How Europe Underdeveloped Africa*.

11. Allen, *Invention of the White Race*, 268–285.

12. Allen, *Invention of the White Race*, 293–340.

13. Gilmore, *Golden Gulag*; and Robinson, *Black Marxism*.

14. Horne, *Apocalypse*, 107–114.

15. Peter H. Wood, "Anatomy of a Revolt," in *Stono: Documenting and Interpreting a Southern Slave Revolt*, ed. Mark M. Smith (Columbia, SC: University of South Carolina Press, 2019), 63.

16. For more on Spanish Florida's influence on slave revolt in the early British colonies through a study of the Stono rebellion, see Horne, *Counter-Revolution of 1776*, 110–135.

17. Wood, "Anatomy of a Revolt," 64.

18. "Lieutenant Governor Bull's Eyewitness Account," in *Stono: Documenting and Interpreting a Southern Slave Revolt*, ed. Mark M. Smith (Columbia, SC: University of South Carolina Press, 2019), 16–17.

19. Wood, "Anatomy of a Revolt," 63–64.

20. "An 'Act for the Better Ordering and Governing of Negroes and Other Slaves,'" in Smith, *Stono*, 20–27.

21. "'Act for the Better Ordering,'" 21.

22. "'Act for the Better Ordering,'" 21.

23. "'Act for the Better Ordering,'" 26–27.

24. "'Act for the Better Ordering,'" 26.

25. Hadden, *Patrols*, 138.

26. Hadden, 17.

27. Requiring permanent occupancy also embodied the convergence of white alliance policing and settler colonialism. The enslaver was expected to be a permanent settler occupier, which is discussed in greater detail in chapter 2 in the context of Florida and the Seminole insurgencies against settler planters.

28. Higginson, "Nat Turner's Insurrection," 175.

29. Nat Turner, quoted in Angela Davis, "Political Prisoners, Prisons, and Black Liberation," in *Imprisoned Intellectuals: America's Political Prisoners Write on Life, Liberation, and Rebellion*, ed. Joy James (New York: Rowman & Littlefield, 2002), 67.

30. Garnet, "Address to the Slaves." See also William Lloyd Garrison's response to Turner's insurrection: "The Insurrection" *Liberator*, September 3, 1831, 143, https://fair-use.org/the-liberator/1831/09/03/the-insurrection.phtml.

31. Breen, *Land Shall Be Deluged*, 2.

32. Allmendinger, *Nat Turner and the Rising*, 78, 212. See also the call from Virginia's General Assembly for the fortification and better arming of state and local militias: "Address to the General Assembly of Virginia," 1831, Nat Turner Project, www.natturnerproject.org/governor-message-general-assembly-1831. A report from the *Richmond Enquirer* shared that

> a meeting of the citizens in Upperville and vicinity in Fauquier County, was held . . . for the purpose of taking into consideration the late disasters of Southampton and North Carolina. They came to a resolution 'that the large and frequent meetings of the slaves in this neighborhood and other parts of the county (some of them for purposes unknown to us) call for more vigilance on our part than has hitherto been observed. . . . The increasing boldness and insolence of the negroes generally of late we consider also as another reason why our attention should be drawn towards them.' They therefore organized themselves into light companies of patrols—and resolved that each member of the association should keep in constant readiness a musket or fowling piece—and recommended to the Commandants of the Regiments and magistrates throughout the County, and the Commonwealth, to carry into immediate effect every part of the Patrol Law.

October 7, 1831, Nat Turner Project, www.natturnerproject.org/richmond-enquirer-oct-7-patrol-law.

33. Oates, *Fires of Jubilee*, 88.

34. After citizens of Northampton County delivered a petition asking for free persons of color to be removed from the area, the General Assembly passed An Act Concerning the County of Northampton, which removed many free Black residents and relocated them to Liberia. March 5, 1832, Nat Turner Project, www.natturnerproject.org/blank-cmaj.

35. This same grassroots fundraising for counterrevolution is discussed in chapter 2; settlers of California raised funds for volunteer militias.

36. Fanon, *Wretched of the Earth*, 41–52.

37. For more on this argument, see Leonard L. Richards, *Gentlemen of Property and Standing: Anti-abolition Mobs in Jacksonian America* (Oxford: Oxford University Press, 1970).

38. Richards, 124; and Silas Niobeh Crowfoot, "Community Development for a White City: Race Making, Improvementism, and the Cincinnati Race Riots and Anti-Abolition Riots of 1829, 1836, and 1841" (PhD diss., Portland State University, 2010), 338.

39. Richards, *Gentlemen of Property*, 125–126; and Crowfoot, "Community Development," 346.

40. Crowfoot, "Community Development," 350–351.

41. Crowfoot, 353.

42. Crowfoot, 354–355.

43. Crowfoot, 363.

44. "Anti-Abolition Meeting," *Cincinnati Enquirer*, September 25, 1841, quoted in Crowfoot, "Community Development," 371. See also Richards, *Gentlemen of Property*, 129.

45. Richards, *Gentlemen of Property*, 123–129.

46. Du Bois writes: "But even the poor white, led by the planter, would not have kept the black slave in nearly so complete control had it not been for what may be called the Safety Valve of Slavery; and that was the chance which a vigorous and determined slave had to run away to freedom." *Black Reconstruction*, 13.

47. Sinha, *Slave's Cause*, 382.

48. For more on how the enslaved served as the major source of collateral in slavery capitalism, see Johnson, *River of Dark Dreams*, 86–87.

49. Sinha, *Slave's Cause*, 527–542.

50. See Jesse Olsavsky, *The Most Absolute Abolition: Runaways, Vigilance Committees, and the Rise of Revolutionary Abolitionism, 1835–1861* (Baton Rouge: Louisiana State University Press, 2022).

51. Gautham Rao, "The Federal 'Posse Comitatus' Doctrine: Slavery, Compulsion, and Statecraft in Mid- Nineteenth-Century America," *Law and History Review* 26, no. 1 (Spring, 2008): 1–56.

52. Rao, 20–26.

53. Sinha, *Slave's Cause*, 382.

54. Sinha, *Slave's Cause*, 390–391, 500.

55. See Fugitive Slave Act, § 7 (September 18,1850), http://hrlibrary.umn.edu /education/slaveact1850.html.

56. Sinha, *Slave's Cause*, 501. See also Fugitive Slave Act, § 5.

57. See Fugitive Slave Act, § 5.

58. Rao cites a petition from the Maryland legislature that argued if enslavers "could not rely upon the attendance and aid of the 'posse comitatus,'" the Fugitive Slave Law would be ineffectual. "Federal 'Posse Comitatus' Doctrine," 37.

59. *Blake*'s publication history is complex. Jerome McGann, who has edited the recent corrected edition of *Blake*, notes that the novel was published in "two serial versions, one incomplete, the other problematic in several ways. These are the twenty-six-chapter version that appeared in the *Anglo-African Magazine (AAM)* in 1859, and the seventy-four-chapter version that came out in the *Weekly Anglo-African (WAA)* in 1861–1862." See Martin R. Delany, *Blake; or, The Huts of America: A Corrected Edition*, ed. Jerome J. McGann (Cambridge, MA: Harvard University Press, 2017), xxxiii. See also Martin Delany, *Blake: Or, the Huts of America*, ed. Floyd Miller (1859; Boston: Beacon Press, 1970).

60. In October 1859, three months after *Blake* was first serialized in the *Anglo-African Magazine* (January to July 1859), John Brown's raid seized Harper's Ferry. A year earlier, in May 1858, at Chatham, Canada, Delany had helped Brown—who was coplanning the action with Harriet Tubman—recruit and prepare for the campaign. In the end, though, Delany did not participate himself.

61. Martin Delany, "Letter to J. H. Kagi, Chatham, August 16, 1858," in "John Brown Insurrection: The Brown Papers: Copied from the Originals at Charlestown by Order of the Executive Department of the State of Virginia," November 16, 1859, reprinted in *Calendar of Virginia State Paper and Other Manuscripts from January 1, 1836, to April 15, 1869* (Richmond: H. W. Flournoy, 1893), II:291–292.

62. Robert Levine, *Martin Delany, Frederick Douglass, and the Politics of Representative Identity* (Chapel Hill: University of North Carolina Press, 1997), 183.

63. Frank (Francis) A. Rollin, *The Life and Public Service of Martin R. Delany* (1868; Boston: Lee and Shepard, 1883), 76.

64. Delany, "Annexation of Cuba," in *Martin R. Delany*, ed. Levine, 165.

65. Delany, *Blake*, ed. McGann, 40.

66. For more on this shift in the Union's strategy, see Sinha, *Slave's Cause*, 579–585.

67. Grant Shreve argues that while ostensibly about slave uprising, *Blake* "is the most sophisticated and capacious expression of [Delany's] thinking from within emigrationism." "The Exodus of Martin Delany" *American Literary History* 29, no. 3 (2017): 450. Robert Levine argues that Delany was averse to serving under a white "Moses" like Brown and, following the Chatham convention, published *Blake* to revive arguments for emigration that he had

articulated in previous essays and speeches earlier in the decade. *Martin Delany, Frederick Douglass*, 183, 203. In the introduction to his corrected edition of *Blake*, Jerome McGann contends that "Delany wrote and published *Blake* as part of an argument for black emigration to Africa and as part of a scheme to raise money for his emigration project." *Blake*'s pro-emigrationist vision, McGann suggests, considers insurrection, especially in relation to Brown's campaign, not only "a white word drawn out of white history," but also impractical martyrdom. Introduction to *Blake*, ed. McGann, xxiv–xxv.

68. Related to the focus on emigrationism, hemispheric readings, best embodied by Paul Gilroy and Ifeoma Kiddoe Nwankwo, highlight the novel's unique literary representation of transnational Black resistance and community building in Cuba. Across these emigrationist and hemispheric readings, scholars contend that *Blake* illustrates Delany's rejection of US-bound abolitionism, most notably the position of integrationism embodied by Frederick Douglass. Andy Doolen interprets this rejection to include North American abolition war. *Blake*'s transnational vision of Black revolution, Doolen suggests, sees abolition war exemplified in Nat Turner's insurrection and Brown's campaign as martyrdom for "the original principles of American white nationalism" that Delany sought to avoid through his emigrationism beyond North America. Paul Gilroy, *The Black Atlantic: Modernity and Double Consciousness* (Cambridge, MA: Harvard University Press, 1993); Ifeoma C. K. Nwakwo, "The Promises and Perils of US African-American Hemispherism: Latin America in Martin Delany's *Blake* and Gayl Jones's *Mosquito*," *American Literary History* 18, no. 3 (2006): 579–599; and Andy Doolen, "Be Cautious of the Word 'Rebel': Race, Revolution, and Transnational History in Martin Delany's *Blake; or, The Huts of America*," *American Literature* 81, no. 1 (2009): 174.

69. Jackson, *American Radicals*, 213.

70. While scholars believe suspending the novel's serialization demonstrates Delany's retreat from insurgent struggle for emigration in Africa, there is another possible explanation when it is understood in relation to John Brown's campaign. In the summer of 1858, shortly after the Chatham Convention, Lysander Spooner, a Boston attorney and anarchist theorist, published the circular "A Plan for the Abolition of Slavery," which called for Northern abolitionists to raid the South and unite with the enslaved and nonslaveholder whites to wage war to overthrow slavery. When Brown learned of the circular,

he asked Spooner to suspend its publication, fearing that it would tip the hand of Brown's impending Virginia plan that depended on deception and surprise as a guerrilla raid. While it can only be speculated, perhaps Brown communicated a similar message to Delany about *Blake*? Delany was promoting his novel at literary festivals in New York City up until at least March 1859. Writing for *Frederick Douglass' Paper*, James McCune Smith covered a festival in honor of Delany on March 14, 1859, in New York City at which Delany read from *Blake* to festivalgoers. Delany had also written William Lloyd Garrison the previous month asking for help in securing a book publisher for *Blake*. This activity appears to indicate enthusiasm for supporting the full serialization of the novel. It is perplexing that he would suspend the novel's serialization after only twenty-eight chapters for reasons of making a trip to West Africa. See Reynolds, *John Brown*, 100–101; Robert E. McGlone, *John Brown's War against Slavery* (Cambridge: Cambridge University Press, 2009), 243; John Stauffer, *Black Hearts of Men*, 182; and Delany, "Letter for Garrison, 19 Feb 1859," in Levine, *Martin Delany: Documentary Reader*, 219–220.

71. Brigitte Fielder, Cassander Smith, and Derrick R. Spires, Introduction to "*Weekly Anglo-African* and *The Pine and Palm*: Excerpts 1861–1862," *Just Teach One: Early African American Print*, no. 4 (Spring 2018): i–xvi, https://jtoaa.americanantiquarian.org/welcome-to-just-teach-one-african-american/weekly-anglo-african-and-the-pine-and-palm/.See also Benjamin Fagan, *The Black Newspaper and the Chosen Nation* (Athens: University of Georgia Press, 2016), 124–125.

72. Thomas Hamilton, "The Nat Turner Insurrection," *Anglo-African Magazine*, December 1859, in Stauffer and Trodd, *Tribunal*, 192–193.

73. Benjamin Fagan, "*Blake* and the Black Newspaper," *American Periodicals: A Journal of History & Criticism* 28, no. 1 (2018): 78–79. See also Fagan, *Black Newspaper and the Chosen Nation*, 119–141.

74. Quoted in Victor Ullman, *Martin R. Delany: The Beginnings of Black Nationalism* (Boston: Beacon Press, 1971), 198.

75. James M. Mason, *Senate Select Committee Report on the Harper's Ferry Invasion*, 36th Cong., 1st Sess., S. Rep. Com. No. 278 (June 15, 1860), 99. For more on Realf in relation to Delany, see McGlone, *John Brown's War*, 233–235.

76. Rollin, *Life of Martin R. Delany*, 85–90. For more on Brown and Delany's plans to create an abolition state in Kansas territory and its contradictions

related to Indigenous self-determination, see Walkiewicz, "Kansas Bleeds in Cuba," in *Reading Territory*, 112–150.

77. See Reynolds, *John Brown*, 262–263; Du Bois, *John Brown*, 190–203; and McGlone, *John Brown's War*, 233–235. Hannah Geffert also suggests that Brown sought Delany's help not only because his leadership would help mobilize veterans of the Underground Railroad for Brown's plan, but also because Delany was from Jefferson County, Virginia, home to Harper's Ferry. Delany had also lived in Chambersburg, Pennsylvania, where Brown staged the raid. Delany had an intimate knowledge of the local terrain that would have provided essential intelligence for planning the raid. "John Brown and His Black Allies: An Ignored Alliance." *Pennsylvania Magazine of History and Biography* 126, no. 4 (2002): 598.

78. Gilroy, *Black Atlantic*, 20.

79. Delany, *Blake*, ed. McGann, 124.

80. Delany, *Blake*, ed. McGann, 102.

81. Delany, *Blake*, ed. McGann, 91.

82. Delany, *Blake*, ed. McGann, 95.

83. Delany, *Blake*, ed. McGann, 94.

84. Delany, *Blake*, ed. McGann, 97.

85. For more on the dispersal of the white population in slavery as a policing force, see Johnson, *River of Dark Dreams*, 209–243.

86. Delany, *Blake*, ed. McGann, 97.

87. Delany, *Blake*, ed. McGann, 112.

88. Delany, *Blake*, ed. McGann, 111.

89. Delany, *Blake*, ed. McGann, 111, 112.

90. Delany writes elsewhere: "The whole country is solemnly bound, in one confederated band, to riddle his breast with ten thousand balls. . . . [H]e is, with one universal voice, denounced in this country, as a rebel, insurrectionist, cut-throat; and all the powers of despotism, America in the foremost rank, sallies forth in one united crusade against him." "True Patriotism," *North Star*, December 8, 1848, in Levine, *Martin R. Delany: Documentary Reader*, 140.

91. Roger Whitlow reads this supernatural fugitivity as a weakness in representation. "The Revolutionary Black Novels of Martin R. Delany and Sutton Griggs," *Melus* 5, no. 3 (Autumn 1978): 28.

92. Delany, *Blake*, ed. McGann, 84.

93. Delany, *Blake*, ed. McGann, 70.

94. McGann, Introduction, xvi.

95. Britt Rusert, "Delany's Comet: Fugitive Science and the Speculative Imaginary of Emancipation." *American Quarterly* 65, no. 4 (2013): 820. For Rusert's book-length study on Delany and the broader context of nineteenth-century Black authors writing against scientific racism, see Britt Rusert, *Fugitive Science: Empiricism and Freedom in Early African American Culture* (New York: New York University Press, 2017).

96. Rusert, "Delany's Comet," 821.

97. Delany, *Blake*, ed. McGann, 113. The novel also shows how the one area in North America immune to white alliance policing is the Great Dismal Swamp, which is also represented through the speculative mode.

98. For more on the La Escalera slave conspiracy see Delany, *Blake*, ed. McGann, 326. On the novel's part 2 as speculative, Jennifer Brittan writes, "The inventions and anachronisms of the second half of the novel produce the kind of alternative history we associate with speculative fiction." See "Martin R. Delany's Speculative Fiction and the Nineteenth-Century Economy of Slave Conspiracy," *Studies in American Fiction* 46, no. 1 (2019): 79–102. See also Alex Zamalin, *Black Utopia: The History of an Idea from Black Nationalism to Afrofuturism* (New York: Columbia University Press, 2019).

99. See Fredric Jameson, *Archaeologies of the Future: The Desire Called Utopia and Other Science Fictions* (New York: Verso, 2005), xiii.

100. Delany, *Blake* ed. McGann, 277.

101. Gerald Horne, *Race to Revolution: The United States and Cuba During Slavery and Jim Crow* (New York: Monthly Review Press, 2014).

102. Delany, *Blake*, ed. McGann, 64.

103. Jeffory Clymer reads *Blake* as playing up these fears to suggest that annexation was causing revolt, not preventing it. "Martin Delany's *Blake* and the Transnational Politics of Property," *American Literary History* 15, no. 4 (2003): 709–731.

104. Delany, *Blake*, ed. McGann, 196.

105. Delany, *Blake*, ed. McGann, 245–247.

106. In this way, the novel also anticipates Horne's analysis of whiteness, which he argues emerged as an "alliance among Europeans of various class

backgrounds, all bound by petrified unity in reaction to the prospect of a slave rebellion that would liquidate them all." *Apocalypse*, 24.

107. Marx and Engels, "Manifesto of the Communist Party."

108. See Marx, *Capital*, 876.

109. Marx closely followed the Civil War and wrote about the role slave rebellion and abolition played in galvanizing European worker movements in the North and in Europe. After John Brown's raid on Harper's Ferry, Marx writes to Engels: "In my view, the most momentous thing happened in the world today is the slave movement—on the one hand, in America, started by the death of [John] Brown, and in Russia, on the other. . . . Should the affair grow serious by and by, what will become of Manchester?" See Karl Marx, "Marx to Engels, January 11, 1860," in *The Civil War in the United States*, ed. Angela Zimmerman (1937; New York: International Publishers, 2016), 17.

110. See Marx, *Capital*, 414.

111. See Karl Marx, "Marx, on Behalf of the International Working Men's Association, to President Abraham Lincoln," November 22, 1864, in *The Civil War in the United States*, ed. Angela Zimmerman (1937; New York: International Publishers, 2016), 154.

112. Marx, "President Lincoln," in Zimmerman, *Civil War in the United States*, 276.

113. Scholars believe Delany either didn't finish the novel, perhaps intentionally, or if he did, the last chapters detailing the insurrection have been lost. See Jared McGann, "Editor's Note," in *Blake*, ed. McGann, xxxv.

114. Delany, *Blake*, ed. McGann, 313.

115. Delany, *Blake*, ed. McGann, 312.

116. Delany, *Blake*, ed. McGann, 312.

117. Delany, *Blake*, ed. McGann, 313.

118. Susan Kay Gillman also reads *Blake*'s nonending as a productive gesture, arguing that it signals a "clarion call for future liberation." See "The Epistemology of Slave Conspiracy," *MFS Modern Fiction Studies* 49, no. 1 (Spring 2003): 111; and Alex Moskowitz, "The Racial Economy of Perception: Reading Black Sociality in the Nineteenth Century," *Novel: A Forum on Fiction* 56, no. 1 (May 2023): 1–20.

119. Moskowitz, "Racial Economy of Perception," 17.

120. Karl Marx, *Germany Ideology*, 1845, 2000, pt. 1, § A, Marxist Internet Archive, https://www.marxists.org/archive/marx/works/1845/german-ideology/.

121. See Stefano Harney and Fred Moten, *The Undercommons: Fugitive Planning and Black Study* (New York: Minor Compositions, 2013), 42–43.

2. ANTICOLONIAL WAR AND SETTLER MASS MILITARISM

1. Peter Linebaugh and Marcus Rediker, *The Many-Headed Hydra: Sailors, Slaves, Commoners, and the Hidden History of the Revolutionary Atlantic* (Boston: Beacon Press, 2013), 24.

2. Linebaugh and Rediker, *Many-Headed Hydra*, 34.

3. Linebaugh and Rediker, 33.

4. Iyko Day, "Eco-Criticism and Primitive Accumulation," in *After Marx: Literature, Theory, and Value in the Twenty-First Century*, ed. Colleen Lye and Christopher Nealon (Cambridge: Cambridge University Press, 2023); Day, *Alien Capital*; Dunbar-Ortiz, *Indigenous Peoples' History*; Estes, *Our History Is the Future*; and Glen S. Coulthard, *Red Skin, White Masks: Rejecting the Colonial Politics of Recognition* (Minneapolis: University of Minnesota Press, 2014); Barker, *Red Scare*; and Karuka, *Empire's Tracks*.

5. Estes et al., *Red Nation Rising*, 20.

6. Dunbar-Ortiz, *Indigenous Peoples' History*, 58.

7. John Grenier, *The First Way of War: American War Making on the Frontier, 1607–1814* (Cambridge: Cambridge University Press, 2005), 13.

8. Grenier, 32.

9. Grenier, 32–39.

10. Grenier, 41.

11. Grenier, 44.

12. Horne, *Counter-Revolution of 1776*. Similarly, Dunbar-Ortiz explains how British policies that restrained settler colonial expansion and settlers' ability to wage wars to destroy competing Indigenous nations are what, in part, motivated American settlers to revolt for their own nation-state. *Indigenous Peoples' History*, 74–76.

13. Winona LaDuke, *All Our Relations: Native Struggles for Land and Life* (Chicago: Haymarket Books, 2016), 45; and Monaco, *Second Seminole War*, 2.

14. LaDuke, *All Our Relations*, 47.

15. Monaco, *Second Seminole War*, 3.

16. Monaco, 118.

17. Monaco, 21–25.

18. Monaco, 47–49.

19. Monaco, 54.

20. Monaco, 55–58.

21. Monaco, 58.

22. Monaco, 54–59.

23. Ryan P. Hovatter, "The Florida Volunteers: Territorial Militia in the Opening of the Second Seminole War" (Master's thesis, US Army Command and General Staff College, 2021), 83–84.

24. Monaco, *Second Seminole War*, 60–61.

25. Monaco, 73–80.

26. Monaco, 110–112, 123–125.

27. LaDuke, *All Our Relations*, 52–59.

28. Monaco, *Second Seminole War*, 116.

29. Laurel Clark Shire, *The Threshold of Manifest Destiny: Gender and National Expansion in Florida* (Philadelphia: University of Pennsylvania Press, 2016), 14–16.

30. Shire, 138–144.

31. Shire, 156.

32. Shire, 164.

33. Shire, 169–171.

34. Shire, 178.

35. Shire, 178.

36. *An Authentic Narrative of the Seminole War; and of the Miraculous Escape of Mrs. Mary Godfrey, and Her Four Female Children: Annexed Is a Minute Detail of the Horrid Massacres of the Whites, by the Indians and Negroes, in Florida, in the Months of December, January and February* (New York: Printed for D. F. Blanchard and others, 1836).

37. Samuel Warner, *Authentic and Impartial Narrative of the Tragical Scene Which Was Witnessed in Southampton County (Virginia) on Monday the 22d of August Last, when Fifty- Five of Its Inhabitants (Mostly Women and Children) Were Inhumanly Massacred by the Blacks! Communicated by Those Who Were Eye Witnesses of the Bloody Scene, and Confirmed by the Confessions of Several of the Blacks while under Sentence of Death* (New York: Printed for Warner & West, 1831).

38. *Narrative of the Massacre, by the Savages, of the Wife & Children of Thomas Baldwin* (New York: Martin & Perry, 1836).

39. Alexander Mazzaferro, "'A Nat Turner in Every Family': Exemplarity and Exceptionality in the Print Circulation of Slave Revolt," *J19: The Journal of Nineteenth-Century Americanists* 10, no. 2 (Fall 2022): 267–303. See also Jim Cusick, "Hidden Meanings in a Second Seminole War Pamphlet," *University of Florida Special & Area Studies Collections Blog*, n.d., https://ufsasc.domains.uflib .ufl.edu/hidden-meanings-second-seminole-war-pamphlet-florida/.

40. Walkiewicz, *Reading Territory*, 87.

41. *Authentic Narrative of the Seminole War*, 3.

42. See Michele Currie Navakas, *Liquid Landscape: Geography and Settlement at the Edge of Early America* (Philadelphia: University of Pennsylvania Press, 2017), 105.

43. *Authentic Narrative of the Seminole War*, 10.

44. *Authentic Narrative of the Seminole War*, 12.

45. Mazzaferro, "'Nat Turner in Every Family,'" 295.

46. Navakas, *Liquid Landscape*, 105–111.

47. See also Brigitte Fielder's reading of the Blanchard pamphlet in which she highlights how it mobilizes "white innocence" and "vulnerability" to conceal how white settlers are "beneficiaries of the settler colonialist violence done to Native people." At the same time, the scene also expresses a "cross-racial sympathy" that could "be described as a shared relation not to power but to place" in the "fugitive space" of the swamp in which Godfrey and her children are hiding. *Relative Races: Genealogies of Interracial Kinship in Nineteenth-Century America* (Durham, NC: Duke University Press, 2020), 195–200, Kindle.

48. *Authentic Narrative of the Seminole War*, 5–7.

49. Mary Rowlandson, *A Narrative of the Captivity and Restoration of Mrs. Mary Rowlandson* (Cambridge, MA, 1682).

50. *Authentic Narrative of the Seminole War*, 6–11

51. Walkiewicz, *Reading Territory*, 90.

52. *Authentic Narrative of the Seminole War*, 24.

53. Treaty of Guadalupe Hidalgo, 1848, National Archives, www.archives .gov/milestone-documents/treaty-of-guadalupe-hidalgo.

54. For histories of the US colonization of California, see Brendan C. Lindsay, *Murder State: California's Native American Genocide, 1846–1873* (Lincoln:

University of Nebraska Press, 2012); Benjamin Madley, *An American Genocide: The United States and the California Indian Catastrophe, 1846–1873* (New Haven, CT: Yale University Press, 2016); Jack D. Forbes, *Native Americans of California and Nevada*, rev. ed. (Happy Camp, CA: Naturegraph Publishers, 1993); and Clifford E. Trafzer and Joel R. Hyer. *Exterminate Them: Written Accounts of the Murder, Rape, and Slavery of Native Americans during the California Gold Rush, 1848–1868* (East Lansing: Michigan State University Press, 1999). Madley notes that "during 1849, more than 65,000 emigrants—often heavily armed, experienced with paramilitary organizations, and full of fear and hatred toward Indians—arrived in California." *American Genocide*, 84.

55. Madley, *American Genocide*, 3; and Damon B. Akins and William J. Bauer Jr., *We Are the Land* (Oakland: University of California Press, 2021), 128.

56. Akins and Bauer, *We Are the Land*, 133.

57. Akins and Bauer, 139.

58. Akins and Bauer, 141. See also Bill Tripp, "Our Land Was Taken. But We Still Hold the Knowledge of How to Stop Mega-Fires," *Guardian*, September 16, 2020, www.theguardian.com/commentisfree/2020/sep/16/california-wildfires-cultural-burns-indigenous-people.

59. Akins and Bauer note that it is estimated that between 1850 and 1863 US settlers held between ten and twenty thousand Indigenous people in slavery. *We Are the Land*, 141–142.

60. Akins and Bauer, 135.

61. Akins and Bauer, 128–131.

62. See the case in which Pomo workers coordinated to kill their settler bosses, Andrew Kelsey and Charles Stone, and Cahuilla leaders who attacked J. J. Warner's ranch. Akins and Bauer, *We Are the Land*, 136, 150.

63. Akins and Bauer, 151–153.

64. See William Edward Evans, "The Garra Uprising: Conflict Between San Diego Indians and Settlers in 1851," *California Historical Society Quarterly* 45, no. 4 (1966): 339–349; Lindsay, *Murder State*, 155–161; and Akins and Bauer, *We Are the Land*, 150–151.

65. Joshua Bean, quoted in Lindsay, *Murder State*, 158–159.

66. Madley, *American Genocide*, 12.

67. See Forbes, *Native Americans of California*. See also Joanne Barker, who cites Forbes's observation of the mass character of the US conquest of

California in support of her argument that the state's strategy of characterizing Indigenous resistance as terrorism receives broad public support as a legacy of this mass character. *Red Scare*, 29.

68. Madley, *American Genocide*, 174.

69. Akins and Bauer, *We Are the Land*, 137.

70. Lindsay, *Murder State*, 209.

71. Lindsay, 210.

72. Lindsay writes that "the volunteer company, composed of citizen-soldiers who elected their captain and lieutenants, was the epitome of democracy in martial form," 149.

73. "Racism and the Law," 1862, Digital History Online Archive, www.digital history.uh.edu/disp_textbook.cfm?smtid=3&psid=17.

74. For sources on the life of Glanton, see Ralph A. Smith, "Glanton, John Joel," rev. Sloan Rodgers, in *Handbook of Texas* (1952; Texas State Historical Association, 1952, 2024), www.tshaonline.org/handbook/entries/glanton-john -joel; Samuel E. Chamberlain, *My Confession: Recollections of a Rogue* (New York: Harper & Brothers, 1956); and Lindsay, *Murder State*, 137–144. Cormac McCarthy's *Blood Meridian* (New York: Random House, 1985) novelizes the story of the Glanton gang and their mercenary violence in Mexico.

75. Lindsay, *Murder State*, 139.

76. Lindsay, 140–141.

77. Madely writes: "Ranger militia operations provided a widely publicized state endorsement of Indian killing, communicating an unofficial grant of legal impunity for Indian killing, and eroding cultural and moral barriers to the homicide and mass murder of Indians. Simultaneously, the money, arms, and material showered on ranger militias inspired vigilantes to mount their own Indian-hunting operations in hopes of becoming similarly well-supplied and well-funded ranger militia companies. By funding, arming, and supplying militias—and, moreover, allowing them to kill Indians—state and federal officials increased the frequency, size, lethality, and geographic scope of Indian-hunting operations." *American Genocide*, 175.

78. John Rollin Ridge, *The Life and Adventures of Joaquín Murieta: The Celebrated California Bandit*, ed. Hsuan L. Hsu (1854; New York: Penguin Books, 2018). See also John Rollin Ridge, *The Life and Adventures of Joaquín Murieta, the Celebrated California Bandit* (1854; Norman: University of Oklahoma Press, 1955).

79. Hsuan L. Hsu, introduction to *Life and Adventures of Joaquín Murieta*, xv–xvi.

80. Ridge, *JM*, ed. Hsu, 117.

81. James W. Parins, *John Rollin Ridge: His Life and Works* (Lincoln: University of Nebraska Press, 2004).

82. Russell Thornton, "Cherokee Population Losses During the Trail of Tears: A New Perspective and a New Estimate," *Ethnohistory* 31, no. 4 (1984): 289–300.

83. For histories that center Murieta's anticolonial rebellion, see Pedro G. Castillo and Albert Camarillo, *Furia y Muerte: Los Bandidos Chicanos* (Los Angeles: Aztlán Publications, 1973); and Eric Hobsbawm, *Bandits* (New York: New Press, 2000). Castillo and Camarillo argue that "forced into a life that was outside of the newly imposed Anglo-American law," Murieta's rebellion "was a banditry in the form of retribution and for the purpose of survival" (2). Hobsbawm analyzes Murieta as a peasant revolutionary. For a complete historical account of Joaquín Murieta, see Bruce S. Thornton's *Searching for Joaquín: Myth, Murieta, and History in California* (San Francisco: Encounter Books, 2003).

84. As critics have noted, there were at least five men named Joaquín who were wanted for alleged crimes against US settlers at the time. For more on this, see Thornton, *Searching for Joaquín*.

85. Quoted in Luis Leal, introduction to *Life and Adventures of the Celebrated Bandit Joaquin Murrieta: His Exploits in the State of California*, by. Ireneo Paz, trans. Francisco A. Lomelí and Miguel R. López (Houston: Arte Publica Press, 2001), xiii.

86. For more on the historical and literary origins of Three-Fingered Jack as a Jamaican maroon, see Erica Stevens, "Three-Fingered Jack and the Severed Literary History of John Rollin Ridge's *The Life and Adventures of Joaquín Murieta*," *ESQ* 61, no. 1 (2015): 73–112.

87. Settlers offered showings of Murieta's head for $1 as a macabre colonial spectacle. See the flyer advertising one of these showings in Stockton, California: "Head of Joaquin Murrieta," Tessa: Digital Collections of the Los Angeles Public Library, https://tessa2.lapl.org/digital/collection/photos/id/101082. See also Timothy Donahue, "Joaquín's Head: Theatrical Punishment, Public Address, and Novelistic Politics in the United States–Mexico Borderlands," *J19* 4, no. 2 (2016): 391–417.

88. See Frank Latta, *Joaquín Murrieta and His Horse Gangs* (Santa Cruz: Bear State Books, 1980); and Alyssa Pereira, "One of SF's Earliest Cons Was a Fake Doctor and His Horrific 'Museum of Anatomy,'" *San Francisco Gate*, May 29, 2018, www.sfgate.com/sfhistory/article/Dr-louis-j-Jordan-museum-anatomy-san-francisco-12945116.php.

89. Hsu, introduction, xvi.

90. Louis Owens writes that the novel "stands as a fascinating testimony to the conflicts and tensions within the mixed blood author, who moves easily inside the dominant culture but cannot forget or forgive the denigration by that culture of his indigenous self." *Other Destinies: Understanding the American Indian Novel* (Norman: University of Oklahoma Press, 1994), 32–33.

91. For a summary of how scholarly criticism has characterized *Joaquín Murieta* as a novel of either resistance or assimilation, see Sean Teuton, "The Indigenous Novel," in *The Oxford Handbook of Indigenous American Literature*, ed. James H. Cox and Daniel Heath Justice (Oxford: Oxford University Press, 2014), 318–331. For readings that interpret *Joaquín Murieta* as a novel of assimilation, see Peter G. Christensen, "Minority Interaction in John Rollin Ridge's *The Life and Adventures of Joaquín Murieta*," *Melus* 17, no. 2 (1992), 61–72; John Lowe, "Joaquín Murieta, Mexican History, and Popular Myths of Freedom," *Journal of Popular Culture* 35, no. 2 (2001): 25–39; John Carlos Rowe, "Highway Robbery: 'Indian Removal,' the Mexican-American War, and American Identity in *The Life and Adventures of Joaquín Murieta*," *Novel: A Forum on Fiction* 31, no. 2 (1998): 149–173; and Joe Goeke, "Yellow Bird and the Bandit: Minority Authorship, Class, and Audience in John Rollin Ridge's *The Life and Adventures of Joaquín Murieta*," *Western American Literature* 37, no. 4 (2003): 453–478. For readings that interpret *Joaquín Murieta* as a novel of resistance, see Owens, *Other Destinies*; Cheryl Walker, *Indian Nation: Native American Literature and Nineteenth-Century Nationalisms* (Durham, NC: Duke University Press, 1997); Jesse Alemán, "Assimilation and the Decapitated Body Politics in *The Life and Adventures of Joaquín Murieta*," *Arizona Quarterly* 59. 1 (2004): 71–98; Maria Mondragon, "'The (Safe) White Side of the Line': History and Disguise in John Rollin Ridge's *The Life and Adventures of Joaquín Murieta, the Celebrated California Bandit*," *American Transcendental Quarterly* 8, no. 3 (1994), 173–187; Molly Crumpton Winter, "Culture-Tectonics: California Statehood and John Rollin Ridge's *Joaquín Murieta*," *Western American Literature* 43, no. 3 (2008): 259–276; and James H. Cox, *Muting White Noise:*

Native American and European American Novel Traditions (Norman: University of Oklahoma Press, 2006).

92. Shelley Streeby, *American Sensations: Class, Empire, and the Production of Popular Culture* (Berkeley: University of California Press, 2002), 263.

93. Ridge, *JM*, ed. Hsu, 7.

94. My reading of the novel's formal structure builds on Owen's early reading, in which he argues, "Ridge's *Joaquín Murieta* can be seen as intensely dialogic, a hybridized narrative within which the author is in dialogue with himself, within which two distinct linguistic consciousnesses, two kinds of discourse, coexist in a 'dialogically agitated and tension-filled environment.'" *Other Destinies*, 35. Lori Merish similarly reads the novel's form in terms of hybridization: "Written about the shifting (inter)national borderland of California, Ridge's novel enacts cultural hybridization in its very medium of expression, defying literary classification and foregrounding the instability of formal, generic, and linguistic cultural boundaries." "Print, Cultural Memory, and John Rollin Ridge's *The Life and Adventures of Joaquín Murieta, the Celebrated California Bandit*," *Arizona Quarterly* 59, no. 4 (2003): 52.

95. John Havard studies Ridge's representation of Murieta's elitism, arguing that "in speaking for the concerns of Mexicans and the Cherokee, Ridge advocates for a world in which exceptional, cosmopolitan peoples of color have the opportunity to rise to the social and economic rank warranted by their elite capacities," and that "against the identity-based ideologies he saw at work in Cherokee Removal, the laws of 1850s California, and sensation fiction, Ridge reproclaims the Enlightenment message that access to a liberal way of life should be open to all." "John Rollin Ridge's *Joaquín Murieta*: Sensation, Hispanicism, and Cosmopolitanism," *Western American Literature* 49, no. 4 (2015): 323, 343.

96. Ridge, *JM*, ed. Hsu, 8.

97. Ridge, *JM*, ed. Hsu, 8.

98. Ridge, *JM*, ed. Hsu, 9.

99. Ridge, *JM*, ed. Hsu, 9.

100. David Drysdale examines how the language of bandit and outlaw was used to racialize Mexican insurgency. The racializing of Mexican insurgency as criminal legitimized counterinsurgent violence. Drysdale argues that Ridge's novel depicts how counterinsurgent violence shapes the meanings of

US citizenship and US state sovereignty. "Ridge's *Joaquín Murieta*: Banditry, Counterinsurgency, and Colonial Power after Guadalupe-Hidalgo," *Canadian Review of American Studies* 46, no. 1 (2016): 62–85.

101. Ridge, *JM*, ed. Hsu, 10.

102. Ridge, *JM*, ed. Hsu, 11–12.

103. Ridge, *JM*, ed. Hsu, 12.

104. Ridge, *JM*, ed. Hsu, 13.

105. See Rowe, "Highway Robbery," 159; and Havard, "Ridge's *Joaquín Murieta*," 338.

106. Ridge, *JM*, ed. Hsu, 136.

107. Mark Rifkin reads the novel's ending as a warning to readers of the potential for future unrest among the populations that US settler colonialism dominates: "Instead of generating anything resembling a program for change, the effect of the novel's deferral of (political) resolution and multiplication of implicit referents is to leave the reader with a sense of the (geopolitical) porousness of the nation and the potential for violence that inheres in the existence of numerous conquered, alienated, and racialized collectivities within U.S. borders." "'For the Wrongs of Our Poor Bleeding Country': Sensation, Class, and Empire in Ridge's *Joaquín Murieta*," *Arizona Quarterly* 65, no. 2 (2009): 40.

108. Ridge, *JM*, ed. Hsu, 14.

109. Ridge, *JM*, ed. Hsu, 95–96.

110. Ridge, *JM*, ed. Hsu, 65–66.

111. Ridge, *JM*, ed. Hsu, 23–24.

112. Cheryl Walker argues that Chinese laborers in the novel serve as an allegory for Indigenous people "who were also slaughtered in large numbers even when they did not resist." *Indian Nation*, 129–130.

113. Ridge, *JM*, ed. Hsu, 56.

114. Ridge, *JM*, ed. Hsu, 84–85.

115. Ridge, *JM*, ed. Hsu, 125–126.

116. Ridge, *JM*, ed. Hsu, 67–69.

117. Ridge, *JM*, ed. Hsu, 29–30.

118. Alemán, "Assimilation and Decapitated Body Politics," 87.

119. Alemán writes, "*Murieta* undermines its author's ostensible assimilationist position and reveals instead the cultural and physical violence American

ideologies perform on individual and collective racial bodies that emulate American ideals." "Assimilation and Decapitated Body Politics," 73–74, 91.

120. Ridge, *JM*, ed. Hsu, 15.

121. Ridge, ed. Hsu, *JM*, 15.

122. Ridge, ed. Hsu, *JM*, 127.

3. WHITE INSURGENCY

1. Du Bois, *Black Reconstruction in America.*

2. Union Republican Congressional Committee, *Homes for the Homeless: What the Republican Party Has Done for the Poor Man* (Washington, DC: Great Republic Office, 1868), /www.loc.gov/ resource/rbpe.2050240b.

3. Union Republican Congressional Committee, *Homes for the Homeless.*

4. Hannah L. Anderson, "That Settles It: The Debate and Consequences of the Homestead Act of 1862," *History Teacher* 45, no. 1 (November 2011): 120.

5. Union Republican Congressional Committee, *Homes for the Homeless.*

6. Here I build on the work of Walter Johnson, who explores white equality in his study of Thomas Hart Benton. See *The Broken Heart of America: St. Louis and the Violent History of the United States* (New York: Basic Books, 2020), 41–52.

7. Eric Foner, *Free Soil, Free Labor, Free Men: The Ideology of the Republican Party before the Civil War* (Oxford: Oxford University Press, 1971), 19–20.

8. Roediger, *Wages of Whiteness*; and Joel Olson, *The Abolition of White Democracy* (Minneapolis: University of Minnesota Press, 2004).

9. Foner, *Free Soil, Free Labor,* 14–17.

10. Du Bois, "The White Worker," in *Black Reconstruction*; and Roediger, *Wages of Whiteness.*

11. Foner, *Free Soil, Free Labor,* 32.

12. Roediger, *Wages of Whiteness,* 66–73.

13. Marx writes, "So long . . . as the worker can accumulate for himself—and this he can do so long as he remains in possession of his means of production—capitalist accumulation and the capitalist mode of production are impossible. The class of wage-labourers essential to these is lacking." *Capital,* 933.

14. Marx, *Capital,* 934.

15. For more on how free labor ideology proponents considered public lands a safety valve for managing class conflict, see Foner, *Free Soil, Free Labor*, 27.

16. Dunbar-Ortiz, *Indigenous Peoples' History*, 82.

17. Johnson, *River of Dark Dreams*, 24.

18. John Suval, *Dangerous Ground: Squatters, Statesmen, and the Antebellum Rupture of American Democracy* (New York: Oxford University Press, 2022), 43.

19. Suval, 22.

20. Suval, 24–26.

21. Dunbar-Ortiz, *Indigenous Peoples' History*, 99.

22. Dunbar-Ortiz, *Indigenous Peoples' History*, 107–110.

23. Suval, *Dangerous Ground*, 26.

24. Suval, 41.

25. Suval, 28.

26. For more on Thomas Hart Benton's aggressive support for white equality, see Johnson, *Broken Heart of America*, 41–52; 113–115.

27. Quoted in Suval, *Dangerous Ground*, 25.

28. James W. Covington, "The Armed Occupation Act of 1842," *Florida Historical Quarterly* 40, no. 1 (July 1961): 45.

29. Glen Boggs, "Free Florida Land: Homesteading for Good Title," *Florida Bar Journal* (January 2009): 14.

30. Covington, "Armed Occupation Act," 42.

31. Quoted in Covington, 42.

32. Quoted in Covington, 45.

33. Covington, 163.

34. Marx and Engels, "Manifesto of the Communist Party," 54.

35. Mark A. Lause, *Young America: Land, Labor, and the Republican Community* (Urbana: University of Illinois Press, 2005), 3.

36. Lause, 19.

37. Roediger, *Wages of Whiteness*, 71–73.

38. See the circular "Vote Yourself a Farm," distributed by the *True Workingman*, January 24, 1846, quoted in *A Documentary History of American Industrial Society: Labor Movement*, ed. John R. Commons, Ulrich B. Phillips, Eugene A. Gilmore, Helen L. Sumner, and John B. Andrews (Cleveland, OH: Arthur H. Clark, 1910), 305–307.

39. "Vote Yourself a Farm."

40. Lause, *Young America*, 31–35, 46, 110, 234.

41. Lause, 80.

42. Foner, *Free Soil, Free Labor*, 265–268; and Johnson, *Broken Heart of America*.

43. Lause, *Young America*, 46.

44. Johnson, *Broken Heart of America*; Foner, *Free Soil, Free Labor*, 266–274.

45. Stephen C. Foster, "Republican Land Policy—Homes for the Million." April 24, 1860, in *Landmark Debates in Congress: From the Declaration of Independence to the War in Iraq*, ed. Stephen W. Stathis (Washington, DC: CQ Press, 2008), 160.

46. Foster, "Republican Land Policy," 157.

47. Foster, "Republican Land Policy," 158.

48. Johnson, *River of Dark Dreams*, 363–365.

49. Johnson, *River of Dark Dreams*, 14–15.

50. William Walker, *War in Nicaragua* (Mobile, AL: S. H. Goetzel, 1860), 23.

51. Walker, 22.

52. Robert E. May, *Manifest Destiny's Underworld: Filibustering in Antebellum America* (Chapel Hill: University of North Carolina Press, 2002).

53. Walker, *War in Nicaragua*, 62.

54. Walker, 21–22.

55. Walker, 21–22.

56. Walker, 23.

57. Walker, 430.

58. May, *Manifest Destiny's Underworld*, 97.

59. May, 99.

60. May, 100.

61. Johnson writes further that "these were men who had been circulated through the commercial economy of the 1850s and been washed up on its hard shoals without anything but their own sense of having been done wrong— their own sense that they deserved something better. They were incomplete and aggrieved white men in search of a stake in the future, for which they could exchange their own race- and sex-based sense of entitlement." *River of Dark Dreams*, 389.

62. Walker, *Du Bow's Review*, 1857, quoted in Johnson, *River of Dark Dreams*, 393.

63. Johnson, *River of Dark Dreams*, 393.

64. "Nicaragua was a place," writes Johnson, "where wounded white men might, in victory, repair themselves and become once again whole, their personal and racial destiny completed by the addition of a black slave; or where, in defeat, they might sink back into the somnolent condition of the lesser races." *River of Dark Dreams*, 394.

65. Walker, *War in Nicaragua*, 25.

66. Walker, 25.

67. William Walker, "Nicaragua: Speech of General WM. Walker," *New York Times*, February 2, 1858.

68. Walker.

69. Walker.

70. Walker.

71. See Horne, *Counter-Revolution of 1776*.

72. Walker, "Walker the Filibuster," *Liberator*, July 3, 1857.

73. Johnson, *River of Dark Dreams*, 376.

74. An Act for Enrolling and Calling Out the National Forces, and for Other Purposes. 37th Cong., 3d. Sess., Cong. Rec., chs. 74, 75 (March 3, 1863).

75. Iver Bernstein, *The New York City Draft Riots: Their Significance for American Society and Politics in the Age of the Civil War* (New York: Oxford University Press, 1991).

76. Adrian Cook, *The Armies of the Streets: The New York City Draft Riots of 1863* (Lexington: University Press of Kentucky, 1974).

77. Bernstein, *Draft Riots*, 18.

78. Leslie M. Harris, *In the Shadow of Slavery: African Americans in New York City, 1626–1863*. (Chicago: University of Chicago Press, 2003), 280–282.

79. Bernstein, *Draft Riots*.

80. Bernstein, 29.

81. Cook, *Armies of the Streets*, 134.

82. Cook, 88–90, 129; and Bernstein, *Draft Riots*, 21.

83. Cook, 72–73, 123–126.

84. Cook, 176.

85. Cook, 175.

86. Cook, 177–180.

87. Cook, 197.

88. Cook, 174.

89. Bernstein, *Draft Riots*, 114–123.

90. Cook, *Armies of the Streets*, 205–206.

4. ABOLITION SHOOTS BACK

1. Jackson, *Force and Freedom*, 87–90.

2. According to Louis Decaro's study, Green first met Brown in early April 1859 during one of the visits Brown made to Douglass's home in Rochester en route to New York. Louis A. Decaro Jr., *The Untold Story of Shields Green: The Life and Death of a Harper's Ferry Raider* (New York: New York University Press, 2022), 31–32.

3. Osborne Perry Anderson, *A Voice from Harper's Ferry: A Narrative of Events at Harper's Ferry* (Boston, 1861).

4. Frederick Douglass, *The Life and Times of Frederick Douglass: His Early Life as a Slave, His Escape from Bondage, and His Complete History* (Hartford, CT: Park, 1883), 276–279.

5. For more on how Black thinkers have understood Brown, see Brigitte Fielder, "Black Madness, White Violence, and John Brown's Legacy," *American Literary History* 35, no. 4 (2021): 1799–1809.

6. John Brown, "Note to Jailer," in Stauffer and Trodd, *Tribunal*, 73.

7. Du Bois, *John Brown*, 254.

8. For studies that focus on abolition war, see Sinha, *Slave's Cause*; Jackson, *American Radicals*; and McGlone, *John Brown's War*.

9. Marx and Engels, "The Manifesto of the Communist Party."

10. Amilcar Cabral, "The Weapon of Theory," Havana, 1966, Marxist Internet Archive, www.marxists.org/subject/africa/cabral/1966/weapon-theory.htm.

11. Du Bois, *John Brown*, 71.

12. Du Bois, *John Brown*, 87.

13. Sinha, *Slave's Cause*, 500.

14. Frederick Douglass, "Speech: Frederick Douglass on John Brown," Boston, 1860, https://blackagendareport.com/speech-frederick-douglass-john-brown-1860.

15. Delany, *Martin R. Delany*, 183–184.

16. Stauffer, *Black Hearts of Men*, 163.

17. Quoted in Stauffer, *Black Hearts*; and James McCune, *Frederick Douglass Paper*, August 8, 1856, 252.

18. William Wells Brown, "John Brown and the Fugitive Slave Law," *Independent*, March 10, 1870, https://archive.wvculture.org/history/jbexhibit/ww brown.html.

19. John Brown, "Words of Advice," in Stauffer and Trodd, *Tribunal*, 8.

20. See Wynter, "Unsettling the Coloniality"; and Hartman, *Scenes of Subjection*.

21. Robert Williams and Mabel Williams, *Negroes with Guns* (New York: Marzani & Munsell, 1962); and Fanon, *Wretched of the Earth*.

22. Brown, "Words of Advice," 9.

23. Brown, "Words of Advice," 10.

24. Brown, "John Brown and the Fugitive Slave Law."

25. Richard J. Hinton, *John Brown and His Men* (New York: Funk & Wagnalls, 1894), 66.

26. "Brown was tremendously affected by the Haitian Revolution and Nat Turner's rebellion," writes Jackson. "Such events changed the way he perceived slavery's probable demise. As a result, he studied insurrectionary warfare and became well versed about the island of Saint-Domingue and its inhabitants' success in defeating the French. Haiti's influence did not end with the early slave rebellions of the nineteenth century." Jackson also points out that "throughout Brown's extensive travel to cities such as Boston, Rochester, Chicago, Concord, Philadelphia, Oberlin, Providence, New York, and Canada, he sought black guidance and support. And it was during his meetings and visits that Brown was mentored and counseled. Only through these relationships could Brown begin and complete his vision." *Force and Freedom*, 86, 89.

27. Franklin B. Sanborn, *The Life and Letters of John Brown: Liberator of Kansas and Martyr of Virginia* (Boston: Robert Brothers, 1891), 136.

28. James Redpath, *The Public Life of Capt. John Brown* (Boston: Thayer and Eldridge, 1860), 206.

29. Du Bois, *John Brown*, 204.

30. Reynolds, *John Brown*, 87.

31. Douglass, *Life and Times*, 239.

32. Du Bois, *John Brown*, 208.

33. Douglass, *Life and Times*, 239.

34. For more on how Fanon theorizes the dialectics of colonized peoples' revolt against the colonizer and how this compels a recognition of their humanity, see Geo Maher's pivotal reading of Fanon's dialectics. *Decolonizing Dialectics* (Durham, NC: Duke University Press, 2017).

35. Douglass, *Life and Times*, 239.

36. Karl Marx, "The Nature and Growth of Capital," in *Wage Labour and Capital*, n.d., Marxist Internet Archive, www.marxists.org/archive/marx/works/1847/wage-labour/ch05.htm.

37. Douglass, *Life and Times*, 239.

38. Douglass, *Life and Times*, 239.

39. Quoted in Redpath, *Public Life*, 204.

40. Quoted in Redpath, *Public Life*, 204.

41. For Southern responses to Brown's raid, see Stauffer and Trodd, "Southern Responses," in *Tribunal*, 233–345.

42. See Jackson, *Force and Freedom*, 101–102.

43. For a comprehensive study of the lives of the Black members of Brown's group, see Eugene L. Meyer, *Five for Freedom: The African American Soldiers in John Brown's Army* (Chicago: Lawrence Hill Books, 2018).

44. Meyer, *Five for Freedom*, 53.

45. See Marx, *Class Struggles in France*; Marx, *The Civil War in France*, 1871, Marxist Internet Archive, www.marxists.org/archive/marx/works/1871/civil-war-france/.

46. This changed at the onset of the Civil War, when many exiled European communists joined the abolition war cause, becoming leaders in the Union Army. See Zimmerman, introduction to *Civil War in the United State*, xxii.

47. Anderson, *Voice from Harper's Ferry*, 33–34.

48. Anderson, 34.

49. Anderson, 34.

50. Anderson, 35.

51. Anderson, 31.

52. Anderson, 39.

53. Hamilton, "Nat Turner Insurrection," 192–193.

54. Fielder, Smith, and Spires, introduction to "*Weekly Anglo-African and The Pine and Palm.*" See also Benjamin Fagan, *The Black Newspaper and the Chosen Nation* (Athens: University of Georgia Press, 2016).

55. Benjamin Fagan, "Emancipated Illustrated," in *Visions of Glory: The Civil War in Word and Image*, ed. Kathleen Diffley and Benjamin Fagan (Athens: University of Georgia Press, 2019), 99–100.

56. Fagan, 102–104.

57. John Brown, "Provisional Constitution and Ordinances for the People of the United States," in Stauffer and Trodd, *Tribunal*, 27.

58. Reynolds, *John Brown*, 114.

59. Quoted in Redpath, *Public Life*, 204.

60. Lenin defined the dual power of the revolutionary party in terms of "a revolutionary dictatorship, i.e., a power directly based on revolutionary seizure, on the direct initiative of the people from below, and not on a law enacted by a centralised state power." V. I. Lenin, "Dual Power," *Pravda*, no. 28 (April 9, 1917), www.marxists.org/archive/lenin/works/1917/apr/09.htm. For Lenin's theory of the revolutionary party, see V. I. Lenin, *What Is to Be Done?*, 1902, Marxist Internet Archive, www.marxists.org/archive/lenin/works/1901/witbd/.

61. V. I. Lenin, *State and Revolution* (1918; Chicago: Haymarket Books, 2014), 62.

62. Anderson, *Voice from Harper's Ferry*, 36.

63. Anderson, 40.

64. Reynolds, *John Brown*, 187–191.

65. Sinha, *Slave's Cause*, 548.

66. Reynolds, *John Brown*, 168–174.

67. Reynolds, 175.

68. Quoted in Reynolds, 195.

69. Quoted in Reynolds, 174.

70. John Brown, "Old Brown's Parallels," *New York Tribune*, January 28, 1859, https://archive.wvculture.org/history/jbexhibit/parallels.html.

71. Brown, "Old Brown's Parallels."

72. Du Bois, *John Brown*, 146.

73. Du Bois, 147.

74. Du Bois, 147.

75. Reynolds, *John Brown*, 204.

76. Reynolds, 12.

77. See Brown, "Provisional Constitution"; and John Brown, "Interview with Senator Mason and Others," in Stauffer and Trodd, *Tribunal*.

78. Brown, "Provisional Constitution," 37.

79. Reynolds, *John Brown*, 263–264. For more on the Chatham Convention's deliberations, see also Richard Realf's testimony before the Senate committee investigating the Harper's Ferry raid in Jason M. Mason, *Senate Select Committee Report on the Harper's Ferry Invasion*, 90–113; McGlone, *John Brown's War*, 233–241; and Anderson, *Voice from Harper's Ferry*, 7–13.

80. Jackson, *Force and Freedom*, 105.

81. Beverly Lowry, *Harriet Tubman: Imagining a Life.* (New York: Doubleday, 2007), 235.

82. James Hamilton, "John Brown in Canada," *Canadian Magazine*, December 1894.

83. Kristen Tegtmeier Oertel, *Harriet Tubman: Slavery, the Civil War, and Civil Rights in the Nineteenth Century* (New York: Routledge, 2016), 45.

84. Quoted in Sara Bradford, *Harriet: The Moses of Her People* (New York: Geo. R. Lockwood & Son, 1897), 117.

85. Lowry, *Harriet Tubman*, 250.

86. Lee shows how Tubman's militancy has been hidden in the open through strategies of overrepresenting and memorializing her as a feminized charity worker. Butch Lee, *Jailbreak Out of History: The Re-Biography of Harriet Tubman* (Montreal: Kersplebedeb Publishing, 2015), 7, 5.

87. Fanon, *Wretched of the Earth*.

88. Humez, *Harriet Tubman*, 25.

89. Bradford, *Scenes in the Life*, 20.

90. Bradford, 20.

91. Bradford, 36.

92. Bradford, 14–15.

93. Douglass, *Life and Times*, 238.

94. Bradford, *Scenes in the Life*, 80.

95. Tubman told Bradford she completed nineteen raids, but some historians believe there were fewer. Of course, underground activity does not always leave a record for historians.

96. Du Bois, *Black Reconstruction*, 13.

97. Du Bois, "The General Strike," in *Black Reconstruction*.

98. Oertel, *Harriet Tubman*, 47.

99. Bradford, *Scenes in the Life*, 25.

100. Bradford, 25.

101. Du Bois, *Black Reconstruction*, 13–15.

102. See Marx, "The Working Day," in *Capital*, 340–411; and "The General Law of Capitalist Accumulation," in *Capital*, 762–854.

103. This was Marx and Engels's vision of the European proletariat in 1848 when they published the *Communist Manifesto*.

104. Frederick Douglass, "The Mission of the War: A Lecture," *New York Tribune*, January 14, 1864.

105. Oertel, *Harriet Tubman*, 59.

106. Bradford, *Scenes in the Life*, 39.

107. Bradford, 39–41.

108. See Tubman's letter to Sanborn in Bradford, 42.

109. Bradford, 42.

110. Bradford, 42.

111. Walter Rodney, "Marxism and Third World Ideology," in *Decolonial Marxism: Essays from the Pan-African Revolution* (London: Verso Books, 2022), 52–73.

112. Du Bois, *John Brown*, 226–300.

113. Reynolds, *John Brown*, 82.

114. Central Intelligence Agency, "Honoring Harriet Tubman: A Symbol of Freedom and an Intelligence Pioneer," September 7, 2022, www.cia.gov/stories/story/honoring-pioneer-harriet-tubman/.

115. Lenin, *State and Revolution*, 41.

CONCLUSION. WHITE COUNTERREVOLUTION TODAY

1. Marx, *Capital*, 793–799.

2. For critical studies of capitalism's accumulation crisis, see Gilmore, *Golden Gulag*; Mike Davis, *Planet of Slums* (London: Verso, 2006); Frederic Jameson, *Representing Capital: A Commentary on Volume One* (London, Verso, 2013); and Giovanni Arrighi, *The Long Twentieth Century: Money, Power, and the Origins of Our Times* (London: Verso, 1994).

3. Wynter, "Unsettling the Coloniality," 321.

4. Grace Manthey, Frank Esposito, and Amanda Hernandez, "Despite 'Defunding' Claims, Police Funding Has Increased in Many US Cities," *ABC News*, October 16, 2022, https://abcnews.go.com/US/defunding-claims-police -funding-increased-us-cities/story?id=91511971. President Biden's fiscal year 2023 budget proposal drastically expanded police funding. See Peter Nickeas, "'The Answer Is Not to Defund': Here's What's in President Biden's Increased Budget for Policing," *CNN*, March 31, 2022, www.cnn.com/2022/03/31/us/biden-police -budget-increase/index.html.

5. Timothy Pratt, "The Real Cost of 'Cop City' under Question after Atlanta Approves $67m for Project," *Guardian*, June 9, 2023, www.theguardian .com/us-news/2023/jun/09/cop-city-cost-atlanta-city-council.

6. Defend the Atlanta Forest Campaign, "Defend the Atlanta Forest," https://defendtheatlantaforest.org/.

7. Natasha Lennard, "Police Shot Atlanta Cop City Protester 57 Times, Autopsy Finds," *Intercept*, April 20, 2023, https://theintercept.com/2023/04/20 /atlanta-cop-city-protester-autopsy/.

8. Christopher E. Bruce and Hina Shamsi, "RICO and Domestic Terrorism Charges against Cop City Activists Send a Chilling Message" *ACLU*, September 21, 2023, www.aclu.org/news/free-speech/rico-and-domestic-terrorism -charges-against-cop-city-activists-send-a-chilling-message; and Fulton County Superior Court, indictment, August 29, 2023, www.fultonclerk.org/Document Center/View/2156/CRIMINAL-INDICTMENT.

9. Is Your Life Better, "Cop Cities, USA," https://isyourlifebetter.net/cop -cities-usa/.

10. Nick Estes and Jaskiran Dhillon, *Standing with Standing Rock: Voices from the #NoDAPL Movement* (Minneapolis: University of Minnesota Press, 2019).

11. See Anne Spice, "Unis'tot'en Camp: No Access Without Consent w/ Anne Spice," *Red Nation Podcast*, December 16, 2019.

12. See Tara Houska, "Line 3 Ain't over w/ Tara Houska," *Red Nation Podcast*, September 13, 2021.

13. Uahikea Maile, "On Being Late: Cruising Mauna Kea and Unsettling Technoscientific," *American Indian Culture and Research Journal* 45, no. 1 (2021): 95–121.

14. Marx, "The Secret of Primitive Accumulation," in *Capital*, 873–940.

15. Valerie Volcovici, "Trump Advisors Aim to Privatize Oil-Rich Indian Reservations," *Reuters*, December 5, 2016.

16. Day, "Eco-Criticism and Primitive Accumulation," 51. Ali Kadri also studies the relationship between accumulation and waste in contemporary capitalism, arguing that the contradictions of accumulation's crisis are resolved through wars that treat populations as disposable. *The Accumulation of Waste: A Political Economy of Systemic Destruction* (Boston: Brill, 2023).

17. Researching the American-Israeli Alliance and Jewish Voice for Peace, *Deadly Exchange Research Report*, September 2018, https://deadlyexchange.org /wp-content/uploads/2019/07/Deadly-Exchange-Report.pdf.

18. Abdul Alkalimat, *The History of Black Studies* (London: Pluto Press, 2021); and Martha Biondi, *The Black Revolution on Campus* (Berkeley: University of California Press, 2014).

19. Maher, *World without Police*, 22.

20. Department of Defense, *The United States Department of Defense (DoD) Agency Financial Report (AFR) for Fiscal Year (FY) 2022*, 12, https://comptroller .defense.gov/Portals/45/Documents/afr/fy2022/DoD_FY22_Agency_Financial _Report.pdf.

21. George Jackson, *Blood in My Eye* (1972; Baltimore, MD: Black Classic Press, 1990).

22. Oliver O'Connell, "Capitol Riot: Trump Supporters Shown Beating Officer Michael Fanone under 'Blue Lives Matter' Flag," *Independent*, October 20, 2021, www.the-independent.com/news/world/americas/crime/blue -lives-matter-capitol-riot-b1942063.html.

23. Southern Poverty Law Center, "Oath Keepers," www.splcenter.org /fighting-hate/extremist-files/group/oath-keepers.

24. For a recent study of the relationship between imperialism and fascism today, see Alyosha Goldstein and Simón Ventura Trujillo, *For Anti-Fascist Futures: Against the Violence of Imperial Crisis* (New York: Common Notions, 2022).

25. For more on how insurgent fascism aligns with the state in counter-revolution against anti-imperialism and abolition, see Alberto Toscano's study of George Jackson and Angela Davis's analysis of US fascism. Toscano, "The Returns of Racial Fascism," in *For Anti-Fascist Futures: Against the Violence of the Imperial Crisis*, ed. Alyosha Goldstein and Simón Ventura Trujillo (Brooklyn: Common Notions 2022). Toscano expands on these ideas in his

recent *Late Fascism: Race, Capitalism and the Politics of Crisis* (London: Verso Books, 2023).

26. Kathleen Belew, *Bring the War Home: The White Power Movement and Paramilitary America* (Cambridge, MA: Harvard University Press, 2018), 104.

27. See Don Hamerquist, J. Sakai, and Mark Salotte, *Confronting Fascism: Discussion Documents for a Militant Movement* (Montreal: Kersplebedeb Publishing, 2002).

28. For an overview of contemporary insurgent fascist ideologies and movements, see Matthew N. Lyons, *Insurgent Supremacists: The U.S. Far Right's Challenge to State and Empire* (Richmond, BC: PM Press, 2018).

29. Michael Quinn Sullivan and Kyle Rittenhouse, *Kyle Rittenhouse Acquitted* (self-published, 2023), Kindle, 102.

30. Sullivan, 59.

31. Sullivan, 105.

32. Sullivan, 104.

33. Sullivan, 113.

34. Rittenhouse characterizes white protesters as "outside agitators," using a common trope of white policing: "Some people were looking for reasons to do bad things as a cover. They were looking to vandalize property. They were looking to set businesses on fire. They just needed an excuse." Sullivan, *Kyle Rittenhouse*, 10.

35. Sullivan, 101.

36. For analysis of insurgent neofascism's aims of capturing the state, see Lyons, *Insurgent Supremacists*; Hamerquist, Sakai, and Salotte, *Confronting Fascism*; and Kali Akuno, "How to Withstand the Neo-Fascists' Conquest of Power," *Hood Communist Blog*, February 3, 2022, https://hoodcommunist.org /2022/02/03/how-to-withstand-the-neo-fascists-conquest-of-power/.

37. For more on the relationship between settler gun violence and modern-day mass shootings, see Roxanne Dunbar-Ortiz, *Loaded: A Disarming History of the Second Amendment* (San Francisco: City Lights Books, 2018).

38. Estes et al., *Red Nation Rising*, 9.

39. See Xtn Alexander and Matthew N. Lyons, *Three Way Fight: Revolutionary Politics and Antifascism* (Oakland, CA: PM Press, 2024); Hamerquist, Sakai, and Salotte, *Confronting Fascism*; and *Three Way Fight: An Insurgent Blog on the Struggle against the State and Fascism*, n.d., threewayfight.blogspot.com/.

40. For more on how critique and study have been captured by counterinsurgency, see Dylan Rodríguez, "Insurgency and Counterinsurgency," *Black Agenda Report*, November 2, 2022, https://blackagendareport.com/insurgency-and-counterinsurgency-interview-dylan-rodriguez.

41. Brown, "Interview with Senator Mason," 44–53.

42. Sanborn, *Life and Letters*, 571–572.

43. Sanborn, *Life and Letters*, 572.

44. Brown, "Interview with Senator Mason," 52.

Bibliography

PRIMARY SOURCES

An Act Concerning the County of Northampton. March 5, 1832. Nat Turner Project. www.natturnerproject.org/blank-cmaj.

An Act for Enrolling and Calling Out the National Forces, and for Other Purposes. 37th Cong., 3d. Sess., Cong. Rec., chs. 74, 75 (March 3, 1863).

"An 'Act for the Better Ordering and Governing of Negroes and Other Slaves.'" In *Stono: Documenting and Interpreting a Southern Slave Revolt*, edited by Mark M. Smith. Columbia, SC: University of South Carolina Press, 2019.

An Act Providing for the Relief of Such of the Inhabitants of Saint Domingo, Resident within the United States, as May Be Found in Want of Support. 6 Stat. Ch. 2 (February 12, 1794).

"Address to the General Assembly of Virginia." 1831. Nat Turner Project. www.natturnerproject.org/governor-message-general -assembly-1831.

Anderson, Osborne Perry. *A Voice from Harper's Ferry: A Narrative of Events at Harper's Ferry*. Boston, 1861.

An Authentic Narrative of the Seminole War; and of the Miraculous Escape of Mrs. Mary Godfrey, and Her Four Female Children: Annexed Is a Minute Detail of the Horrid Massacres of the Whites, by the Indians and Negroes, in Florida, in the Months of December, January and February. New York: Printed for D. F. Blanchard and others, 1836.

Brown, John. "Interview with Senator Mason and Others," October 18, 1859. In *The Tribunal: Responses to John Brown and the Harpers Ferry Raid*, edited by John Stauffer and Zoe Trodd, 44–53. Cambridge, MA: Harvard University Press, 2012.

———. "Old Brown's Parallels." *New York Tribune*, January 28, 1858. https://archive.wvculture.org/history/jbexhibit/parallels.html.

———. "Provisional Constitution and Ordinances for the People of the United States." In Stauffer and Trodd, *Tribunal*, 26–37.

———. "Words of Advice." In Stauffer and Trodd, *Tribunal*, 7–9.

Brown, William Wells. "John Brown and the Fugitive Slave Law." *Independent*, March 10, 1870. https://archive.wvculture.org/history/jbexhibit/wwbrown .html.

Chamberlain, Samuel E. *My Confession: Recollections of a Rogue.* New York: Harper & Brothers, 1956.

Defend the Atlanta Forest Campaign. "Defend the Atlanta Forest." https://defendtheatlantaforest.org/.

Delany, Martin. *Blake: Or, the Huts of America.* Edited by Floyd Miller. Boston: Beacon Press, 1970. First published 1859.

———. *Blake; or, The Huts of America: A Corrected Edition.* Edited by Jerome J. McGann. Cambridge, MA: Harvard University Press, 2017.

———. "The Condition, Elevation, Emigration, and Destiny of the Colored People of the United States." In *Martin R. Delany: A Documentary Reader*, edited by Robert S. Levine, 189–216. Chapel Hill: University of North Carolina Press, 2003.

———. "Letter for Garrison, 19 Feb 1859." In Levine, *Martin R. Delany*, 219–220.

———. "Letter to J. H. Kagi, Chatham, August 16, 1858." In "John Brown Insurrection: The Brown Papers: Copied from the Originals at Charlestown by Order of the Executive Department of the State of Virginia," November 16, 1859, reprinted in *Calendar of Virginia State Paper and Other Manuscripts from January 1, 1836, to April 15, 1869*, 11:291–292. Richmond: H. W. Flournoy, 1893.

————. *Martin R. Delany: A Documentary Reader.* Edited by Robert S. Levine. Chapel Hill: University of North Carolina Press, 2003.

————. "Political Destiny of the Colored Race." In Levine, *Martin R. Delany,* 245–279.

————. "True Patriotism." *North Star,* December 8, 1848. In Levine, *Martin R. Delany,* 137–140.

Department of Defense. *The United States Department of Defense (DoD) Agency Financial Report (AFR) for Fiscal Year (FY) 2022.* https://comptroller.defense.gov/Portals/45/Documents/afr/fy2022/DoD_FY22_Agency_Financial_Report.pdf.

Douglass, Frederick. *The Life and Times of Frederick Douglass: His Early Life as a Slave, His Escape from Bondage, and His Complete History.* Hartford, CT: Park, 1883.

————. "The Mission of the War: A Lecture." *New York Tribune,* January 14, 1864.

————. "Speech: Frederick Douglass on John Brown." Boston, 1860. https://blackagendareport.com/speech-frederick-douglass-john-brown-1860.

Foster, Stephen C. "Republican Land Policy—Homes for the Million," April 24, 1860. In *Landmark Debates in Congress: From the Declaration of Independence to the War in Iraq,* edited by Stephen W. Stathi, 157–160. Washington, DC: CQ Press, 2008.

The Fugitive Slave Act. September 18, 1850. http://hrlibrary.umn.edu/education/slaveact1850.html.

Garnet, Henry Highland. "An Address to the Slaves of the United States of America." In *Electronic Texts in American Studies Libraries at University Nebraska–Lincoln.* 1843. https://digitalcommons.unl.edu/etas/8/.

Garrison, William Lloyd. "The Insurrection." *Liberator,* September 3, 1831, 143. https://fair-use.org/the-liberator/1831/09/03/the-insurrection.phtml.

Hamilton, James. "John Brown in Canada." *Canadian Magazine,* December 1894.

Hamilton, Thomas. "The Nat Turner Insurrection." *Anglo-African Magazine,* December 1859. In Stauffer and Trodd, *Tribunal,* 192–193.

Head of Joaquin Murrieta. Tessa: Digital Collections of the Los Angeles Public Library. https://tessa2.lapl.org/digital/collection/photos/id/101082.

Higginson, Thomas Wentworth. "Nat Turner's Insurrection." *Atlantic,* August 1861. www.theatlantic.com/magazine/archive/1861/08/nat-turners-insurrection/308736.

"Lieutenant Governor Bull's Eyewitness Account." In *Stono: Documenting and Interpreting a Southern Slave Revolt*, edited by Mark M. Smith, 16–17. Columbia, SC: University of South Carolina Press, 2019.

Marx, Karl. "Marx, on Behalf of the International Working Men's Association, to President Abraham Lincoln," November 22, 1864. In *The Civil War in the United States*, edited by Angela Zimmerman, 153–154. New York: International Publishers, 2016. First published 1937.

———. "Marx to Engels, January 11, 1860." In Zimmerman, *Civil War in the United States*, 17–18.

Mason, Jason M. *Senate Select Committee Report on the Harper's Ferry Invasion.* June 15, 1860. 36th Cong., 1st Sess., S. Rep. Com. No. 278.

Narrative of the Massacre, by the Savages, of the Wife & Children of Thomas Baldwin. New York: Martin & Perry, 1836.

Patterson, Williams. "To George Washington from William Patterson et al.," January 30, 1794. Founders Online. Founders Online, National Historical Publications & Records Commission. https://founders.archives.gov/documents/Washington/05-15-02-0120.

"Petition from the Citizens of Hanover County." December 11 and 14, 1831. Nat Turner Project. www.natturnerproject.org/petition-hanover-county.

"Petition from Women of Augusta County to the Hon. the General Assembly of the State of Virginia." January 19, 1832. Nat Turner Project. www.natturner project.org/petition-augusta-county.

"Racism and the Law." 1862. Digital History Online Archive. www.digital history.uh.edu/disp_textbook.cfm?smtID=3&psid=17.

Researching the American-Israeli Alliance and Jewish Voice for Peace. Deadly Exchange Research Report. September 2018. https://deadlyexchange.org/wp-content/uploads/2019/07/Deadly-Exchange-Report.pdf.

Richmond Enquirer, The. October 7, 1831. Nat Turner Project. www.natturner project.org/richmond-enquirer-oct-7-patrol-law.

Ridge, John Rollin. *The Life and Adventures of Joaquín Murieta, the Celebrated California Bandit.* Norman: University of Oklahoma Press, 1955. First published 1854.

———. *The Life and Adventures of Joaquín Murieta: The Celebrated California Bandit.* Edited by Hsuan L. Hsu. New York: Penguin Books, 2018.

Rowlandson, Mary. *A Narrative of the Captivity and Restoration of Mrs. Mary Rowlandson.* Cambridge, MA, 1682.

Smith, James McCune. *Frederick Douglass Paper*, August 8, 1856, 252.

Treaty of Guadalupe Hidalgo. 1848. National Archives. www.archives.gov /milestone-documents/treaty-of-guadalupe-hidalgo.

Turner, Nat. *The Confessions of Nat Turner: The Leader of the Late Insurrection in Southampton, VA.* Edited by Thomas Grey. Baltimore, MD: Lucas & Deaver, 1831.

Union Republican Congressional Committee. *Homes for the Homeless: What the Republican Party Has Done for the Poor Man.* Washington, DC: Great Republic Office, 1868. https://tile.loc.gov/storage-services/service/rbc/rbpe/rbpe20 /rbpe205/2050240b/2050240b.pdf.

"Vote Yourself a Farm." Distributed by the *True Workingman*, January 24, 1846. Quoted in *A Documentary History of American Industrial Society: Labor Movement*, edited by John R. Commons, Ulrich B. Phillips, Eugene A. Gilmore, Helen L. Sumner, and John B. Andrews, 305–307. Vol. 7. Cleveland, OH: Arthur H. Clark, 1910.

Walker, William. "Nicaragua: Speech of General WM. Walker." *New York Times*, February 2, 1858.

———. "Walker the Filibuster." *Liberator*, July 3, 1857.

———. *War in Nicaragua.* Mobile, AL: S. H. Goetzel, April 1860.

Warner, Samuel. *Authentic and Impartial Narrative of the Tragical Scene Which Was Witnessed in Southampton County (Virginia) on Monday the 22d of August Last, When Fifty-Five of Its Inhabitants (Mostly Women and Children) Were Inhumanly Massacred by the Blacks! Communicated by Those Who Were Eye Witnesses of the Bloody Scene, and Confirmed by the Confessions of Several of the Blacks while under Sentence of Death.* New York: Printed for Warner & West, 1831.

OTHER WORKS CITED

Akins, Damon B., and William J. Bauer Jr. *We Are the Land.* Oakland: University of California Press, 2021.

Akuno, Kali. "How to Withstand the Neo-Fascists' Conquest of Power." *Hood Communist Blog*, February 3, 2022. https://hoodcommunist.org/2022/02/03 /how-to-withstand-the-neo-fascists-conquest-of-power/.

Alemán, Jesse. "Assimilation and the Decapitated Body Politics in *The Life and Adventures of Joaquín Murieta.*" *Arizona Quarterly* 59, no. 1 (2004): 71–98.

Alexander, Xtn, and Matthew N. Lyons. *Three Way Fight: Revolutionary Politics and Antifascism*. Oakland, CA: PM Press, 2024.

Alkalimat, Abdul. *The History of Black Studies*. London: Pluto Press, 2021.

Allen, Theodore. *The Invention of the White Race*. Vol. 2. London: Verso, 1994.

Allmendinger, David F., Jr. *Nat Turner and the Rising in Southampton County*. Baltimore, MD: Johns Hopkins University Press, 2014.

Anderson, Hannah L. "That Settles It: The Debate and Consequences of the Homestead Act of 1862." *History Teacher* 45, no. 1 (November 2011): 117–137.

Arrighi, Giovanni. *The Long Twentieth Century: Money, Power, and the Origins of Our Times*. London: Verso, 1994.

Barker, Joanne. *Red Scare: The State's Indigenous Terrorist*. Oakland: University of California Press, 2021.

Belew, Kathleen. *Bring the War Home: The White Power Movement and Paramilitary America*. Cambridge, MA: Harvard University Press, 2018.

Bernstein, Iver. *The New York City Draft Riots: Their Significance for American Society and Politics in the Age of the Civil War*. New York: Oxford University Press, 1991.

Biondi, Martha. *The Black Revolution on Campus*. Oakland: University of California Press, 2014.

Boggs, Glen. "Free Florida Land: Homesteading for Good Title." *Florida Bar Journal* (January 2009): 11–18.

Bradford, Sarah. *Harriet: The Moses of Her People*. New York: Geo. R. Lockwood & Son, 1897.

———. *Scenes in the Life of Harriet Tubman*. Auburn, NY: W. J. Moses, 1869.

Breen, Patrick H. *The Land Shall Be Deluged in Blood: A New History of the Nat Turner Revolt*. Oxford: Oxford University Press, 2015.

Brittan, Jennifer C. "Martin R. Delany's Speculative Fiction and the Nineteenth-Century Economy of Slave Conspiracy." *Studies in American Fiction* 46, no. 1 (2019): 79–102.

Brownstein, Lewis. "The Concept of Counterrevolution in Marxian Theory." *Studies in Soviet Thought* 22, no. 3 (August 1981): 175–192.

Bruce, Christopher E., and Hina Shamsi. "RICO and Domestic Terrorism Charges against Cop City Activists Send a Chilling Message." ACLU. September 21, 2023. www.aclu.org/news/free-speech/rico-and-domestic-terrorism-charges-against-cop-city-activists-send-a-chilling-message.

Bruyneel, Kevin. *Settler Memory: The Disavowal of Indigeneity and the Politics of Race in the United States*. Chapel Hill: University of North Carolina Press, 2021.

Burden-Stelly, Charisse. *Black Scare/Red Scare: Theorizing Capitalist Racism in the United States*. Chicago: University of Chicago Press, 2023.

Cabral, Amilcar. "The Weapon of Theory." Havana, 1966. Marxist Internet Archive. www.marxists.org/subject/africa/cabral/1966/weapon-theory.htm.

Castillo, Pedro G., and Albert Camarillo. *Furia Y Muerte: Los Bandidos Chicanos*. Los Angeles: Aztlán Publications, 1973.

Central Intelligence Agency. "Honoring Harriet Tubman: A Symbol of Freedom and an Intelligence Pioneer." September 7, 2022. www.cia.gov/stories /story/honoring-pioneer-harriet-tubman/.

Christensen, Peter G. "Minority Interaction in John Rollin Ridge's *The Life and Adventures of Joaquín Murieta*." *Melus* 17, no. 2 (1992): 61–72.

Clinton, Catherine. *Harriet Tubman: The Road to Freedom*. London: Little Brown, 2004.

Clymer, Jeffory A. "Martin Delany's *Blake* and the Transnational Politics of Property." *American Literary History* 15, no. 4 (2003): 709–731.

Cook, Adrian. *The Armies of the Streets: The New York City Draft Riots of 1863*. Lexington: University Press of Kentucky, 1974.

Coulthard, Glen S. *Red Skin, White Masks: Rejecting the Colonial Politics of Recognition*. Minneapolis: University of Minnesota Press, 2014.

Covington, James W. "The Armed Occupation Act of 1842." *Florida Historical Quarterly* 40, no. 1 (July 1961): 41–52.

Cox, James H. *Muting White Noise: Native American and European American Novel Traditions*. Norman: University of Oklahoma Press, 2006.

Crowfoot, Silas Niobeh. "Community Development for a White City: Race Making, Improvementism, and the Cincinnati Race Riots and Anti-Abolition Riots of 1829, 1836, and 1841." PhD diss., Portland State University, 2010.

Cusick, Jim. "Hidden Meanings in a Second Seminole War Pamphlet." *University of Florida Special & Area Studies Collections Blog*, n.d. https://ufsasc .domains.uflib.ufl.edu/hidden-meanings-second-seminole-war-pamphlet -florida/.

Davidson, Adenike Marie. *The Black Nation Novel: Imagining Homeplaces in Early African American Literature*. Chicago: Third World Press, 2008.

Davis, Angela. "Political Prisoners, Prisons, and Black Liberation." In *Imprisoned Intellectuals: America's Political Prisoners Write on Life, Liberation, and Rebellion*, edited by Joy James, 62–77. New York: Rowman & Littlefield, 2002.

Davis, Mike. *Planet of Slums*. London: Verso, 2006.

Day, Iyko. *Alien Capital: Asian Racialization and the Logic of Settler Colonial Capitalism*. Durham, NC: Duke University Press, 2016.

———. "Eco-Criticism and Primitive Accumulation." In *After Marx: Literature, Theory, and Value in the Twenty-First Century*, edited by Colleen Lye and Christopher Nealon, 40–54. Cambridge: Cambridge University Press, 2023.

Decaro, Louis A., Jr. *The Untold Story of Shields Green: The Life and Death of a Harper's Ferry Raider*. New York: New York University Press, 2022.

Donahue, Timothy. "Joaquín's Head: Theatrical Punishment, Public Address, and Novelistic Politics in the United States–Mexico Borderlands." *J19: The Journal of Nineteenth-Century Americanists* 4, no. 2 (2016): 391–417.

Doolen, Andy. "Be Cautious of the Word 'Rebel': Race, Revolution, and Transnational History in Martin Delany's *Blake; or, The Huts of America*." *American Literature* 81, no. 1 (2009): 153–179.

Drysdale, David J. "Ridge's *Joaquín Murieta*: Banditry, Counterinsurgency, and Colonial Power after Guadalupe-Hidalgo." *Canadian Review of American Studies* 46, no. 1 (2016): 62–85.

Du Bois, W. E. B. *Black Reconstruction in America*. New York: The Free Press, 1998. First published 1935.

———. *John Brown*. New York: International Publishers, 1996. First published 1909.

Dunbar-Ortiz, Roxanne. *An Indigenous Peoples' History of the United States*. Boston: Beacon Press, 2014.

———. *Loaded: A Disarming History of the Second Amendment*. San Francisco: City Lights Books, 2018.

Estes, Nick. *Our History Is the Future: Standing Rock versus the Dakota Access Pipeline, and the Long Tradition of Indigenous Resistance*. London: Verso, 2019.

Estes, Nick, and Jaskiran Dhillon. *Standing with Standing Rock: Voices from the #NoDAPL Movement*. Minneapolis: University of Minnesota Press, 2019.

Estes, Nick, and Roxanne Dunbar-Ortiz. "Examining the Wreckage." *Monthly Review* 72, no. 3 (July–August, 2020). https://monthlyreview.org/2020/07/01/examining-the-wreckage/#en7backlink.

Estes, Nick, Melanie Yazzie, Jennifer Nez Denetdale, and David Correia. *Red Nation Rising: From Bordertown Violence to Native Liberation*. New York: PM Press, 2021.

Evans, William E. "The Garra Uprising: Conflict between San Diego Indians and Settlers in 1851." *California Historical Society Quarterly* 45, no. 4 (1966): 339–349.

Fagan, Benjamin. *The Black Newspaper and the Chosen Nation*. Athens: University of Georgia Press, 2016.

———. "*Blake* and the Black Newspaper." *American Periodicals: A Journal of History & Criticism* 28, no. 1 (2018): 78–80.

Fanon, Frantz. *The Wretched of the Earth*. New York: Grove Press, 1965.

Fielder, Brigitte. "Black Madness, White Violence, and John Brown's Legacy." *American Literary History* 35, no. 4 (2021): 1799–1809.

———. *Relative Races: Genealogies of Interracial Kinship in Nineteenth-Century America*. Durham, NC: Duke University Press, 2020. Kindle.

Fielder, Brigitte, Cassander Smith, and Derrick R. Spires. Introduction to "*Weekly Anglo-African* and *The Pine and Palm*: Excerpts 1861–1862." *Just Teach One: Early African American Print*, no. 4 (Spring 2018): i–xvi. https://jtoaa.americanantiquarian.org/welcome-to-just-teach-one-african-american/weekly-anglo-african-and-the-pine-and-palm/.

Finch, Martha L. *Dissenting Bodies: Corporealities in Early New England*. New York: Columbia University Press, 2010.

Foner, Eric. *Free Soil, Free Labor, Free Men: The Ideology of the Republican Party before the Civil War*. Oxford: Oxford University Press, 1971.

Forbes, Jack D. *Native Americans of California and Nevada*. Rev. ed. Happy Camp, CA: Naturegraph Publishers, 1993.

Geffert, Hannah N. "John Brown and His Black Allies: An Ignored Alliance." *Pennsylvania Magazine of History and Biography* 126, no. 4 (2002): 591–610.

Gillman, Susan Kay. "The Epistemology of Slave Conspiracy." *MFS Modern Fiction Studies* 49, no. 1 (Spring 2003): 101–123.

Gilmore, Ruth Wilson. *Golden Gulag: Prisons, Surplus, Crisis, and Opposition in Globalizing California*. Berkeley: University of California Press, 2007.

Gilroy, Paul. *The Black Atlantic: Modernity and Double Consciousness*. Cambridge, MA: Harvard University Press, 1993.

Goeke, Joe. "Yellow Bird and the Bandit: Minority Authorship, Class, and Audience in John Rollin Ridge's *The Life and Adventures of Joaquín Murieta*." *Western American Literature* 37, no. 4 (2003): 453–478.

Goldstein, Alyosha, and Simón Ventura Trujillo. *For Anti-Fascist Futures: Against the Violence of Imperial Crisis*. New York: Common Notions, 2022.

Greenberg, Kenneth S. *Nat Turner: A Slave Rebellion in History and Memory*. Oxford: Oxford University Press, 2003.

Grenier, John. *The First Way of War: American War Making on the Frontier, 1607–1814*. Cambridge: Cambridge University Press, 2005.

Hadden, Sally. *Slave Patrols: Law and Violence in Virginia and the Carolinas*. Cambridge, MA: Harvard University Press, 2001.

Hamerquist, Don, J. Sakai, and Mark Salotte, *Confronting Fascism: Discussion Documents for a Militant Movement*. Montreal: Kersplebedeb Publishing, 2002.

Hampton, Fred. "You Can Murder a Liberator, but You Can't Murder Liberation." April 27, 1969. Marxist Internet Archive. www.marxists.org/archive/hampton/1969/04/27.htm.

Harney, Stefano, and Fred Moten. *The Undercommons: Fugitive Planning and Black Study*. New York: Minor Compositions, 2013.

Harootunian, Harry. *Marx after Marx: History and Time in the Expansion of Capitalism*. New York: Columbia University Press, 2015.

Harris, Cheryl. "Whiteness as Property." *Harvard Law Review* 106, no. 8 (June 1993): 1707–1791.

Harris, Leslie M. *In the Shadow of Slavery: African Americans in New York City, 1626–1863*. Chicago: University of Chicago Press, 2003.

Hartman, Saidiya V. *Scenes of Subjection: Terror, Slavery, and Self-Making in Nineteenth-Century America*. Oxford: Oxford University Press, 1997.

Havard, John. "John Rollin Ridge's *Joaquín Murieta*: Sensation, Hispanicism, and Cosmopolitanism." *Western American Literature* 49, no. 4 (2015): 321–349.

Heatherton, Christina. *Arise! Global Radicalism in the Era of the Mexican Revolution*. Oakland: University of California Press, 2022.

Hernández, Bernadine Marie. *Border Bodies: Racialized Sexuality, Sexual Capital, and Violence in the Nineteenth-Century Borderlands*. Chapel Hill: University of North Carolina Press, 2022.

Hinton, Richard J. *John Brown and His Men*. New York: Funk & Wagnalls.

Hobsbawm, Eric. *Bandits*. New York: New Press, 2000.

Holden, Vanessa M. *Surviving Southampton: African American Women and Resistance in Nat Turner's Community*. Champaign: University of Illinois Press, 2021.

Horne, Gerald. *The Apocalypse of Settler Colonialism: The Roots of Slavery, White Supremacy, and Capitalism in 17th Century North America and the Caribbean*. New York: Monthly Review Press, 2018.

———. *The Counter Revolution of 1836: Texas Slavery and Jim Crow and the Roots of U.S. Fascism*. New York: International Publishers, 2022.

———. *The Counter-Revolution of 1776: Slave Resistance and the Origins of the United States of America*. New York: New York University Press, 2016.

———. *The Dawning of the Apocalypse: The Roots of Slavery, White Supremacy, Settler Colonialism, and Capitalism in the Long Sixteenth Century*. New York: Monthly Review Press, 2020.

———. *Race to Revolution: The United States and Cuba During Slavery and Jim Crow*. New York: Monthly Review Press, 2014.

Houska, Tara. "Line 3 Ain't over w/ Tara Houska." *Red Nation Podcast*, September 13, 2021.

Hovatter, Ryan P. "The Florida Volunteers: Territorial Militia in the Opening of the Second Seminole War." Master's thesis, US Army Command and General Staff College, 2021.

Hsu, Hsuan L. Introduction to *The Life and Adventures of Joaquín Murieta: The Celebrated California Bandit*, edited by Hsuan L. Hsu, xvi. New York: Penguin Books, 2018.

Humez, Jean McMahon. *Harriet Tubman: The Life and the Life Stories*. Madison: University of Wisconsin Press, 2003.

Ignatiev, Noel. *How the Irish Became White*. New York: Routledge, 1995.

———. *Treason to Whiteness Is Loyalty to Humanity*. London: Verso, 2022.

Jackson, George. *Blood in My Eye*. Baltimore, MD: Black Classic Press, 1990. First published 1972.

Jackson, Holly. *American Radicals: How Nineteenth-Century Protest Shaped the Nation*. New York: Crown, 2019.

Jackson, Kellie Carter. *Force and Freedom: Black Abolitionists and the Politics of Violence*. Philadelphia: University of Pennsylvania Press, 2019.

James, C. L. R. *The Black Jacobins: Toussaint L'Ouverture and the San Domingo Revolution*. New York: Random House, 1963.

Jameson, Frederic. *Archaeologies of the Future: The Desire Called Utopia and Other Science Fictions*. New York: Verso, 2005.

———. *Representing Capital: A Commentary on Volume One*. London, Verso, 2013.

Johnson, Walter. *The Broken Heart of America: St. Louis and the Violent History of the United States*. New York: Basic Books, 2020.

———. *River of Dark Dreams: Slavery and Empire in the Cotton Kingdom*. Cambridge, MA: Harvard University Press, 2013.

Kadri, Ali. *The Accumulation of Waste: A Political Economy of Systemic Destruction*. Boston: Brill, 2023.

Karuka, Manu. *Empire's Tracks: Indigenous Nations, Chinese Workers, and the Transcontinental Railroad*. Oakland: University of California Press, 2019.

Kornbluh, Anna. "Totality." *Victorian Literature and Culture* 47, no. 3 (2019): 671–678.

Koshy, Susan, Jodi Byrd, Brian Jordan Jefferson, and Lisa Marie Cacho. *Colonial Racial Capitalism*. Durham, NC: Duke University Press, 2022.

LaDuke, Winona. *All Our Relations: Native Struggles for Land and Life*. Chicago: Haymarket Books, 2016.

Latta, Frank. *Joaquín Murrieta and His Horse Gangs*. Santa Cruz: Bear State Books, 1980.

Lause, Mark A. *Young America: Land, Labor, and the Republican Community*. Urbana: University of Illinois Press, 2005.

Leal, Luis. Introduction to *Life and Adventures of the Celebrated Bandit Joaquin Murrieta: His Exploits in the State of California*, by Ireneo Paz, translated by Francisco A. Lomelí and Miguel R. López, xi–xciv. Houston: Arte Público Press, 2001.

Lee, Butch. *Jailbreak Out of History: The Re-Biography of Harriet Tubman*. Montreal: Kersplebedeb Publishing, 2015.

Lenin, V. I. "Dual Power." *Pravda*, no. 28 (April 9, 1917). www.marxists.org /archive/lenin/works/1917/apr/09.htm.

———. *The State and Revolution*. Chicago: Haymarket Books, 2014. First published 1918.

———. *What Is to Be Done?* 1902. Marxist Internet Archive. www.marxists.org /archive/lenin/works/1901/witbd/.

Lennard, Natasha. "Police Shot Atlanta Cop City Protester 57 Times, Autopsy Finds." *Intercept*, April 20, 2023. https://theintercept.com/2023/04/20/atlanta -cop-city-protester-autopsy/.

Levine, Robert. *Martin Delany, Frederick Douglass, and the Politics of Representative Identity*. Chapel Hill: University of North Carolina Press, 1997.

Lindsay, Brendan C. *Murder State: California's Native American Genocide, 1846–1873*. Lincoln: University of Nebraska Press, 2012.

Linebaugh, Peter, and Marcus Rediker, *The Many-Headed Hydra: Sailors, Slaves, Commoners, and the Hidden History of the Revolutionary Atlantic*. Boston: Beacon Press, 2013.

Losurdo, Domenico. *Class Struggle: A Political and Philosophical History*. New York: Palgrave Macmillan, 2016.

Lowe, John. "Joaquín Murieta, Mexican History, and Popular Myths of Freedom." *Journal of Popular Culture* 35, no. 2 (2001): 25–39.

Lowe, Lisa. *The Intimacies of Four Continents*. Durham, NC: Duke University Press, 2015.

Lowry, Beverly. *Harriet Tubman: Imagining a Life*. New York: Doubleday, 2007.

Lukács, György. *The Historical Novel*. Lincoln: University of Nebraska Press, 1983.

———. *History and Class Consciousness: Studies in Marxist Dialectics*. Cambridge, MA: MIT Press, 1971.

Lyons, Matthew N. *Insurgent Supremacists: The U.S. Far Right's Challenge to State and Empire*. Richmond, BC: PM Press, 2018.

Madley, Benjamin. *An American Genocide: The United States and the California Indian Catastrophe, 1846–1873*. New Haven, CT: Yale University Press, 2016.

Maher, Geo. *Anticolonial Eruptions: Racial Hubris and the Cunning of Resistance*. Oakland: University of California Press, 2022.

———. *Decolonizing Dialectics*. Durham, NC: Duke University Press, 2017.

———. *A World without Police: How Strong Communities Make Cops Obsolete*. London: Verso, 2021.

Maile, Uahikea. "On Being Late: Cruising Mauna Kea and Unsettling Technoscientific." *American Indian Culture and Research Journal* 45, no. 1 (2021): 95–121.

Manthey, Grace, Frank Esposito, and Amanda Hernandez. "Despite 'Defunding' Claims, Police Funding Has Increased in Many US Cities." *ABC News*, October 16, 2022. https://abcnews.go.com/US/defunding-claims-police-funding -increased-us-cities/story?id=91511971.

Marx, Karl. *Capital: A Critique of Political Economy*. Vol. 1. New York: Vintage Books, 1977.

———. *The Civil War in France*. 1871. Marxist Internet Archive. www.marxists .org/archive/marx/works/1871/civil-war-france/.

———. *The Class Struggles in France, 1848 to 1850*. 1850, 1895. Marxist Internet Archive. https://www.marxists.org/archive/marx/works/1850/class-struggles -france/.

———. *Germany Ideology*. 1845, 2000. Marxist Internet Archive, Part 1, Section A. www.marxists.org/archive/marx/works/1845/german-ideology/.

———. *Grundisse: Foundations of the Critique of Political Economy*. New York: Penguin, 1973. First published 1939.

———. "The Nature and Growth of Capital." In *Wage Labour and Capital*. n.d. Marxist Internet Archive. www.marxists.org/archive/marx/works/1847 /wage-labour/ch05.htm.

Marx, Karl, and Frederick Engels. "Manifesto of the Communist Party." 1848. Marxist Internet Archive. www.marxists.org/archive/marx/works/download /pdf/Manifesto.pdf.

May, Robert E. *Manifest Destiny's Underworld: Filibustering in Antebellum America*. Chapel Hill: University of North Carolina Press, 2002.

Mazzaferro, Alexander. "'A Nat Turner in Every Family': Exemplarity and Exceptionality in the Print Circulation of Slave Revolt." *J19: The Journal of Nineteenth-Century Americanists* 10, no. 2 (Fall 2022): 267–303.

McCarthy, Cormac. *Blood Meridian*. New York: Random House, 1985.

McGann, Jerome. Introduction to Martin Delany, *Blake; or, The Huts of America: A Corrected Edition*, edited by Jerome J. McGann, xxiv–xxv. Cambridge, MA: Harvard University Press, 2017.

McGlone, Robert E. *John Brown's War against Slavery*. Cambridge: Cambridge University Press, 2009.

McGowan, James A., and William Kashatus. *Harriet Tubman: A Biography*. London: Greenwood, 2011.

Merish, Lori. "Print, Cultural Memory, and John Rollin Ridge's *The Life and Adventures of Joaquín Murieta, the Celebrated California Bandit*." *Arizona Quarterly* 59, no. 4 (2003): 31–70.

Meyer, Eugene L. *Five for Freedom: The African American Soldiers in John Brown's Army*. Chicago: Lawrence Hill Books, 2018.

Monaco, C. S. *The Second Seminole War and the Limits of American Aggression*. Baltimore, MD: Johns Hopkins University Press, 2018.

Mondragon, Maria. "'The (Safe) White Side of the Line': History and Disguise in John Rollin Ridge's *The Life and Adventures of Joaquín Murieta, the Celebrated California Bandit*." *American Transcendental Quarterly* 8, no. 3 (1994): 173–187.

Moskowitz, Alex. "The Racial Economy of Perception: Reading Black Sociality in the Nineteenth Century." *Novel: A Forum on Fiction* 56, no. 1 (May 2023): 1–20.

Navakas, Michele Currie. *Liquid Landscape: Geography and Settlement at the Edge of Early America*. Philadelphia: University of Pennsylvania Press, 2017.

Nichols, Robert. *Theft Is Property! Dispossession and Critical Theory*. Durham, NC: Duke University Press, 2019.

Nickeas, Peter. "'The Answer Is Not to Defund': Here's What's in President Biden's Increased Budget for Policing." *CNN*, March 31, 2022. www.cnn.com /2022/03/31/us/biden-police-budget-increase/index.html.

Nwakwo, Ifeoma C. "The Promises and Perils of US African-American Hemispherism: Latin America in Martin Delany's *Blake* and Gayl Jones's *Mosquito*." *American Literary History* 18, no. 3 (2006): 579–599.

Oates, Stephen B. *The Fires of Jubilee: Nat Turner's Fierce Rebellion*. New York: Harper Perennial, 1975.

O'Connell, Oliver. "Capitol Riot: Trump Supporters Shown Beating Officer Michael Fanone under 'Blue Lives Matter' Flag." *Independent*, October 20, 2021. www.the-independent.com/news/world/americas/crime/blue-lives -matter-capitol-riot-b1942063.html.

Oertel, Kristen Tegtmeier. *Harriet Tubman: Slavery, the Civil War, and Civil Rights in the Nineteenth Century*. New York: Routledge, 2016.

Olsavsky, Jesse. *The Most Absolute Abolition: Runaways, Vigilance Committees, and the Rise of Revolutionary Abolitionism, 1835–1861*. Baton Rouge: Louisiana State University Press, 2022.

Olson, Joel. *The Abolition of White Democracy*. Minneapolis: University of Minnesota Press, 2004.

Orihuela, Sharad B. "The Black Market: Property, Freedom, and Martin Delany's *Blake; or, The Huts of America*." *J19: The Journal of Nineteenth-Century Americanists* 2, no. 2 (2014): 273–300.

Owens, Louis. *Other Destinies: Understanding the American Indian Novel*. Norman: University of Oklahoma Press, 1994.

Palombo, Nick. "Delving into Martin Delany. 'To Stay or To Go?': The 1854 National Emigration Convention." Colored Conventions Project. Accessed October 24, 2022. https://coloredconventions.org/emigration-debate/martin-delany/.

Parins, James W. *John Rollin Ridge: His Life and Works*. Lincoln: University of Nebraska Press, 2004.

Pereira, Alyssa. "One of SF's Earliest Cons Was a Fake Doctor and His Horrific 'Museum of Anatomy.'" *San Francisco Gate*, May 29, 2018.

Pratt, Timothy. "The Real Cost of 'Cop City' under Question after Atlanta Approves $67m for Project." *Guardian*, June 9, 2023. www.theguardian.com/us-news/2023/jun/09/cop-city-cost-atlanta-city-council.

Rao, Gautham. "The Federal 'Posse Comitatus' Doctrine: Slavery, Compulsion, and Statecraft in Mid-Nineteenth-Century America." *Law and History Review* 26, no. 1 (Spring 2008): 1–56.

Redpath, James. *The Public Life of Capt. John Brown*. Boston: Thayer and Eldridge, 1860.

Reynolds, David. *John Brown, Abolitionist: The Man Who Killed Slavery, Sparked the Civil War, and Seeded Civil Rights*. New York: Random House, 2005.

Richards, Leonard L. *Gentlemen of Property and Standing: Anti-Abolition Mobs in Jacksonian America*. Oxford: Oxford University Press, 1970.

Rifkin, Mark. "'For the Wrongs of Our Poor Bleeding Country': Sensation, Class, and Empire in Ridge's *Joaquín Murieta*." *Arizona Quarterly* 65, no. 2 (2009): 27–56.

Robinson, Cedric J. *Black Marxism: The Making of the Black Radical Tradition*. Chapel Hill: University of North Carolina Press, 1983, 2020.

Rodney, Walter. *Decolonial Marxism: Essays from the Pan-African Revolution*. London: Verso Books, 2022.

———. *How Europe Underdeveloped Africa*. London: Verso, 2018. First published 1972.

Rodríguez, Dylan. "Insurgency and Counterinsurgency." *Black Agenda Report*, November 2, 2022. https://blackagendareport.com/insurgency-and-counter insurgency-interview-dylan-rodriguez.

———. *White Reconstruction: Domestic Warfare and the Logics of Genocide*. New York: Fordham University Press, 2021.

Roediger, David. "Accounting for the Wages of Whiteness: US Marxism and the Critical History of Race." In *Class, Race, and Marxism*, 47–72. London: Verso, 2019.

———. *The Wages of Whiteness: Race and the Making of the American Working Class*. London: Verso, 1991.

Rollin, Frank (Francis) A. *The Life and Public Service of Martin R. Delany*. Boston: Lee and Shepard, 1883. First published 1868.

Rowe, John Carlos. "Highway Robbery: 'Indian Removal,' the Mexican-American War, and American Identity in *The Life and Adventures of Joaquín Murieta*." *Novel: A Forum on Fiction* 31, no. 2 (1998): 149–173.

Rusert, Britt. "Delany's Comet: Fugitive Science and the Speculative Imaginary of Emancipation." *American Quarterly* 65, no. 4 (2013): 799–829.

———. *Fugitive Science: Empiricism and Freedom in Early African American Culture*. New York: New York University Press, 2017.

Sanborn, Franklin B. *The Life and Letters of John Brown: Liberator of Kansas and Martyr of Virginia*. Boston: Robert Brothers, 1891.

Saxton, Alexander. *The Rise and Fall of the White Republic: Class Politics and Mass Culture in Nineteenth-Century America*. London: Verso, 1990.

Shire, Laurel Clark. *The Threshold of Manifest Destiny: Gender and National Expansion in Florida*. Philadelphia: University of Pennsylvania Press, 2016.

Shirley, Neal, and Saralee Stafford. *Dixie Be Damned: 300 Years of Insurrection in the American South*. Chico, CA: AK Press, 2015.

Shreve, Grant. "The Exodus of Martin Delany." *American Literary History* 29, no. 3 (2017): 449–473.

Singh, Nikhil Pal. "On Race, Violence, and So-Called Primitive Accumulation." *Social Text* 34, no. 3 (2016): 27–50.

———. *Race and America's Long War*. Oakland: University of California Press, 2017.

———. "The Whiteness of Police." *American Quarterly* 66, no. 4 (2014): 1097.

Sinha, Manisha. *The Slave's Cause: A History of Abolition*. New Haven, CT: Yale University Press, 2016.

Smith, Ralph A., "Glanton, John Joel." Revised by Sloan Rodgers. In *Handbook of Texas*. Texas State Historical Association, 2024. www.tshaonline.org/handbook/entries/glanton-john-joel. First published 1952.

Southern Poverty Law Center. "Oath Keepers." www.splcenter.org/fighting
-hate/extremist-files/group/oath-keepers.

Spice, Anne. "Unis'tot'en Camp: No Access without Consent w/ Anne Spice."
Red Nation Podcast, December 16, 2019.

Stauffer, John. *The Black Hearts of Men: Radical Abolitionists and the Transformation of Race*. Cambridge, MA: Harvard University Press, 2002.

Stauffer, John, and Zoe Trodd. *The Tribunal: Responses to John Brown and the
Harpers Ferry Raid*. Cambridge, MA: Harvard University Press, 2012.

Stevens, Erica. "Three-Fingered Jack and the Severed Literary History of John
Rollin Ridge's *The Life and Adventures of Joaquín Murieta*." *ESQ* 61, no. 1 (2015):
73–112.

Streeby, Shelley. *American Sensations: Class, Empire, and the Production of Popular
Culture*. Berkeley: University of California Press, 2002.

Sullivan, Michael Q., and Kyle Rittenhouse. *Kyle Rittenhouse Acquitted*. Self-
published, 2023. Kindle.

Suval, John. *Dangerous Ground: Squatters, Statesmen, and the Antebellum Rupture
of American Democracy*. New York: Oxford University Press, 2022.

Teuton, Sean. "The Indigenous Novel." In *The Oxford Handbook of Indigenous
American Literature*, edited by James H. Cox and Daniel Heath Justice, 318–
331. Oxford: Oxford University Press, 2014.

Thornton, Bruce S. *Searching for Joaquín: Myth, Murieta, and History in California*.
San Francisco: Encounter Books, 2003.

Thornton, Russell. "Cherokee Population Losses during the Trail of Tears: A
New Perspective and a New Estimate." *Ethnohistory* 31, no. 4 (1984): 289–300.

Toscano, Alberto. *Late Fascism: Race, Capitalism and the Politics of Crisis*. London: Verso Books, 2023.

———. "The Returns of Racial Fascism." In *For Anti-Fascist Futures: Against the
Violence of the Imperial Crisis*, edited by Alyosha Goldstein and Simón Ventura Trujillo, 243–255. Brooklyn: Common Notions, 2022.

Trafzer, Clifford E., and Joel R. Hyer. *Exterminate Them: Written Accounts of the
Murder, Rape, and Slavery of Native Americans during the California Gold Rush,
1848–1868*. East Lansing: Michigan State University Press, 1999.

Tripp, Bill. "Our Land Was Taken: But We Still Hold the Knowledge of How to
Stop Mega-Fires." *Guardian*, September 16, 2020. www.theguardian.com

/commentisfree/2020/sep/16/california-wildfires-cultural-burns-indigenous
-people.

Ullman, Victor. *Martin R. Delany: The Beginnings of Black Nationalism*. Boston:
Beacon Press, 1971.

Veracini, Lorenzo. *Settler Colonialism: A Theoretical Overview*. London: Palgrave
Macmillan, 2010.

Villard, Oswald Garrison. *John Brown, 1800–1859: A Biography Fifty Years After*.
Boston: Houghton Mifflin, 1910.

Volcovici, Valerie. "Trump Advisors Aim to Privatize Oil-Rich Indian reservations." *Reuters*, December 5, 2016.

Walker, Cheryl. *Indian Nation: Native American Literature and Nineteenth-Century
Nationalisms*. Durham, NC: Duke University Press, 1997.

Walkiewicz, Kathryn. *Reading Territory: Indigenous and Black Freedom, Removal,
and the Nineteenth-Century State*. Chapel Hill: University of North Carolina
Press, 2023.

Wang, Jackie. *Carceral Capitalism*. Cambridge, MA: MIT Press, 2018.

Whitlow, Roger. "The Revolutionary Black Novels of Martin R. Delany and
Sutton Griggs." *Melus* 5, no. 3 (Autumn 1978): 26–36.

Williams, Robert, and Mabel Williams. *Negroes with Guns*. New York: Marzani
& Munsell, 1962.

Winter, Molly Crumpton. "Culture-Tectonics: California Statehood and John Rollin Ridge's *Joaquín Murieta*." *Western American Literature* 43, no. 3 (2008): 259–276.

Wolfe, Patrick. "Settler Colonialism and the Elimination of the Native." *Journal
of Genocide Research* 8, no. 4 (2006): 387–409.

Wood, Peter H. "Anatomy of a Revolt." In *Stono: Documenting and Interpreting a
Southern Slave Revolt*, edited by Mark M. Smith, 59–72. Columbia, SC: University of South Carolina Press, 2019.

Wynter, Sylvia. "Unsettling the Coloniality of Being/Power/Truth/Freedom:
Towards the Human, after Man, Its Overrepresentation—an Argument."
CR: The New Centennial Review 3, no. 3 (2003): 257–337.

Zamalin, Alex. *Black Utopia: The History of an Idea from Black Nationalism to Afrofuturism*. New York: Columbia University Press, 2019.

Zimmerman, Angela. Introduction to *The Civil War in the United States*, xi–xxx.
New York: International Publishers, 2016. First published 1937.

Index

Abiaka, 99

abolition democracy, 36

abolitionists: African colonization movement, 16; anti-abolitionist groups, 56–57, 165–66; anti-slavery organizations, growth of in 1830s, 53–54; Frank Sanborn, 10–11, 207–8, 218, 220; Fugitive Slave Act, as motivation for activists, 176–77; George Jackson, 37, 233–34; Henry Highland Garnet, 15, 50, 177; James McCune Smith, 67, 170, 177–78; James Redpath, 67; John Hinton, 180; land reform and, 149; William Lloyd Garrison, 50, 160–61; William Wells Brown, 180. *See also* Brown, John; Chatham

Convention (1858); Delany, Martin; Tubman, Harriet

abolition movement: emancipated Blacks as humane Africans, 104–5, 107; fugitivity, anti-abolition mobs, and slave catcher whiteness, 53–57; Martin Delany and, 63–66. *See also* Brown, John

abolition terror as tactic, 198–203

abolition war: as anti-capitalist project, 30–32, 222–23; Black print culture and, 66–69; Canada West community, support for John Brown, 207–8; class contradictions between enslavers and nonenslavers, 152–53; contemporary applications of, 37; crisis of slavery abolition war (*continued*)

capital, Tubman on, 216–17, 220–22; dialectics of, 195–97; fugitive slaves as future Black army, 185–86; fugitivity, anti-abolition mobs, and slave catcher whiteness, 53–57; in Gaza, 228–29; Harper's Ferry uprising as political success, 182; John Brown on need for Black militancy, 178–81; John Brown's vision and, 1–5; the "John Brown Way," 175–89; Martin Delany and, 63–66; Martin Delany's *Blake* and abolition war endings, 82–84; Martin Delany's *Blake* and abolition war planning, 69–77; as means to abolish racialized class society, 173–75; modern-day state repression and surplus labor, 230–33; in modern-day US protest movements, 224–30; Nat Turner's view of, 13–18; New York City's anti-abolition insurgency, *162*, *163–67*; Osborne Anderson and the dictatorship of abolition, 189–93; "Provisional Constitution and Ordinances for the People of the United States" (Brown), 3, 196, 205; Reconstruction era policies, 133–38; settler mass militarism in Florida, 146–47; Stono rebellion (1739), 45–48; theoreticians of, 243–47; treason to whiteness and, 77–82; "Turning the Tables on the Overseer," dictatorship of abolition and, 193–206, *194*, *199*, *200*, *206*; Underground Railroad as key project of, 57–58; use of term, 3–4; white alliance policing and, 12–18; white counterrevolution as

reactionary and anticipatory, 24; white insurgent fascism, 233–43. *See also* Brown, John; Tubman, Harriet; Underground Railroad; white counterrevolution

accumulation crisis of capitalism. *See* capitalism

Act Concerning Volunteer or Independent Companies (1850), 114

Act for the Better Ordering and Governing of Negroes and Other Slaves (Negro Act) (1740), 46–48

Act for the Government and Protection of Indians (1850), 111

African colonization, 16, 150, 259n30

Aid the Suffering and Indigent Inhabitants of Florida Act (1836), 100

Akins, Damon, 110–11, 112, 115

Alachua region, Spanish Florida, 96

Alemán, Jesse, 128

Alleghenies, 182–83

Allen, Theodore, 27–28, 42–43

Alton, Illinois, 53

American Radicals (Jackson), 31

Amistad rebellion, 170

Anderson, Osborne, 36, *187*, 189–93, 196, 198, 201

Andrew, John, 218

Anglo-African Magazine, 66–67; "Turning the Tables on the Overseer," publication of, 193–206, *194*, *199*, *200*, *206*

Anishinaabe, 227–28

anti-capitalism: abolition war as form of class struggle, 84, 222–23; abolition war theoreticians, 175, 243–47; Indigenous anticolonial war as proletarian struggle, 87; liberation movements as,

California: Act Concerning Volunteer or Independent Companies (1850), 114; colonization of Indigenous California, 88–89, 109–18; gold rush, 109; Indigenous land defense and Mexican anticolonialism, 34–35; Indigenous slavery in, 110–11; *Joaquín Murieta* (Ridge), 118–32; militia groups, financing of, 115, 117; statehood (1850), 5; vigilante violence in, 113–18

Canada West community, 206, 207

capitalism: abolition war as anti-capitalist project, 222–23; abolition war theoreticians, 243–47; accumulation crisis, COVID-19 pandemic and, 225; Caribbean sugar production as center of capitalism, 44; class of the unwaged and, 226; deindustrialization and, 235–36; Global South, US imperialism and, 232–33; Indigenous land, extractive industries and, 227–28; Jamestown and the Virginia Company, 86; liberation raids as strike against reproduction of capitalism, 212–22; Marx on accumulation crisis of capitalism, 32, 225; Marx on capitalism's reproduction and expansion, 24–27; Marx on capital shedding of labor from production, 32, 215–16, 225; Marx on settler colonialism and proletarianization, 139–41; maturation of, 25–26; modern-day state repression and surplus labor, 229–33, 240; "normal capitalism" as racial capitalism, 44–45; Second Seminole War of Florida, effect on economy, 96–97; white alliance

policing and, 230–31; white equality and, 135–38; white insurgent fascism, rise of, 233–43. *See also* US racial capitalism; wars of capital accumulation

captivity narratives, 106

Caribbean: Cuba, Conspiracy of the Ladder (1843–1844), 74; slavery in, 43–44; sugar production in, 44; threat of Black abolition war, 146

cattle ranching, 111–12, 127

Cazenovia Fugitive Slave Law Convention (1850), 177

Central America, William Walker's filibustering in, 153–62

Chambersburg, Pennsylvania, 171

Charleston, South Carolina, 241–42

Charlottesville, Virginia, 229

Chatham Convention (1858), 63–64, 66, 68–69, 185–86, 189, 196, 204

Chatham Tri-Weekly Planet, 68

Cherokee, 34–35, 118–19; Andrew Jackson's Indian removal policies, 88–89; *Joaquín Murieta* (Ridge), 120–32; New Echota Treaty (1835), 119; Trail of Tears, 119

Chochuma, Mississippi, 143–44

Choctaw, 143–44

Cincinnati, Ohio: anti-abolition riots in, 53, 54–57; Black Codes (1807), 55–56

Cincinnati Anti-Slavery Society, 54–55

Cinqué, Joseph, 170

civil rights: abolition and anticolonialism, civil rights frameworks and, 30, 173; John Brown's abolitionism and, 204

class struggles, 7–9, 256n7, 257n16; abolition and anticolonial wars as, 4;

class struggles (*continued*)
abolition war as anti-capitalist project, 222–23; abolition war as means to abolish racialized class society, 173–75; abolition war theoreticians, 243–47; Civil War, inflation and class antagonism, 163; crisis as opening for worker revolution, 215–17, 220–22; between enslavers and nonenslavers, 152–53; Jamestown colony and the allure of Indigenous way of life, 85–87; Marxism as a science for understanding class struggle, 222; modern-day otherness of the unwaged, 225–26; Nat Turner's rebellion and class war of slavery, 17–18; Osborne Anderson and the dictatorship of abolition, 190–93; Seminole society and, 94–95; settler mass militarism and, 88; settler solidarity, forging of, 124; slavery as, 3; "Turning the Tables on the Overseer," dictatorship of abolition and, 193–206, *194, 199, 200, 206*; white insurgent fascism, 233–43; white racial pride as safety valve for class conflict, 43–44. *See also* proletarian struggles

Clay, Henry, 142
Clinch, Duncan, 97
Clymer, Jeffory, 79
Coacooche (Wildcat), 96
Coastal GasLink Pipeline (CGL), 227–28
Cocopahs, 112–13
collective life: in anti-capitalist nineteenth-century America, 30–32; Indigenous governance as incompatible with capitalism, 20–21,

22; white counterrevolution and, 24, 37
colonialism: colonial blind spot, 17; Gaza and, 228–29; Global South, US imperialism and, 232–33; modern-day otherness of the unwaged, 225–26; period of primitive accumulation, 8; William Walker, filibustering in Central America, 153–62. *See also* African colonization; anticolonial war; Indigenous anticolonial wars
Colorado, 109
Colored Orphan Asylum, *162, 163*
Combahee River raid, 10, 213, 218–22, *221*
communism: anti-capitalist nineteenth-century America, 30–32; Brown's "Provisional Constitution" and, 197, 222; dictatorship of abolition over slavery and, 36, 174–75; European communist movement, 190, 222, 244; Karl Marx's theory of, 81, 84; land reform and, 147; Osborne Anderson and, 190
Communist Manifesto (Marx and Engels), 7, 81, 147
community-defense vigilance committees, 5, 58, 59
Confederate States of America, 217–22
The Confessions of Nat Turner (1831), 13–15, 67–68
Conscription Act (1863), 163–64
Conspiracy of the Ladder (La Escalera) (1843–1844), 74
Cook, Adrian, 166
Cop City, 226–27
Copeland, John, 189
Correia, David, 21, 87–88

206. *See also* fugitive flights of enslaved Africans; Underground Railroad

Freedman's Bureau, 133

free labor, definition of, 138, 148

free soil movement, 150

fugitive flights of enslaved Africans: in abolition and anticolonial wars, 3–4; data on, 57; expanding fugitivity and slave catcher whiteness, 57–63, 62*fig*; fugitivity, anti-abolition mobs, and slave catcher whiteness, 53–57; liberation raids as strike against slavery, 212–22; Nat Turner's insurrection, response to, 51–53, 52*fig*; Negro Act (Act for the Better Ordering and Governing of Negroes and Other Slaves) (1740), 46–48; slave catcher whiteness and, 41; supernatural fugitivity, 73–74. *See also* free Blacks; Underground Railroad

Fugitive Slave Act (1793), 58–63, 62*fig*, 176

Fugitive Slave Act (1850), 33, 57, 59–63, 62*fig*

fugitive slave laws, 58–63, 62*fig*

Garnet, Henry Highland, 15, 50, 177

Garra, Antonio, 112–13

Garra uprising (1851), 112–13

Garrison, William Lloyd, 50, 160–61

Gaza, 228–29

Geary, John, 204

Gendron, Payton S., 241–42

genocide: Andrew Jackson's policies and, 143; colonization of Indigenous California, 109–18; John Brown and abolition war, 246–47; modern-day mass shootings, motivations for,

241–42; in Palestine, 228, 229; as response to slave revolts, 16; settler violence and, 35; "white genocide" theory, 241–42

Georgia, 119

Gillman, Susan, 83

Gilmore, Wilson, 44

Gilroy, Paul, 69

Glanton, John Joel, 116–17

Global North, 232–33

Global South, 232–33

governance: California, settler democracy and volunteer militias, 114–15; Indigenous forms of, 85–87; Jamestown colony and the allure of Indigenous way of life, 85–87; of Seminole, 94–95

Great Black Way, Appalachian Mountains, 182–83

Great Britain: intention to abolish slavery in the colonies, 92–93

Great Dismal Swamp maroon society, 5; Nat Turner and, 13, 49–53, 49*fig*, 52*fig*

"great replacement theory," 241–42

Greeley, Horace, 165, 190

Green, Shields, 171–72, 189, 191, 198

Grenier, John, 90, 92

Grey, Thomas, 13–15

guerrilla tactics: fugitivity, insurgent power of, 57–58; in Haitian Revolution, 38–39; Harriet Tubman's role in Civil War, 217–22; irregular warfare, 89–91; Nat Turner's insurrection, 12–13, 49–53, 49*fig*, 52*fig*; in Second Seminole War of Florida, 98, 102; Underground Railroad as guerrilla

transcontinental railroad and settler colonialism, 19–20; white counter-revolution as reactionary and anticipatory, 24. *See also* Seminole War of Florida, Second (1836–1842)

Indigenous culture: colonization of California and, 111–12; Jamestown colony and the allure of Indigenous way of life, 85–87

Indigenous land. *See* settler colonialism

The Invention of the White Race (Allen), 27–28, 42–43

Ireland, British colonization of, 43–44

Irish immigrants, 167

Irish national liberation struggle, 8

irregular warfare, defined, 89–90

Israel, 228–29

Jackson, Andrew, 18; Cherokee removal, 119; Indian Removal Act (1830), 95, 143; Indian removal policies, 88; Pre-emption Act (1830), 143; support of squatters' demand for white equality, 142–43; Thomas Hart Benton and, 144–47

Jackson, George, 37, 233–34

Jackson, Holly, 31

Jackson, Kellie Carter, 170, 181, 205

Jamaica, slavery in, 43–44

James, C. L. R., 8, 38–39

Jameson, Fred, 74

Jamestown, 85–86

January 6, 2021, attack on the Capitol, 234–35

Jefferson, Thomas, 142, 150

Jesup, Thomas, 98

Joaquín Murieta (Ridge), 34, 89, 118–32, 241, 281nn94–95

Johnson, Walter, 4, 152–53, 157, 161

Jones v. Van Zandt (1846), 59

Kagi, John, 63, 68, 171, 185–86, 196–97

Kansas-Nebraska Act (1854), 150

Kansas territory: Battle of Osawatomie (1856), 1–5, 66, 200–204; John Brown, abolition war and, 176, 199–202; Treaty of Guadalupe Hidalgo (1848), 109

Karuka, Manu, 8, 19–20, 21, 22, 87

Kenosha, Wisconsin, 236–40

King Philip's War (Pan-Indian War) (1675), 91

Ku Klux Klan (KKK), 236

Kumeyaay, 112–13

labor: Bacon's rebellion (1676) and, 43–44; Black worker vanguardism, 179–81, 190–93; bond laborers, 27, 43–44; counterrevolution and free labor, 27–30; crisis as opening for worker revolution, 215–17, 220–22; European labor and aspirations for white equality, 35–36, 43–44; exploitation of wage labor, 138–41; free labor, definition of, 138, 148; fugitivity as blow to enslaver's wealth, 57–63, 62*fig*; homestead utopianism, 135; Indigenous workers and slavery in California, 110–11, 112; Jamestown colony leaders and retention of labor, 85–87; labor of settlers, value conferred by, 151–53; liberation raids as strike against slavery, 212–22; Marx on capitalism's reproduction and

George Floyd murder, protests over, 224–30, 236–40; modern-day state repression and, 230–33; Negro Act (1740) and early formation of policing, 47–48; Oath Keeper members and, 234–35; posse comitatus doctrine and, 59–60. *See also* settler mass militarism; white alliance policing

Polish national liberation struggle, 8

political economy, Indigenous forms of, 85–87

political theater, 179, 191–93, 201, 203–4

posse comitatus doctrine, 58, 59–60, 267n58

Powhatan Confederacy, 85–86

Preemption Act (1830), 143

preemption doctrine, 142

Prigg, Edward, 59

Prigg v. Pennsylvania (1837), 58–59

prison guard whiteness, 41; slave revolt and, 42–45; Stono rebellion (1739), 45–48

proletarian internationalism, 80–81

proletarianization, process of, 139–41, 149

proletarian struggles: crisis as opening for worker revolution, 215–17, 220–22; Indigenous anticolonial war as proletarian struggle, 87; Osborne Anderson and the dictatorship of abolition, 190–93; "Turning the Tables on the Overseer," dictatorship of abolition and, 193–206, *194, 199, 200, 206. See also* class struggles

proslavery forces. *See* enslavers; planter class

protests, criminalization of, 226–30

Provincial Freeman, 190

Provisional Constitution (John Brown), 3, 196, 205

"Provisional Constitution and Ordinances for the People of the United States" (Brown), 3, 196, 205

Quechan, 112–13, 116–17

race. *See* Blackness; US racial capitalism; whiteness

racial capitalism, defined, 44–45. *See also* US racial capitalism

rancher class: Indigenous people of California, ranch raids by, 111–12

ranging, 90–92, 114–18, 278n77

Realf, Richard, 68, 181

Reconstruction, 23, 133, 262n52

Reconstruction Acts, 133

recursive dispossession, 261n47

Rediker, Marcus, 85–86

The Red Nation Rising (Estes et al.), 21

Redpath, James, 67

religion, as tool to deradicalize the enslaved, 71

Republican Party, founding of, 150–51

retributive violence, 16, 21, 113–18

revolution and crisis, 215–17, 220–22

revolutionary nationalism, 183

Reynolds, David, 196, 204, 222

Reynolds, George J., 205

Richards, Leonard, 57

Ridge, John, 119, 281nn94–95

Ridge, John Rollin, 34, 89, 118–32, 241

Ridge, Major, 119

Rittenhouse, Kyle, 236–40

Robinson, Cedric, 8, 44

Rodney, Walter, 8, 42, 222

centralism of action strategy, 213–15; "The General of All of Us," 206–12, *210, 211*

Turner, Nat, 12–18, 33, 165, 259n30; *Confessions,* 67–68; Haitian Revolution, study of, 181; insurrection of and white alliance policing, 49–53, *49fig*, *52fig*, 58; rebellion of, as flashpoint to white alliance policing, 41

Tuscarora, 5

Tuscarora War (1711), 92

Tustenugge, Halpatter (Alligator), 96

Uncle Tom's Cabin (Stowe), 9–10, 178

Underground Railroad, 5, 33, 36, *62fig*, 171; Cincinnati anti-abolition riots and, 54–57; as flashpoint to white alliance policing, 41; Fugitive Slave Laws and expanding slave catcher whiteness, 57–63, *62fig*, 176; fugitivity, anti-abolition mobs, and slave catcher whiteness, 53–57; as guerrilla campaign, 17–18; Harper's Ferry uprising, planning of, 182–84; Harriet Tubman and, 9–11, 206–12, *210, 211*; John Brown and, 178; as key project of abolition wars, 57–58; liberation raids as strike against slavery, 212–22; Subterranean Pass Way, 182

United States annexation of Cuba, 74–75

Unite the Right rally (2017), 229

universities, US military funding and, 232

US Army, California militias and, 114–15

US Civil War, 193–94; abolition war and the push to Civil war, 204; Black print culture and, 67; crisis of slavery capital and, 217–22; Enrollment (Conscription) Act (1863), 163–64; Harriet Tubman's role in, 217–22; Martin Delany and, 64–65; Reconstruction era policies following, 133–38

US Constitution: Fifteenth Amendment, 133; Fourteenth Amendment, 133; Thirteenth Amendment, 133

US racial capitalism: abolition war as anti-capitalist project, 222–23; abolition war as means to abolish racialized class society, 173–75; in anti-capitalist nineteenth-century America, 30–32; Bacon's rebellion (1676) and, 42–43; *Blake,* abolition war and treason to whiteness, 79–81; counterrevolution and free labor, 27–30; fugitivity as blow to enslaver's wealth, 57–63, *62fig*; Gerald Horne on the pan-European unity of whiteness, 23–24, 40–41; Haitian Revolution, white solidarity with enslavers, 39–40; Harriet Tubman on, 208–9; Jamestown colony and the allure of Indigenous way of life, 85–87; John Brown on destabilizing capital accumulation, 184–85; liberation raids as strike against slavery, 212–22; Marx on capitalism's reproduction and expansion, 24–27; mass protests in summer of 2020, 224–30; as mode of repression, 3–4; modern-day state repression and surplus labor, 230–33; Nat Turner's view of, 13–18; Osborne Anderson and the dictatorship of abolition, 190–93; Reconstruction and the power of Black labor, 23; transcontinental railroad and, 19–20;

white insurgency (*continued*)
    and, 133–38; from land reform to
    homestead utopianism, 147–53; New
    York City's anti-abolition insurgency,
    162, 163–67; squatter vanguard,
    141–46; wage labor in settler colonies,
    138–41. *See also* white counter-
    revolution
white insurgent fascism, 233–43
white nationalism, 261n46; contempo-
    rary forms of, 36; modern-day mass
    shootings, motivations for, 241–42;
    white insurgent fascism, 233–43
whiteness: abolition war and treason to
    whiteness, 77–82; bourgeois human-
    ity, modern definitions of, 178;
    construction of, 42–43; counterrevolu-
    tion and free labor, 27–30; European
    labor and aspirations for white
    equality, 35–36; expanding fugitivity
    and slave catcher whiteness, 57–63,
    62fig; as a form of psychological
    compensation, 28–29; Horne on the
    Pan-European unity of whiteness,
    23–24; modern-day state repression
    and, 231; Second Seminole War as
    undermining the myth of white
    supremacy, 95–96; settler solidarity
    and crimes against Indigenous
    persons, 115–17, 124; slave revolt and

prison guard whiteness, 42–45; as tool
    of social control over working class,
    27–28; as vehicle for deradicalizing
    the white proletariat, 29–30; white
    labor and capital, relationship
    between, 167–69
"white slavery," white worker grievances
    and, 28–29, 148
Wilderson, Major James, 55
Williams, Mabel, 178
Williams, Robert, 178
Williams, William, 165
Winslow, Edward, 18
Wise, Henry, 245
Withlacoochee, Battle of, 97
Wituwamat, 18–19
women: expansionist domesticity of
    settler families, 100; sex trafficking of
    Indigenous women and children, 111.
    See also Tubman, Harriet
working-class, evolution of, 139–41
working-class unity: Bacon's rebellion
    (1676) and the privileged status of
    whiteness, 43–44; counterrevolution
    and free labor, 27–30
Wynter, Sylvia, 8, 44, 178, 226
Wyoming, 109

Yazzie, Melanie, 21, 87–88
Yuma, 116

Founded in 1893,
UNIVERSITY OF CALIFORNIA PRESS
publishes bold, progressive books and journals
on topics in the arts, humanities, social sciences,
and natural sciences—with a focus on social
justice issues—that inspire thought and action
among readers worldwide.

The UC PRESS FOUNDATION
raises funds to uphold the press's vital role
as an independent, nonprofit publisher, and
receives philanthropic support from a wide
range of individuals and institutions—and from
committed readers like you. To learn more, visit
ucpress.edu/supportus.

www.ingramcontent.com/pod-product-compliance
Lightning Source LLC
Chambersburg PA
CBHW020823270326
41928CB00006B/416